Small Stream Fly-Fishing

Jeff Morgan

Small-Stream Fly-Fishing

Jeff Morgan

Frank Amato
PORTLAND

Dedication

To my Grandparents, Gordon and Mary Morgan, who always found time to encourage my fly-fishing addiction.

Acknowledgements

This book is the product of the contributions of many. A big thanks goes to Gary Muck and Jack Lynch, who offered sage criticism on repeated drafts of this book. I also would like to thank my mom and dad, Gary Muck, Jeff Dieter and Jim Schollmeyer for their photographic contributions to this book. I know that this book sometimes may seem critical of fly shops, but John, Shirley, and Jack Hagan at Northwest Flyfishing Outfitters and Don Nelson at River City Fly Shop have been invaluable tutors on how to treat all people with respect and conduct business in an ethical and honest manner. They gave me many opportunities when my youth would have disqualified me in the eyes of many shop owners. Thanks to Scott Richmond for being an excellent editor on my Westfly articles and for offering creative insights on the broader world of the flyfishing industry, as well as editing on parts of the entomology section of this text. Finally, thanks to my many fly-tying clients who provided me with enough employment to bring this project to fruition.

About the Author

Jeff Morgan is a professional fly tier, fly tying columnist for Westfly.com, and author of *An Angler's Guide to the Oregon Cascades*. He is currently working on a new book examining the diversity of trout prey and making fly-fishing presentations throughout the West. Jeff is currently a Ph.D. candidate in American History at Stanford University and lives in San Francisco, California.

All inquiries should be addressed to:
Frank Amato Publications, Inc. • P.O. Box 82112 • Portland, Oregon 97282
503-653-8108 • www.amatobooks.com

Fly Photography: Jim Schollmeyer
Photography: Jeff Morgan unless noted
Photography on pages 59, 79, 81, 83, 95, 97 Barry and Cathy Beck
Back Cover Photography: Jim Repine
Book Design: Jerry Hutchinson
ISBN: 1-57188-346-0
UPC: 0-81127-00180-4
Printed in Hong Kong
1   3   5   7   9   10   8   6   4   2

Contents

Chapter 1
Small-Stream Fly-Fishing and the Great American Myth

Americans like big things. Not a day passes when you don't see a mammoth SUV cruising down the highway, a group of shoppers leaving one of the myriad warehouse food stores, or a half-empty 64 oz. Double Big Gulp sitting on the curb. Everyone seems to want to live in big houses with three-car garages, mired in the sprawling suburbs with their wide streets and electronics superstores. Thousands of steak houses across the country offer a free dinner to the person who can scarf down the 64, 72, or 80 oz. steak. "American Pie," "Stairway to Heaven," "November Rain" and hundreds of other marathon songs reverberate around Earth, and beyond, riding the waves of American radio stations.

This complex pervades all aspects of American life, it trickles over to our recreational habits, and even the quiet sport of fly-fishing. What angler doesn't feel their heart pound over the thought of the June salmonfly emergence, while the September mahogany dun emergence elicits nary a flutter. How many anglers would die to be on the Madison during the October spawning run of three-pound brown trout from Hebgen Lake, yet won't even glance up from this page when their friend announces people are catching a bunch of eight-inch brookies in the creek across town. And show me the angler that would trade their 9' 9" Loomis GLX for a petite 6' 6" slow-action cane rod.

Nowhere is this complex more evident than in anglers' choices on where to fish. Every day anglers flood to the broad waters of the Deschutes, Madison, San Juan, Sacramento, Missouri, Delaware, and Battenkill. On their way they drive or fly over hundreds of smaller streams, ranging from first-order alpine trickles to thirty-foot-wide canyon torrents. The broad-river dreams have crushed the small-stream reality surrounding them. Since these small streams were not lauded in newspapers, magazines, books, or on the Internet, they do not support good fishing, right?

The origins of American fly-fishing can be traced back to the colonial era, when British Army officers wet their lines on small New England brook-trout streams. Anglers in turn-of-the-century Pennsylvania and Appalachia were elated with their mountain brookies and valley brown trout. Angling books in the pre-Vietnam era discuss small streams with far more regularity than today. For most of the long history of fly-fishing, most flies were flung on streams less than fifteen-meters wide.

For many decades, these streams satisfied all the needs of anglers, so the question must be broached: When and why did we move onto large streams? Why were small streams dismissed by the best anglers and left to lie fallow for young and learning anglers?

Sure, stocking practices and the influx of tailwater fisheries have opened up many large streams that were previously devoid of trout (like the Green, Bighorn, or San Juan). However the shift has had a lot more to do with the recent transformation of fly-fishing from a family or regional tradition into a multi-national sector of the economy. Magazines can't sell much advertising when they talk about fishing that can be done in your own backyard. Guides can't feed their families with anglers who are content exploring brushy mountain streams. Rod, reel, and line companies have no market for fast-action rods, advanced drag-systems, and shooting-taper lines when anglers are only looking to make fifteen-foot roll casts. Waders and boots are tough to sell to small-stream anglers who avoid getting in the water whenever possible. None of these interests believe they have anything to gain by an army of anglers interested in fly-fishing secluded small streams.

Now, this isn't a big conspiracy theory, it is just an industry acting in a utilitarian manner, like most do. Nobody blames the parties involved for doing what they do, for if any of us were in their shoes, we'd probably do the same thing. It is not wrong for sectors of the economy to choose not to invest in areas that appear to not be in their best interest. Do you see hotel chains with advertisements for RVs in their rooms? Do construction companies support urban growth restrictions? Of course not and businesses in the flyfishing industry should not be expected to act differently. But anglers need to recognize the real reasons that small streams are the flyfishing equivalent of the "uncle we don't talk about."

As a whole generation of anglers grows up in the New World of fly-fishing, many never get out to small streams. However, they continue to hear about small streams in books, magazines, lectures, and from fishing shops. Most small streams become simplified and stereotyped, a second-class citizen compared to the more unique glamour waters. They fall into a world of angler neglect, and a lack of angler expertise on these waters only reinforces the stereotypes already imposed on them. These anglers go on to perpetuate what I call the American Small-Stream Myth.

Like myths throughout the world, the American Small-Stream Myth is rooted in truths and accurate perceptions. However, as time goes on, and anglers spend less and less time on small streams, the Myth grows more rigid and dogmatic. All small streams are like this, and all small-stream fish act like this, and all small streams require a particular type of equipment, ad infinitum. In time, the American Small-Stream Myth becomes a part of our sport's collective memory, no longer challenged by rational arguments.

Like other myths throughout the world, the American Small-Stream Myth is not one, but a collage of myths, each contributing to the whole generic myth. Here we will discuss each myth, learning in which ways each is accurate, and how each is misleading. Many will be familiar, oft-repeated quotes. Others may be tacit assumptions, unsaid but implied by flyfishing culture and absorbed by the masses.

Myth: Small Streams Contain Small Fish

This myth is the cornerstone for all other small-stream myths. Small fish don't stress your equipment, so small streams should only be fished with cheap reels, short rods, and thick tippets. Small fish aren't smart, so you can catch them on anything with a hook. Small fish. . . (insert your own small-fish myth here).

Despite my apparent iconoclasm, I will be the first to vouch that most small streams do contain smaller fish than large streams. Small streams lack the quality of lies and the quantity of food that larger streams provide, and these factors limit the growth of trout. However, this is a blanket statement. There are certainly small streams that produce more and larger trout than some large streams in their regions. I would take a wild guess based on my small-stream experience and say that 7-12% of small streams produce a similar, or better quality trout, as neighboring larger streams. This seems like a small percentage, but when you consider the sheer quantity of small streams in this country, that makes them far more abundant than "glamour" rivers that receive all the press and pressure. Many of these small streams lie unmolested by anglers who believe the myth that small streams only produce small fish.

Trout grow because they eat more calories than they exert to stay in position. It is that simple. This fish-growth theorem applies to all trout waters throughout the world, yet anglers seem to think that only large streams can grow large fish. I can think of dozens of large streams where trout must exert a tremendous amount of energy for the gain of a few measly insects. The St. Mary's River in northern Montana and Alberta typifies this model. The St. Mary's is a broad, clear, cobble-bottomed river that looks like it is straight out of an issue of Gray's Sporting Journal with the minor exception that it has all the fertility of a bottle of Clorox. Other streams with good biomass may lack adequate holding water. A classic example of this scenario is the Metolius River in central Oregon. This stream has phenomenal biomass and an extremely diverse insect population, but its value as a trout fishery is marginalized by the fact that it lacks sufficient holding water for trout. Trout that live in these poor lies must battle against a charging current, and though they have a great source of food, there are relatively few trout per mile and surprisingly few manage to grow much larger than fifteen inches. Good, but not great.

Big waters may bring crowds pursuing big fish. If you pick the right small stream, you can chase big trout with hardly a soul around.

When ascertaining the big-fish potential of a stream, don't look at the volume of water. Look to see if there is a good balance between fast riffles and shallows that produces insects (caloric input) and deeper, slower water to allow fish security and a place to exert less energy when not feeding actively (caloric export). Fast, infertile streams with wide, rocky riparian zones are poor fish growers (regardless of size) because they violate both aspects of the big fish theorem: they have little food and trout must exert a great amount of energy in order to obtain it.

Clues that a Small Stream has Small Fish

1.) It is heavily pressured by anglers. Catch-and-keep anglers can quickly reduce the average size of fish by keeping all the larger fish. It only takes a handful of anglers catching their limit on a small stream to render it bereft of large fish for the season. Even incidental mortality by hordes of catch-and-release anglers can quickly whittle down a trout population. When heavy pressure is the result of proximity to population centers rather than the existence of a phenomenally productive small stream, small fish are nearly always the quarry.

2.) It is a spawning tributary for a lake or larger river. When this is the case, much of the food base is consumed by fingerlings, which subsequently migrate out of the stream. This increases food competition for resident trout and their number and sizes are reduced.

3.) Streams with a high width-to-depth ratio. These streams are characteristic of glacial or heavy-snowmelt streams of the West. The shallow and fast nature of these streams forces trout to exert a tremendous amount of energy to hold in their lies. Unless the stream is unusually productive, it is difficult for trout to grow very large.

4.) Streams with predominantly slow water. Unless the stream is at a high elevation or receives coldwater inputs (i.e. springs), it is often too warm and too low in dissolved oxygen, to produce enough insects for trout to grow to larger sizes.

All this discussion of "growing" large fish fails to recognize the fact that many small streams harbor large trout

Once one understands the conditions that produce quality trout in small streams, trout are not that difficult to find.

that migrate in and out during the season. Many small streams are spawning grounds for larger fish, and can hold unusually large fish for several months of the year. Other small streams receive trout that are seeking cooler, more oxygenated, or less turbid water during parts of the year. Since most anglers fish large streams and ignore tributaries, these migrations often go unnoticed, undocumented, and unheralded within the local angling community. All over the country, anglers who buy into the small-stream-equals-small-fish myth drive past the best fish of the season just to fish relatively empty large rivers.

I am a big fan of this myth, to the extent that it keeps anglers off some of my favorite streams. It also keeps anglers on big rivers, when their tributaries are more productive. An example of this is in Glacier National Park in Montana, where the big St. Mary's River sees a good chunk of the park tourists' light angling pressure. What is odd about this is that the aforementioned St. Mary's River has few insects or trout. There is hardly a living thing in there, be it fish, insect, or algae. However, a few small tributaries of St. Mary's Lake have a thin, almost unperceivable coating of algae on them. This is all it takes to harbor a small insect population, and subsequently a small trout population. While all the anglers flail the sterile big water, I am plying my trade on ten-foot-wide creeks and finding no shortage of fish.

To throw a wrench in this whole discussion of big and small fish, the definition of big is very subjective. Some anglers won't even raise their rods unless they have a shot at a twenty-inch fish. My thoughts about this are similar to my thoughts about guys that drive monster trucks: they have a serious complex, if you know what I mean. Trophy trout need not be a salve for the ego. Gierach once put it so elegantly, "Maybe your stature as a fly fisherman isn't determined by how big a trout you can catch, but by how small a trout you can catch without being disappointed, and, of course, without losing faith that there's a bigger one in there."

My definition of big, as far as the rest of this book is concerned, is twelve inches and up. In many places this is a trophy, while other small streams can grow trout up to twenty inches, and still others can handle migrant trout even larger. However, since few people can honestly say a foot-long trout is small, this appears to be a viable definition.

Myth: Small Streams are for Beginners and Kids

Maybe it was because many of us learned the basics of this great pastime on a small valley "crick" that we maintain and perpetuate this myth. The fact is, small streams are great places to learn how to fly-fish for a number of reasons: they don't require long casts, the fish are often eager to rise, and they are easily accessible to most anglers regardless of whether they live in the city, suburbs, or country. However, some of the best guides and fishermen I know would rather spend their summer afternoons on a ten-foot-wide brook than on many of the blue-ribbon streams in the region. Why?

Basically, good anglers are extremely efficient when fishing small streams. First of all, the ability to read the water will allow anglers to concentrate their casts to locations that have a high likelihood of holding trout. Such places are very obvious in small streams, where pocket water, boulders, undercut banks, and plunge pools scream out like highlighted text in a college notebook. Most good anglers will eliminate 90% of the water with one quick glance. The same glance on large streams will often get an angler into fish, but it may take many more casts because there is a greater quantity of water to cover. Secondly, the ability to cast accurately (distance is of minuscule importance), will make the most of the ability to read water. Good casters can hit these prime lies with a minimum of casts, and will generate a high cast-to-catch ratio. Besides, these anglers don't suffer the perpetual frustrations that haunt small-stream neophytes: snagging every branch, log, rock, or tuft of grass that litters the stream.

This small-streams-are-for-rookies myth can be misleading, even harmful, to new anglers. As we mentioned before, reading water, approaching fish, and accurate casting are essential for consistent success on small streams.

However, these are three of the most difficult things for a novice to do. To compound the problem even more, many new anglers come in with plenty of ideas of how fly-fishing should be done. I have found the best place to teach beginners how to fly-fish is calf deep in the middle of a run the size of a football field, just blindly lobbing a team of nymphs. This quickly quells bad mental habits before they get fossilized.

Myth: Small Streams are Not Challenging

Certainly, there are some very easy small streams in America, so easy that anyone can catch as many fish as he or she pleases. I have fished hundreds of small streams where the trout couldn't be less concerned with proper angler approach, drag-free drifts, or accurate hatch imitations. These are often fun waters to fish, and many people enjoy spending an afternoon on them. The quantity of these easy streams outnumbers the challenging ones by at least 15 to 1. However, that still leaves tens of thousands of miles of challenging small streams for the discriminate angler. This is significantly more than the mileage of challenging large streams.

Many experienced guides, like Gary Muck, like to challenge themselves by pursuing big fish on small streams.

See pool, cast to pool, catch trout, move on. Simple right? That is the idea many anglers have when they think of the doldrums of small-stream angling. What they fail to see is how immensely boring big-river fishing can be! Roll casting nymphs through a giant, featureless run, pounding miles of banks with hoppers, or repeatedly throwing salmonfly dries under willows requires little imagination or casting creativity. To top this off, effective techniques for big streams have been shared in fly shops and via the Internet and hatch charts are printed in newspapers, magazines, and books. These streams are fished year-round by guides and their clients, so there is no "mysterious" time of year where you have to figure things out on your own.

There are no Cliffs Notes for small streams. Small streams lack fraternities of anglers who freely swap information at coffee shops and sporting goods stores. There are no fly shops along the banks of small streams offering detailed hatch charts and bins full of flies specifically conceived for that body of water. In other words, you are left to your own devices.

The reason many small streams are considered easy is that fly choice makes negligible difference. Fly choice is noticed more on large streams, where fish are not as commonly spooked by approaching, wading, or casting, but pay particular attention to the flies that drift by following an awkward approach. A fish will rise and drift back ten feet

only to snub the hundredth CDC Thorax Upside-Down Dun you drifted past it. On small streams, the opposite is the case. Fish are extremely sensitive to everything prior to the fly coming into their cone of vision. If everything is peachy when the fly drifts into view, they will almost universally take it. The challenge here is to get your fly in front of the fish in a natural manner while remaining undetected. In this way, small streams offer a unique and distinct challenge that is absent from fishing popular water.

Some of the most difficult fishing I have had has been on small streams, and that is why I regard them so highly. Before I make my perennial pilgrimages to Slough Creek and the Lamar River—two potentially difficult streams in Yellowstone National Park—I hop in my car and drive to a small stream near my home to warm up. Eagle Creek is a small stream on the rural outskirts of Portland, Oregon where many families and teenagers go to swim, play in the water, and enjoy summer afternoons. When the shadows advance on the water, the fun-lovers leave, and the trout reclaim the long, slow, shallow pools. These seven- to ten-inch cutthroat will finally gain the courage to rise to the surface to a smorgasbord of small caddis, adult midges, tiny beetles and ants. In the placid waters, the trout have an eternity to inspect whatever is drifting by, their noses just grazing the meniscus.

Usually I will fish this water until sunset, painfully crawling across river rock, maneuvering around trees and

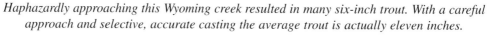

Haphazardly approaching this Wyoming creek resulted in many six-inch trout. With a careful approach and selective, accurate casting the average trout is actually eleven inches.

boulders to gain optimal casting position, and tying on microscopic flies on eye-numbing tippets. Why? Because it's the perfect training for the picky fish on Slough Creek!

Those anglers who choose to hone their angling skills by fishing small streams will be amazed at how well their angling can improve on larger streams. Things that are essential on small streams, like approaching fish and knowing how fish hold in relation to rocks, are often overlooked on larger streams. By doing something repeatedly on a small stream, you ingrain it in your routine, and your large-stream productivity increases.

I believe the greatest testament to the challenge of small streams is that so many anglers believe that they are generally poor fisheries. This results more from the difficulties anglers encounter casting to and catching fish than from an inherent unworthiness of the fishery. Many anglers often walk right up to the water in a small stream, hop in, and start casting randomly. They come without the skills to critically read the water or to execute difficult casts, and they lack a selection of flies that fish well in the harsh conditions of the small stream. The result is obvious: few fish, and almost none of "respectable" size. For some anglers, this is enough, but for most it is a disappointing, frustrating experience. So many of these anglers who suffered through tangled lines and snagged flies simply write-off small streams as little-fish factories and pay them no more notice.

Myth: Small-Stream Fly Selection is Basic
Again, another myth that is founded in a shred of truth. I agree, many small streams can be fished with nothing more than a greased-up Royal Wulff. That is one of their charms. Instead of filling a fly box with hundreds of $2.00 patterns, many of which will only be cast during one short week of the season, all you need for some small streams is a box of standard attractor patterns.

The problem is when anglers make the jump between associating attractor patterns with many small streams and associating attractor patterns to all small streams. This malady afflicts many fly-anglers, and seems particularly acute

The ecological diversity of small streams increases the scope of insects that trout can turn selective to...even this size 2 Mormon cricket may require an imitation!

among many guides and shops who don't fish the small streams of their region. If you subscribe to this theory and walk onto many of the small streams where I like to fish, you could be sorely disappointed.

The reality of small-stream fly selection is almost the opposite of the myth. Since small streams incorporate all aspects of potential habitat and potential insect life, a wide assortment of fly patterns become useful: high-floaters for pocket water, heavy nymphs for pools, streamers for spawning-run fish, parachutes for visibility in low-light conditions, flatwater patterns for slick-surfaced meadow streams, terrestrials for the overhanging willows, and emergers for heavily-pressured trout. Thus, a fly selection based solely on stream structure is much broader on small streams than on large streams.

Then come the bugs. The insect populations are almost always more diverse on small streams than on the larger, more famous waters because there is a greater variety of microhabitats. Large rivers tend to be fairly uniform in structure, thus producing a fairly uniform standing crop of insect life. Tailwater habitats are notorious for this, often producing less than 70 different species of aquatic insects, of which ten are important to trout. While the density of insects on smaller streams is rarely sufficient to allow selective fishing, it can and does happen (often when I am not prepared!), so a wide selection of flies is certainly advantageous.

What about terrestrials? As we will discuss in later sections of this book, terrestrials are much more important to the angler on small streams than on larger rivers because the entire breadth of the stream is in the drop zone for terrestrial bugs. This potentially means another fly box full or ants, beetles, crickets, hoppers, crane flies, inchworms, wasps, bees, cicadas, and alder flies.

It is a common theme among many writers and fishermen to whittle down fly selection to five or ten essential patterns that are "all you need." Following this advice is akin to tying one hand behind your back on the water. I always try to carry as many patterns as I can, up to the point where movement is hindered. The First Axiom of Fly Choice is, "If you don't have it, it is bound to be what the trout want," and it still haunts me every time I try to reduce my fly boxes to only the "basic and essential" patterns.

Myth: Small Streams are Tough to Access
This is what most anglers think, since major roads rarely follow tiny creeks through a mountain pass. Highways and main roads tend to follow larger rivers since they carve out a broader, straighter valley. Any small streams that are encountered by main roads are quickly crossed and left behind, never to be seen again. Many anglers' opinions on small streams are then rooted in the thirty-foot section visible from the road. Since a majority of anglers do not relish the thought of walking great distances from an access point, these streams are rarely fished.

However, once you venture off the highway, you will find many small streams that are followed by county roads and national forest roads. Many small streams offer the easiest access into mountain lake basins, and well-established trails often skirt the banks for several miles. While there is no shortage of small streams that require bushwhacking, many small streams offer access as good as large streams. Accessing many small streams doesn't require any extra sweat or muscle, unless you want to exert it.

You can use the core of truth for this myth of tough access to your advantage. Looking near home you can find waters that are surprisingly empty because of tough access. There is a stream within 25 miles of my home that flows into a larger river that is extremely popular with anglers and summer visitors. With a big reservoir and dozens of campgrounds in the vicinity, few fly-fishermen would come within fifty miles of this area. However, by taking a few dirt roads and a short, one-mile hike, I can cast to wild, thirteen-inch rainbow trout.

Myth: Small Streams Do Not Allow for
Versatile Techniques

"Attractor dry flies are the only thing you need to fish these small streams." This quote, given to me by a guide in West Yellowstone, first made me chuckle, then upon reflection, brought a moment of thought. Is this what the experts really think about small streams? Is this what they are telling beginners?

Many anglers, myself included, relish the opportunity to explore all aspects of fly-fishing. It is those rare opportunities

to sight-nymph, throw streamers to spawners, or lob hoppers at grassy banks that implore me to keep dreaming of the sport during long and rainy Oregon winters. For every technique in this sport, I can think of a small stream within 100 miles of my home where I can put it into practice. In contrast, I can only think of one big trout stream in that proximity. And on that one, the Deschutes, I spend 90% of my time indicator nymphing or fishing dry caddis patterns under the shoreline trees.

The idea that small streams don't allow for diversity in angling styles is anchored in the traditional assumption that small streams require only simple upstream dry-fly fishing. I have gotten into many arguments with people who ask me, "Why do you want to make a simple thing more difficult? If you can just go out and catch some fish with a size 12 Humpy and a seven-foot fly rod, why complicate things?" According to that logic, why do we bother nymphing in rivers when we could still catch some trout on dry flies? Hell, why do we learn to drive cars when we can just as easily walk wherever we are going? Once the association between small streams and "simplicity" is broken, and we look at small streams with a big-stream mentality, then we will be open to all of the possibilities of angling.

Myth: Small Streams Cannot
Support the Fly-Fishing Industry

I have heard this argument pop up dozens of times around fly shops: "We can't get enough people on good small

Many good small streams lie just a few feet from roads, but are overlooked by anglers concentrating on the "glamour waters."

streams to survive." To a degree, this is true. Rod companies that base their current existence on casting further and further surely don't want anglers to shift their attention to small streams. Super-slick coated rocket-taper fly lines don't look as appealing at $50.00 a pop when you are just trying to roll cast twenty feet. Large-arbor reels with fancy drag systems would never be used on small streams. Since small streams (allegedly) don't require diverse fly selections, the big market for imported flies would collapse.

However, this loss would not be the end of the story. A shift in consumer demand would actually create a whole new market for fly-fishing. Some anglers would like high-quality slow-action rods. Other anglers would demand more durable fly lines that could handle beatings on small streams. If there is a shift of interest towards small streams, there will be a market for new attractors and other small-stream flies, as well as older flies that are growing less and less productive on our heavily pressured waters. All these things, thanks to Adam Smith's magic hand, will likely occur if we redirect our angling focus. If anything, a boom in the popularity of small-stream fishing would likely greatly benefit the industry.

When reviewing a rough draft of this book, my friend Jack Lynch offered an idea. He mentioned that a small-stream taper line, which would properly load a 2- to 4-weight rod at fifteen feet, could be a potential new product that would come about with a shift towards small-stream angling. I'm sure there are dozens of potential new products like this that would come onto the market if there was greater emphasis on small-stream angling.

What about fly shops? How can more waters to fish on hurt them? (Having more options is great for the industry: crowded waters thin out, offering a higher-quality experience for those who continue to fish them, and people looking to get away from crowds can find out about more places they can go.) I would personally spend much more of my meager income in shops if I could find high-quality equipment designed for my small-stream fishing. I'm sure many of you reading this would concur.

Myth: Small Streams Do Not Give the Angler Space

Most anglers can easily cast across a small stream, and, on many sections, can jump across them. This results in a situation where angler space is at a premium. A separation of 200 yards between anglers is usually quite sufficient (and cherished) on a large stream. But on a small stream, an angler only 200 yards "ahead" of the direction you are fishing can cause a promising day to quickly deteriorate. If we consider angler pressure in comparison to stream-surface area, a ten-foot-wide stream is as effectively "crowded" as a 100-foot-wide stream when there is 1/10 the number of anglers.

Many people dislike fishing very small streams because they don't allow you to fish with a friend. In order to have enough water to work, you often have to separate yourself from your fishing buddy until the end of the fishing day.

This means that you cannot chat and share flies, information, and snack breaks together. These things are important to many anglers, and missing out on them on small streams is often a deterrent.

The problem of angler space on small streams is a minor one and one that is easily resolved. For instance, there is the "hopscotch" method, where anglers fish apart, but leap frog each other moving upstream, often sharing successful patterns and techniques on each pass. This way you get some solitude, but still have someone nearby to share the highs and lows.

The greatest thing about small streams is that they don't occur in a vacuum. Where there is a good small stream, there are generally more in the area. Geologic and ecological factors that cause trout to appear in abundance generally occur over a certain region, not just isolated in one creek's watershed. Also, productive big rivers often have productive tributaries. Thus, if one creek is crowded, you can simply move onto another stream nearby.

Myth: Small Streams Do Not Have Insect Emergences

Do small streams have aquatic insects? Yes. Do most aquatic insects eventually emerge into adults? Yes. With these two questions answered, are there hatches on small streams? Surprisingly, most anglers would answer "no" to this question.

Why do anglers think there are no hatches on small streams? First of all, it's because there are rarely "blanket hatches" on small streams. With the wide variety of habitat afforded by small streams, even rich streams rarely support enough of one insect to result in thick hatches. Secondly, the types of insects that we usually think of when we say "hatch"—pale morning duns, salmonflies, American grannom, *Hydropsyche* caddis (spotted sedge)—are rarely found on small streams. When the big-water angler tries a small stream during the salmonfly hatch, they are often disappointed by the numbers of naturals they find. This is not a result of low stream productivity, it's simply that this large insect is an anomaly in small creeks. Thirdly, the times of emergence on small streams vary from nearby large streams because of a difference in water temperatures. In Oregon, thousands of anglers chase the golden stonefly emergence on the Deschutes River, eagerly awaiting its arrival in June. However, almost none fish the smaller creeks of the western Cascades during May when this same insect emergence is also thick.

Many anglers fish so that they can match the hatch. The challenge contained in observing fish activity, looking for insects on the surface, selecting a proper imitation, and catching a fish with it, is a real source of joy for these fishermen, and much more desirable than throwing a bunch of nymphs under an indicator. Because these anglers enjoy this type of fishing, they ignore small streams because of the myth that there are no hatch-matching situations on small streams.

Granted, 50% of the time you can drift anything over an actively-feeding small-stream trout—regardless of what insect is emerging—and get a rise. The other 50% of the time, trout will be more likely to respond to a more precise imitation of the natural on which they're feeding.

A few years ago, I fished a small creek in Yellowstone National Park. Because of its location, it is overlooked by most anglers heading to the Yellowstone, Lamar or the Gardner, despite the fact it supports a superb population of ten-inch brook trout. One evening, I spotted a number of fish steadily rising in a riffle below a logjam. Rather than coming to the surface in a random and excitable manner, as we all think is the a priori behavior of small-stream trout, these trout were rising calmly and steadily. Every three seconds, these brook trout would come up and sip a size-16 Glossosoma caddis from the surface. After I carefully moved into position and tied on a size 12 Elk Hair Caddis to my 6X tippet, I succeeded in nothing but putting down the fish. Obviously, these fish weren't the mythical dumb little brook trout that we hear are always finning small streams. I had to change flies three times before I was convinced they weren't going to cooperate with anything less than a close approximation of the natural. Finally, I decided to play their game and tied on a size 16 brown X-Caddis and succeeded in fooling four fish in the ten-inch range. It took forty minutes of changing flies and "pool resting" to land four fish, which I could have caught in five minutes had I paid more attention to what was emerging and how the trout were responding.

Craig Martin, in his book *Mountain Water*, brings up a great anecdote connecting Pascal's wager with hatch matching. Pascal's wager states that a person is a fool not to believe in God, since if there is a God, and you don't believe, you are all squared away with Paradise and "all that jazz." If there is not a God, and you believed, you are no worse for wear. But if there is a God and you didn't believe, you're really up a creek without many fish. This is not so different from pursuing small-stream trout. If you match the natural insects, you can fool fish regardless of whether they are picky or not. However, if the trout are finicky, and you choose to adhere to the venerable Humpy, the only fish that you can fool are the indiscriminate, and usually smaller, ones. Thus, it takes no more effort than good fly selection to catch more fish. If catching fish is a goal—and it is for most of us—then it makes little sense to stock your fly box with nothing but attractors.

Myth: Anglers Don't Like to Fish Small Streams

Certainly there are some anglers who are intimidated by small streams. The fish can be spooky; a misstep being the catalyst for reverse "V's" darting away from the angler. Small streams, with their jumbled corridors of alder and willow, granite and basalt, pose perpetual challenges to the angler's deftness with the rod. Small streams generally lack streamside trails, leaving the angler many opportunities to slip, fall, cut, scrape, and end up looking like a NFL lineman on Monday morning. For these reasons, and others founded and unfounded, the myth has been perpetuated that anglers simply enjoy bigger streams more.

Actual angler surveys contradict this myth. A study done by psychologist Robert Jackson at the University of Wisconsin-LaCrosse revealed that anglers value many things ahead of "catching many fish" or "catching large fish." This survey asked anglers to rate the most important aspects of their fishing experiences. "Catching many fish" and "catching large fish," the alleged reasons why we fish large streams, came in a miserable second to last and last, respectively. The survey revealed that anglers prefer the aesthetic aspects of fly-fishing much more than the results and most, if not all, of the aesthetic aspects are better served on small streams.

The greatest reason anglers do not spend as much time fishing smaller waters is a lack of knowledge. This lack of knowledge is not for a lack of trying. Small streams are not discussed in mainstream angling periodicals, and most regional guidebooks ignore small streams. Shops rarely post info on small streams on their hatch boards, and most fishing reports just lump all small streams into the "other-streams" category. All of this results in a large number of anglers not knowing where to go or what to do. Because there is little serious angling research about small streams, the myths of "Humpies and 4X" prevail, and anglers who follow the same old techniques are coming up with the same old seven-inch trout. There are simply no answers out there for the curious angler looking to expand their horizons.

But the times they are a-changin'.

Chapter 2
Small-Stream Equipment

Equipment for small streams can be as varied as the flies in your box. Some anglers save their old beat-up equipment for use on small streams; others invest in $700 0-weight rods with affixed reels. While any equipment you use on large rivers can be used on small streams, there are some different conditions that small streams pose, and you should be prepared for these things.

I am an ardent gearphobe. I could really care less about scrim, fly line polymers, reel gear technologies, etc., so I will not discuss equipment with the expertise or eloquence of a tackle dealer or manufacturer rep. However, these things are fun to toy with and debate, and being an insectophile, I have a good appreciation for addictions to some of the more tangental aspects of our sport. I would recommend

anglers peruse the works of Charles Meck, John Gierach, and Craig Martin, and consider their recommendations for small-stream tackle as well.

Rods

Like in all other areas of fly-fishing, rod choice for use on small streams is one decision that sparks up plenty of debate. Because of the rapid advancement of materials and design over the past twenty years, choice of rods can be bewildering, even for supposedly easy small streams.

Many people simply fish hand-me-downs or old rods on small streams, perhaps because of nostalgia or just maybe because they don't want to break a good rod chasing little fish. This is all fine and dandy, but rod choice and selection

Small rods are not always perfect for small streams. On an open-canopy stream like this,
a long rod will allow for longer presentations and fewer spooked trout.

can be much more central to your angling experience on small streams than on any other type of stream. Bad rod choice on small streams can leave you backcasting through trees, cramped when you roll cast, unable to use dappling techniques when necessary, or occasionally missing fish because you couldn't cast far enough to reach them.

It is a common occurrence for a potential customer to come into a fly shop and cast the entire gallery of fly rods, then simply buy the rod they can cast the farthest. This is not the approach you should take when buying a small-stream rod. Look for a rod that casts accurately at short distances and also requires little line to load the rod. These two features are much more important to the small-stream angler than casting distance.

Buying a small rod for small streams is the status quo in fly-fishing. If you walk into a shop and ask for a "crick rod," they will quickly steer you to the diminutive end of the rod rack. Rod manufacturers and catalogs trumpet their smaller—shorter than eight feet—rods as "perfect for smaller rivers and creeks." This is true, especially when you are fishing on brushy creeks and small pocket water, where casts rarely exceed thirty feet. However, what about those situations where a thirty-foot cast leaves you thirty feet short of the fish: open meadows, low-water pools, or beaver ponds. Here, a long rod, up to ten feet, is helpful to make long and accurate casts while leaving comfortable spacing between you and the trout.

When I took a trip to Austria and Switzerland in high school, I crossed the Alps where a tiny trickle, the fetal Danube River, meets the road and starts its migration to the Black Sea. All along the river were old Austrian gentlemen armed with suits and twelve- to fourteen-foot-long rods, dappling flies and bait for brown trout and grayling. A long rod is perfect for that kind of fishing, allowing you to cover most of a small stream with a dry fly without making a back-cast. This kind of rod also allowed them to "Czech nymph"—which is more or less a kind of a high-stick nymphing, quite effective on deep runs, and something we'll tackle more in-depth later on. You wouldn't think a rod as wide as the stream is a good idea, but in the right hands, it can be deadly.

When researching this book, I spent a lot of time on small meadow streams in the Rocky Mountains. The seven-foot rods I loved so much on the brushy streams of western Oregon couldn't cast through the wind that howled through those alpine meadows. Trying to fish a hopper at 50 feet was impossible. Heck, fishing it at 25 feet was impossible, and getting within 25 feet of a trout on these streams was angling suicide. The only recourse I had was my 9' 9" six-weight, which despite its heavy construction became my favorite

A medium-fast action rod, 3- to 5-weight floating double-taper line and a click-drag reel create an excellent basic small-stream outfit.

open-canopy rod in my collection. It allowed me to make accurate presentations from upwards of sixty or seventy feet, plopping down a fly on top of a trout while remaining undetected. I found that with this husky rod—one that conventional angling wisdom shuns in small-stream situations—I was catching more and better trout on small creeks.

Some anglers love a 7- to 8-foot bamboo rod for their small-stream fishing. The slow action and short-distance accuracy that they offer is a dream for control freaks on small streams. The aesthetic combination of bamboo rods and small, secluded streams is enough to turn even the most social angler into a hermit.

Besides the length, action, and weight of the rod, another important consideration is whether to get a two-piece rod or four-piece travel rod. When I was a kid, the four-piece rods had the deft touch of a Louisville Slugger, but over the past fifteen years, their quality is nearly on par with two-piecers. The benefits of a four-piece rod are many. They can be easily packed in on a horse or in a backpack, thus eliminating the urge to stop and fish while hiking in to a remote lake or stream. They can also be carried on airplanes, busses, and trains, thus eliminating the risk of your rod arriving in Boston when you land in Bozeman. However, the number of pieces you want your rod to break down to is dictated more by your travel habits than your fishing habits.

Finally, any discussion of small-stream rod selection is incomplete without covering lifetime-warranty rods. If you plan on doing a lot of small-stream fishing, it is worth your while to buy one of these rods. With all the scrambling and crawling and stumbling we do on small streams, a broken rod is pretty much inevitable over the course of ten or so seasons. It is really worth it to invest in these rods, which will put up with all you can dish out in a lifetime of small-stream angling.

Reels

A reel on a small stream is no more than a glorified line-storage unit. You might as well put your spare line in a little hip satchel. It is not that you won't necessarily catch fish that will test your drag, the fish just have nowhere to go. In a large stream, even smaller trout can take line from your reel because of the distance you often hook them at and the subsequent torque exerted on your rod. In a small stream, even trout hooked at a distance cannot run east-west on you unless they go through instant evolution, grow legs, and run off through the alders.

A reel, though it doesn't need a drag system adequate for a tarpon, does need to play out line smoothly. On a stream you are constantly pulling more line from your reel to make a longer cast, reeling the line back on when you walk around, then pulling out more line for your next cast. If the line easily gets caught in the rim or wrapped around the reel seat, it can quickly tear up your line. Also, you never know when you will hook a large trout in a small stream, and when this special moment occurs, it is a pity to allow a bad reel to cost you the trout of the year.

The most important aspect of a small-stream reel is durability. On small streams, rods and reels take a beating that reels that live a posh life in the hands of a big-stream angler could never dream of. Slipping, scrambling, and crawling—three endeavors in which the large-stream angler rarely participates—cause the small-streamer's reel to be dragged, banged, knocked, and pounded against the rocks. A reel that is not durable will last only a season of serious small-stream fishing. The banging and scraping received by a small-stream reel means that you don't want to use your best reels for small streams. There is no reason to pay more than $100 for a small-stream reel. Any more, and you will regret it after replacing it every five years.

If you are a hardcore small-stream devotee, and either bushwhack deep or hike and camp on small streams, it is a good idea to always carry two reels and keep the spare in your car or in your vest.

Lines

Double taper, double taper, double taper. Short casting is the norm on creeks, and the double-taper line is accurate at short distances and is easy to load your rod. Another benefit of the double-taper line is that you can turn them around when the front section gets worn down. Considering how quickly lines can be decimated, this benefit cannot be overemphasized.

Beginning anglers, and many advanced anglers, may prefer a weight-forward line because it is certainly easier to load the rod for short casts. However, it's much more difficult to lay down gently than a double taper, especially at short distances. So, if you are just beginning to fly-fish, try the weight forward, otherwise convert to the double taper for small-stream uses.

A floating fly line is all you need on a small stream, for you rarely cast enough line to utilize the benefits of a sinking or sink-tip line. If you need to fish below the surface, either indicator nymphing or adding a split-shot in front of a streamer should get you deep enough. The only exception to this rule is in the Pacific Northwest, where many large creeks receive a run of summer steelhead, which tend to hold at the bottom of deeper runs and pools. Here I carry a small section of sinking shooting head, which I loop onto the front of my floating line. This lets me get down to the steelies.

Another exception is when you believe you have a good shot at encountering a beaver pond somewhere on your stream. In this situation, if the pond is deeper than five feet, you might want to carry a type II sinking line. Of course, if you are exploring a new stream, you might not know if there is a pond there or not, so it's generally a good idea to carry an extra spool.

A durable fly line is important, and depending on how serious you are with your small-stream fishing, you may want to replace it often. On a big river, the only thing the line usually touches is air and water. Old age and UV damage will render a big-stream fly line unusable before heavy use will. On creeks, it is a different story. Your line is cast over logs and grass and rocks, and wrapped around tree branches and stumps. I replace my creek lines almost every 18 months because they are often cracked and don't float anymore.

Though a perfect floater is not essential on many creeks, I believe it cannot hurt.

The alternative argument to my view is that since fly lines take such a beating on small streams there is no need to invest in a quality floater. A few good anglers that I know save their old lines to spool onto their "creek" spools. Their view is that a perfectly uniform floating line is not that important, since you rarely have that much line on the water. A little sink is acceptable and the dirt and fading on the line help reduce fish-spooking flash. This is certainly a valid argument, and one that an angler on a budget (as most of us are) should consider.

Aside from durability and quality discussions, line color should be considered. I agree with Gary Borger's eloquent defense of dying fly lines so they don't look like they are fresh from Three Mile Island. Bright orange and chartreuse-hued lines have no place in serious small-stream fishing. Sure, you may be able to catch fish with them, but there are untold hundreds (or thousands) of potential fish that those lines prevented you from catching. You may want to dye your lines per Gary's recommendation, but I simply buy buckskin-colored lines or similarly muted colors for my lines.

Leaders and Tippets

While the angling greats of the past have written entire chapters on leader design, I have been a poor student. The taper of my leader is something I rarely have concerned myself with, except when fishing on small streams. Since accuracy is important, both to catch fish and to protect your leader from damage, the makeup of your leader can be critical. I use several different recipes for my leaders, depending on the type of fishing I am doing. Here are my normal choices for leader composition:

If you think lines take a beating on creeks, inspect your tippet closely. Even one fishing trip can render your tippet totally unusable. The impact of hundreds of tiny teeth, dozens of snags, and a couple knots will reduce the strength of your leader significantly. It's always a good idea to put on a new leader (at least the front two sections) at the start of the day, and to check your leader several times during the course of fishing.

To inspect your leader on-stream for defects, carry a tiny zip-lock bag with a couple of cotton balls. Run the cotton balls up and down your tippet to check for tiny nicks and abrasions. The cotton will catch wherever there is damage, giving you a clear picture of the status of your leader.

Since abrasion resistance is a desirable quality of small-stream leaders, look for brands that specialize in this. Though several different brands fish well on creeks, I use Maxima Chameleon on exceptionally brushy small streams. I learned to love this brand when fishing Pacific jetties for rockfish, a type of fishing that saws through most leaders. It has a quite poor strength-to-diameter ratio, but it holds up well when fishing in woody streams where the tippet perpetually drags across logs.

Fluorocarbon leaders are important only when nymphing, and even then it is probably a good idea to keep the expensive fluorocarbon tippet deep in the vest except when fishing a heavily pressured small stream. Fluorocarbon tippets can actually hurt your dry-fly fishing because they have lower stretch than monofilament and in their thinner diameters they float like a cork on the surface. How many trout want to eat a fly attached to a bowline?

Fly Boxes

I like to carry several small fly boxes because I have a tendency to forget them or drop them in the stream. Make sure your fly boxes float; for me, plastic is the only way to go.

A good idea may be to put in strips of magnetic tape in your boxes. This keeps them attached if you stumble, when plain plastic bins are like ejectable seats for your expensive flies.

Nymphing Equipment

Most anglers have a fear of nymphing small streams. Considering that many small streams have highly variable depths, short pockets, and brushy shorelines, this fear is certainly warranted. Nymphing on small streams is very effective if you know when to do it and if you have the proper equipment with you. On small streams, I always carry everything I need to fish nymphs: indicators, weights, and plenty of extra tippet. You never want to be stuck in a situation where nymphing is the only thing that will work, and you shuffle through your vest only to find yourself lacking the proper tools.

For an indicator, I prefer to use a Corkie (a foam float that baitfishermen use for steelhead) with a toothpick to hold it in place. These are inexpensive—about seven for one dollar—which is crucial for small streams, where you are likely to lose many in trees or by snagging on the bottom. I usually carry a selection of sizes, so I can use anything from a pair of big stonefly nymphs to a single, tiny scud—without pulling the indicator under. The color of the indicator is also important. I have found that on heavily fished streams and some small streams, the standard orange, pink, or chartreuse indicator colors tend to spook fish. We've all seen fish rise to indicators while nymphing, and thus tend to think indicators don't alert fish to something awry. What we don't see is that for every fish that rises to our indicator, ten fish swim away either because it is unnatural or else it brings back bad memories. I started to paint my indicators in sky-blue or white to match the sky, or black or brown to match floating bark or debris. My catch rate with nymphs on high-pressure waters skyrocketed. Now I only have a few bright indicators left and they are reserved for swift, deep water where their extreme visibility is required.

For weight, I have now turned entirely to non-toxic split-shot for weighting my flies. I used to use the lead strips that come in those matchbooks, but they were difficult to handle under cold conditions and were cumbersome to cast. Non-toxic shot is more expensive, but better for the environment and you can leave your fly vest around your kids without fear of them turning into the Emperor Nero.

If you plan on nymphing in small streams, you are going to get plenty of snags, tangles, and knots. Often it's easier to make a preemptive strike and cut everything off and re-tie it, rather than to probe, pull, and twist your jumble of flies, weights and indicators for twenty minutes only to find out that you have to cut it all off anyway.

Waders

Waders seem essential to the angler, and many fishermen feel naked without them. Waders are critical because they keep you warm, dry and comfortable while fishing. And although waders should probably never be left out of your gear bag for large streams and lake fishing, they are not as critical for small streams as it may seem.

There is little reason to wear waders on small streams during the warm months, for you rarely wade deeper than your knees. Even if the stream is a little cold, it is usually a refreshing change from the hot summer pursuit. Besides, wet wading puts you in touch with the quarry you are pursuing.

In addition to the experience of wet wading, it is economical and safer. Waders, plus small streams, equals punctures by the dozen. If you want perforated waders then take them for a spin on any wooded small stream, and you'll quickly achieve your goal. If you wear waders through a season of small-stream fishing, you'll have to put "new waders" on your Christmas list each year. Some people I know realize this threat, and wear their old, pre-punched waders for small-stream work. However, since these already leak like the Titanic, you are going to get wet anyway, so why not just wear shorts!

The second important reason to wet wade is for safety. There is a section of the Lamar River below the Lamar Valley (in Yellowstone National Park), where the river shoots down a steep canyon amongst Dodge Neon-sized granite boulders. There is some good fishable water here, but wading is unwise, if not impossible, because of the swift and deep water. To move up and down the stream effectively you have to scale huge boulders and jump rock-to-rock with swift water running underfoot. Waders restrict movement and hinder your jumping ability, thus presenting a serious threat to your safety.

Waders also encourage the angler to get into the water, something that isn't always a good idea. Regardless of which direction you are wading, the easiest way to spook a trout is by being in the water. The reason most anglers don't catch quality fish on small streams is because they spook them before they can even make a presentation. When wearing waders, most anglers lack the discipline to stay out of the water, and for this reason, waders should remain in the car when fishing small streams.

Finally, waders restrict your movement and prevent you from accessing parts of streams. You cannot climb over or under logs and wading is made more difficult because of the increased buoyancy. Bare legs might get scraped up or a little cold, but they are the best tools you have to place you in optimal casting situations.

With all that said, if you get too cold to comfortably fish without waders, there is no shame in wearing them. If waders prolong your day on the water, allowing you to wade deeper without soaking all your clothes, by all means bring them along. Of course, if you fish a small stream that is open during the wintertime then waders are essential, if for nothing less than heat retention. But remember, in small-stream fly-fishing, waders are definitely an optional piece of equipment.

Many small-stream anglers swear by hip waders. The

The ideal small-stream outfit trades waders for good wading boots and breatheable clothing, allowing you to comfortably cover miles of water.

argument is that they are easier to transport, cooler than neoprene chest waders, and cheaper than breathable chest waders. Maybe I was born too late, but I never have, and never will, own hip waders. Either the air (and water) is cold enough to warrant chest waders, or else I haven't needed them.

Boots

Boots can be important on small streams, but they are by no means mandatory. Many people comfortably fish small streams in tennis shoes, especially those with low gradients or uniform bottoms. Mud- and gravel-bottomed valley streams can be traversed with any old pair of sneakers. They are serviceable in low-gradient streams, but when you must fish a stream with algae growth (which includes almost all of them), you might as well wear roller skates. A couple of bruising falls may make the high price of wading boots look a lot cheaper.

Others simply prefer wading sandals, like those used for river rafting. But keep in mind that these were designed so that you can put your feet in the water while drinking beer on a raft, not to wade a knee-deep stretch of pocket water. With no toe or ankle protection, you will rarely make the mistake of wearing these sandals more than once. In addition to the torture they can put your feet through, many of these sandals won't even make it two trips through boulder-strewn streams. My friend bought a pair to wear fishing, only to have the straps break after three hours of wading and fishing. In addition, there are some specialty wading sandals for anglers with studded felt soles, but these still expose your toes and heels to painful encounters with rocks.

If you plan on spending a lot of time in the water, it is wise to invest in good wading boots because they are absolutely essential to your comfort and enjoyment of the stream. Small streams, unlike many large streams, require lots of wading, walking, and scrambling along uncivilized shorelines, all of which is made easier with quality boots. Felt soles are essential when buying boots, and really help to grip algae and moss-covered rocks. However, mud and felt are a bad combination, with felt taking on the properties of the former when they make contact.

I prefer cleated wading boots because they give me total freedom on the stream. They lessen the fear of falling and make it easier to move into optimal casting positions. Cleated boots also eliminate the "would have, could have, should have" excuses that fly when you couldn't move into position for that large trout.

I often wear neoprene booties when I wade, usually just to keep my feet warmer than with socks. They also keep rocks out of your boots, which lengthens any day of angling.

Clothing

Clothing on a small stream should be chosen to match the surroundings. As will be discussed later, small-stream trout are easily spooked, and using clothes that match the riparian vegetation can go a long way towards concealing your approach. Choose earthtones like olive or brown in forests, tans on desert streams, blues or greens on open-meadow streams, and grays on alpine streams or boulder-ridden streams. Full camouflage may be optimal in some places, but you will get weird looks from other anglers.

The clothing you choose, and their materials, are pretty much the same as on larger streams. Quick-drying nylon and other synthetics are great, but cottons will suffice when the sun will help accelerate their drying. Fleece may feel nice on crisp fall days, but it becomes as porous as a wiffle ball when the wind whips up. Wool is a great choice if you are expecting cold weather because it retains heat even after it gets wet.

Long-sleeved fishing shirts with buttons that allow you to button up the sleeves when you get warm are great for all types of fishing, but are an excellent choice on small streams where you may have to do quite a bit of hiking between casts.

I prefer shorts and bare legs for small-stream fishing, because it is easy to tear up long pants and they take much longer to dry off than skin. If you are fishing a stream where you know you probably won't be getting too wet, long pants work just fine. If it is particularly cool and you don't have waders, a pair of polypropylene running tights under your shorts will keep you a little warmer and they'll allow you to dry off quickly. These tights take up almost no room in a daypack, and can be a good idea to take along for emergency purposes.

On many small streams that flow through canyons or heavily-forested lands, daytime temperatures can be surprisingly different than in the surrounding area. One cold creek I fished flowed under a thick canopy of spruce and Douglas firs. The canopy acted like a cooler, retaining the air cooled by the frigid creek. The air temperature at the mouth of the creek was 87°F. A mile up the stream, the air temperature was a relatively frigid 50°F. The moral of this story is to always pack a long-sleeved shirt or rain jacket when venturing up unknown streams.

Also, always keep a change of clothes in the car. If you get deep up a creek, it can be difficult to spot a thunderstorm coming, and the insurance of warm clothes will allow you to fish longer and with fewer worries.

Other Equipment

Rod sling: I use this interesting leather contraption to hold my rod when I need all my appendages to safely navigate around a dangerous section of stream. I used to simply bite the cork handle of my rod when I needed to climb over a logjam or scramble up a cliff, and although this method will suffice, it is hard to keep your balance and easy to drop your rod or break its tip. Holding your rod in such a precarious way will alter your equilibrium and foul your balance, endangering both the safety of yourself and your fly rod. With the rod sling, your rod is safely on your back, positioned so that it will not interfere with your range of motion. The rod is safe and you are free to climb and scramble without interference. This sling can be purchased for $20 at shaverleater.tripod.com.

Fly floatant: Apart from your rod, reel, and flies, nothing is as important as fly floatant on small streams. On larger streams, where you hook fewer fish and your flies drift through slower water, you can get away with extra false casts and changing your fly after each fish. On smaller streams, your fly is attacked by more fish and the rapid water seems like the Yangtze to your fly. Without floatant, you will lose sight of your fly, catch fewer fish, and you'll find it frustrating to have to perpetually put on a new, dry fly.

When it comes to floatants, I always opt for giving my flies a double-dose. I use a permanent floatant, like Gorilla Proof, before I put any dry fly in my small-stream boxes, and then apply a paste floatant before using it on the stream. This combination is much more effective than using one without the other.

I also always carry a container of Top Ride (by Loon Products) a floatant/desiccant that does not affect CDC feathers. (You never know when conditions warrant the use of CDC flies, and without this stuff, you will have to change CDC flies after every fish.) It is also good for sporadic use on standard dry flies, especially when they get really slimy and need cleaning.

For all of its positives, don't believe the hype on the side of the bottle: "Great on Large Dry Flies and Hoppers." If you use it to dry these bulky flies, you'll go through $7 bottles of Top Ride faster than you can believe.

Insect repellant: Small streams often go through a variety of water levels throughout the year, and stagnant pools near streams are breeding grounds for all sorts of mosquitoes and biting flies. The marshy meadow sections of small streams can turn into havens for a myriad of torturous insects. Nothing can be more infuriating than trying to decipher a hatch while insects perpetually buzz around your head like choppers looking for Charlie. A bottle of repellant will keep away most—not all—of your assailants, allowing you to concentrate on fishing.

I once took a group of friends fishing on a small stream in Yellowstone Park for a bachelor-party-fishing-trip. We went down to fish a small stream on a sunny evening. As soon as we were on the water, we noticed our legs were bleeding. There were no visible insects and if we hadn't stopped and inspected our legs, we might have been eaten alive. There were tiny insects, which looked more like dirt or poppy seeds than bugs crawling on our legs. It turns out they were chiggers, and they were vicious little bastards. The groom-to-be left Yellowstone with over two dozen big, red swollen sores on his legs that barely healed before his wedding two weeks later. The rest of us suffered a similar fate. The moral of this tale is that insect repellant is as important as a fly rod or fly box.

Hemostats: Small-stream trout rarely sip insects on the surface, they pounce on them. When trout attack flies with reckless abandon, they can be hooked in a variety of places; eyes, gills, pectoral fins, caudal fin, anus, and the tail are all potential hooking sites. The reason for this is that when the trout rises to your fly and quickly dives, if the fly is not squarely in the mouth (as is often the case with smaller trout), the line gets tangled around fins and other body parts. As you set the hook, you pull the fly from the mouth and across various parts of the body until the hook finds a nice little niche to bury itself in. The hemostat is an invaluable tool to wrench hooks free from difficult piercings, and it is often the best way to get a hook out of you. A hemostat is also useful for de-barbing flies when you misplace your pliers.

Hemostats deserve a place in your vest, on your fly-tying desk, in your car, and anywhere else you can imagine having flies around. Make friends with someone in the health care industry and you can get dozens for free or almost free. They have way too many uses to be left at home.

Thermometer: A thermometer is a luxury piece of equipment for most anglers, but if you have a favorite small stream, it is an invaluable tool for understanding the creek. The thermometer will allow you to start to study the relationships between stream temperatures and hatches, feeding activity, and the migrations on your particular home stream. Once these are understood, a check of the water temperature will give you a good idea of what should work and what might not.

Compass/GPS: When exploring new streams in new country, it is easy to be disorientated. A compass or GPS, along with a laminated map, should allow you to find your way back out to your car. The GPS will also let you mark your favorite spots on streams. More importantly, the GPS will mark points on the trail where you have to hike down to good holes.

Bear bells and bear mace: If you plan on doing any exploring on small streams in the Northern Rocky Mountains where you might share a stream with grizzly bears, these are critical. It you plan on fishing these waters alone, you absolutely need multiple quantities of these items.

The bells let bears know you're coming so that they can get out of the way. Along a stream, where the noise of the water can drown out footsteps and the rustling of brush, a couple pairs of bells are recommended. They make you sound like freakin' Santa Claus walking down the trail, but that is better than sounding like bear food. The number one reason for bear attacks is the surprise encounter, and bells prevent that. I credit bells for my lack of grizzly encounters during my many months of explorations through the Rocky Mountain backcountry. Besides bells, nothing can replace observation of tracks and scat to tell if an area has been recently visited by a grizzly. Also, keep your head up when fishing. A lot of times it is too easy to get into fishing and never look up. I always scan 100 yards ahead, when possible, to see if there will be any trouble ahead.

If bells and observation don't work, then a large can of bear mace (pepper spray) can usually deter or stop an attack. These large (spray-paint sized) cans of pepper spray can

Small-stream fly-fishing can put you in the heart of bear country. Always be aware of natural and human signs!

shoot up to 40 feet for six seconds. However, if you do the math, a bear, at a full 35 m.p.h. charge, will cover that last 40 feet in less than one second. Even if you hit the bear in the eyes, it will usually still run into you before retreating, so don't expect the spray to save you from all damage. It is still better to prevent an attack by observing and wearing bells.

It must be noted that the spray is an attack deterrent not an encounter repellant. DO NOT spray it on yourself or your tent, because the strong scent will likely attract bears from great distances that otherwise would have been ignorant to your presence.

A lot of people say, "I don't think it will work," or "I heard it doesn't work," and subsequently don't carry the stuff. These opinions are based mostly on anecdotal evidence, as all the studies done with them say that the spray prevents further attack in the vast majority of cases.

Sunscreen: Catching a lot of fish during a trip may make a trip seem fantastic, but unless you were adequately lathered up with sunscreen, the short-term memory of the trip will be less than stellar. Always carry a small two-ounce bottle of sunscreen with you, no matter what the size of the water you're fishing.

Polarized glasses: Anyone who fishes with them knows why they are essential. With these glasses you can see fish, the bottom structure for wading, and your fly, even with intense surface glare, and you can continue to see all these things for years to come when a fly comes unexpectedly shooting at your eye. Without polarized glasses, you cannot see fish, you cannot see your fly when fishing in the direction of the sun, and an unexpected fly shooting at your eye will turn you into Sammy Davis Jr. If you don't currently wear polarized glasses, try them—you'll never go back.

Snacks and drinks: During my life as an angler, I have found that I am almost never hungry while I fish. I think that by devoting my attention and focus on fishing, things like food fall on the back burner. However, as soon as the fishing is over, hunger can kick in like lightning. I always pack some beef jerky, nuts, or energy bars, though any food that won't melt or crumble is a good choice. As for a drink, always carry a small, 20 oz. bottle of water or sports drink, especially if your fishing takes you more than a mile from your car. Once on the stream, bury your bottle in the water so that it will cool off while you're fishing.

Food and drink is optional when you are fishing from your car, but anytime you venture more than a couple miles from your car, it becomes much more important. When you get a long way away, it can be easy to get lost or to overextend yourself. Make sure you have some emergency food and water just in case.

Daypack: I used to think this was just an easy way to make fishing extra comfortable. Many trips to remote streams have proven the importance of taking a day pack loaded with some extra food, drink, clothes, maps, and emergency supplies (fire starters, matches, emergency blankets, and flashlight). During the course of a good fishing day, it is easy to get overextended, and the extra stuff you bring in a daypack can keep you comfortable and alive.

Climbing rope: Climbing rope is not a necessity, but if you are planning on going to tough-to-access streams, this can open up some totally virgin water. There is a stream near my house that flows over a waterfall in the Columbia Gorge. The water below the falls is fished heavily by anglers and traversed by dozens of hikers and tourists every day. Above the falls, a trail hovers between 50 and 100 feet above the creek, with a very steep slope carpeted with ferns blocking any unaided descent. Nobody fishes the creek. One day, I decided to hike in with a 100-foot length of rope purchased at a hardware store. I tied it to a tree, and threw the rest down the slope. Then, carefully, I moved down the hill, using the rope to stabilize my descent. I encountered some superb fishing for wild cutthroat in the 7- to 12-inch range. After I was done, I returned to my rope, climbed back up, and hiked back to the car. Ever since that enlightening experience I have packed a length of rope in my truck.

A harness and belaying setup can be useful if you want to access water below sheer cliffs. As cool as this may sound at first, it isn't a great idea because if you are fishing where you need these to get to the water, it is likely that upstream and downstream movement along the stream is virtually impossible.

Vest: Vests are as essential for small-stream fishing as they are for large-stream fishing. Many articles and book chapters lament the virtues of leaving your fishing vest at home when on small streams. They advocate wearing shirts and shorts with lots of pockets, jamming them with all your gear, and walking awkwardly around with things bouncing around everywhere. This is all done in the name of omitting the weight and bulk of the vest. Like walking somewhere because you get too tired driving the car there, this logic makes no sense. It is a tired fantasy to fish a small stream with nothing more than your rod, a box of flies, and a spool of tippet. We all enjoy doing this on occasion, but why treat your small-stream fishing as something less important than your other fishing? By omitting the vest, you do nothing except leave yourself less organized and less prepared. If a fishing vest is so heavy and oppressive that it is a burden to wear, why wear it on a large stream? If it is too heavy, maybe weightlifting should replace fly-fishing as a hobby.

Landing net: It is a rare occurrence for contemporary anglers to be on a stream without the most archaic piece of fishing equipment. The ironic thing is that angler and fish are generally better off without it, especially on small streams. Nets attached to the vest or the belt gravitate towards shoreline trees and brush with magnetic certainty. The elastic cords, unfortunately, win most battles with the foliage, and return the net towards you with supersonic velocity. Many anglers lose fish right at the net because of the awkward contortions required to get a squirming fish at the end of a nine-foot rod

into a net in your other hand. As for the fish, many are needlessly harmed by anglers playing them excessively; so that they glide, exhausted, into the net. Still others are harmed by spinning around in the nets, which causes them undue damage to their scales and gills. (Many anglers think that by using knotless nets they don't harm fish. Whilst this style is preferable to the knotted nylon nets in most sporting goods stores, the fish still can do plenty of damage to themselves.) Nets are one thing that all small-stream anglers should omit from their standard equipment list.

I am not the only one who holds this belief. The English great John Goddard claims it has been a "long, long time" since he last carried a net on a river. Also, some British fish authorities now recommend prohibiting landing nets as a way to increase the survival of released fish. (I will discuss some release techniques later in the book).

Stomach pump: I never have been a fan of stomach pumps, if it is only to figure out what a fish is eating at the moment. If I cannot solve a hatch visually, I will not pump a fish to solve the problem at hand. Why torture a prisoner of war to get his secrets, while reconnaissance will eventually get the same answers? Stomach pumps should not be used as a way to cheat your way into the selective processes of the trout. Careful observation and drift samples will let you solve tough fishing conditions and give you the answers you need without torturing a fish.

Unless you are planning to do a detailed study of a particular stream, keep the stomach pump at home. Stomach pumps should be used by biologists and researchers, and only if they are properly trained in doing so. Improper use of stomach pumps can kill fish, and it is ethically questionable to kill fish for something as trivial as solving a particular hatch.

Chapter 3
Small-Stream Ecology: Rocks, Trees and Fish

After years and years of fishing, when your hair silvers and a good breakfast sounds more appealing than the sunrise spinner fall, you may have several streams you can call your own. The hatches, habitat, fish, water temperatures, trees, grasses, and rocks never occur in absentia, they perform a magical waltz together that you follow in time with your fly rod. Through decades of experience, sown in August heat and February snowstorms, you know the rhythms of the stream and exactly what you need to do to catch fish. This is the special reward that can be achieved over a lifetime of trial and error, or during a couple days with a book on trout-stream ecology.

Stream ecology. Sounds like work. It sounds like something some college student majoring in environmental studies should study, not an angler. Surprisingly, few things can improve your angling success on small streams more than a solid knowledge of stream ecology and entomology. Why would this information be more important on small streams than on large streams? Because factors that influence stream's organic collage—riparian vegetation, water chemistry, solar radiation, substrate makeup, and hydrology—are much more direct and unique on creeks. Big rivers receive water over a vast watershed and all the unique properties of individual creeks are blended into one big homogeneous broth.

Tributary creeks to major rivers can be quite different, though they are in the same geographic area. On a large, famous river I have fished, four very different streams—one spring creek, one glacier-fed stream, one lake-originating creek, and one standard freestone stream—all serve as tributaries. Not surprisingly, they hold different species of fish, which feed on different hatches, and occupy different habitats, though the creeks are only separated by 20 miles. All of these imortant things were caused by conditions considered unimportant by some anglers: primarily geology and plant growth.

Talk of stream ecology is foreign to most angling texts but should not be ignored by anglers. Ernie Schwiebert in his classic *Trout* said, "Understanding the chemistry and biology of a trout stream is becoming indispensable for a modern angler, and in the knowledge of its ecology lie many secrets we could never learn from the fishing itself." Besides just tangential knowledge that ecology can help anglers with, ecology can teach us things that have a direct impact on our fishing, even down to our fly choice. In *Stoneflies for the Angler*, Eric Leiser and Robert Boyle mention that, "Given the correct association of nymphs with specific leaves, the day comes, as crazy as it sounds, when the knowledgeable angler will know what pattern to use simply by identifying the trees along the banks." On small streams, the importance of these things is so critical that it cannot be omitted by any comprehensive text.

Many anglers think this kind of detail is overkill, even those who spend hours arguing the virtues and pitfalls of choosing a Simms vest over one made by Columbia Sportswear. Trout are far more concerned with the shade of trees, rather than the shade of the latest in angling sportswear. Yet, "Why make it more complicated than it has to be?" is the cry from those who wish to revel in their own ignorance.

Knowledge of stream ecology can teach many things that would take years to learn on the water. It can help with everything from approach techniques, to knowing likely hatches, to knowing how a stream responds to a rainstorm. Given a good knowledge of stream ecology, a learned angler can know all of these things about a new stream without even wetting a line. Now knowing all this may not help you catch fish in a particular instance, but knowledge puts the ball in your court.

Small-Stream Geology
This may be the most critical factor in determining how well a stream produces trout, yet book after book ignores the once-removed relationship between rocks and trout.

All trout streams start with a rainstorm. However, not all of their water comes from surface runoff. Much of that water is absorbed by mosses, plants, and organic debris before it can reach a perennial stream. What doesn't run off, or is not absorbed by plants, percolates through the rocks to join the vast system of underground seepages and reservoirs. It is then released through cracks and holes, to flow back into streams, infused with new minerals that enhance production.

If you don't buy this story, check this out. Just think how it may not rain for three months, yet a small stream still flows. Water must be slowly released for this to occur. If no additional water were is infused into the system, the creek would be dry in hours or days. Certain types of rocks, such as igneous (volcanic) rocks, are most likely to see a lot of permeation and release of water. Obviously, this little geological factoid holds major importance for anglers who enjoy fishing in the summertime, yet we still ignore how relevant geology is to our angling.

Rocks are where our trout streams get their character. What minerals the water absorbs from these rocks plays a major role in how productive a trout stream is. What may matter most, in terms of chemistry, is the alkalinity and pH level of the water. Hard waters, those with a high alkalinity, are the best for growing trout. A stream with highly alkaline water may support 20 times the amount of trout and their food supply than a similar stream with acidic water. While it may take a week of fishing to determine the number and size of fish in a stream, this cornerstone element of trout growth and abundance can be revealed to an angler in less than one second with the help of a strip of pH paper. This information will quickly let you know the likelihood of quality fish inhabiting the stream. Learning other aspects of the ecological mix of particular streams is just as simple. Knowing these things can allow the exploring angler to locate productive waters without spending years playing guess-and-check trying to locate productive waters.

In high school, our advanced biology class would take trips to local streams and do water quality surveys. This was my favorite part of the class, and I would usually swap fishing info with my teacher to ensure my position in the Macroinvertebrates group assigned to collect various quantities of trout food. I hated nothing more than having to do time with the Water Chemistry group, fiddling with endless gadgets and meters and doing complicated tests to decipher everything from phosphate levels to dissolved oxygen content.

I learned over time that chemistry is extremely important when it comes to cultivating various kinds of foliage for insects to eat. Nitrates, phosphorus, dissolved oxygen, dissolved carbon dioxide, magnesium, sulfates, chloride and calcium all play their roles, some more important than others. Small changes in the quantity of these elements and compounds rarely will have an immediate effect on trout. Rather, they will cause a change in primary production.

Primary production in stream ecosystems is most often recognized as the growth of algae, the foundation for all other aquatic life in the stream. A stream with good primary production will provide food for more aquatic insects, in turn providing a larger food base for trout. Without the seemingly unimportant presence of algae, most of our trout streams would be bereft of fish. Water chemistry influences this aspect of nature significantly, and an angler can likely tell how large and abundant the trout are in a stream by simply testing the water chemistry.

At 8,000 feet, this small stream would be fishless without an open canopy to spark photosynthesis and a rich layer of algae on the rocks.

For all the hoopla about different chemicals, the limiting factor for primary production on most small streams is actually the amount of available sunlight that reaches the water. You can dump buckets of nitrogen and lime into a stream, yet without sunlight, photosynthesis will not occur. This is why most of the better small streams have rather open canopies where plenty of sunlight can fuel aquatic production. This creates the queer result that small-stream production actually benefits from forest fires and clearcuts in the short-run (1-25 years after occurrence). Many small streams in Yellowstone Park produced their best fish ever in the ten years following the forest fires of 1988.

Besides contributing to the chemistry of a stream, geological types play an important role in how the stream reacts to storms and drought. Storms can wreck havoc on a small stream, turning it into milky sludge within hours of a heavy rainfall. Certain types of rocks, particularly shale and sandstone, do nothing to help this process at all. These rocks are easily eroded and can cloud a stream up quickly. Another thing about these soft rocks, particularly shale, is that a hill or mountain can be perpetually eroding into the stream. This is the case with the Gardner River in Yellowstone. The huge ridge to the east of the stream is slowly eroding into the river, causing it to be perpetually off-color and prone to milkiness after a storm. For many anglers, this is a turn off, but for others it is a gold mine. Anglers in-the-know are aware that where this kind of perpetual erosion occurs, a disproportionate number of terrestrial worms and crane fly larvae get washed into the stream and heavily contribute to the trout diet.

Another geological feature that is important to anglers is glaciers. Glacier-fed streams take on the inverse behavior of most small streams: they get cloudy during hot, dry weather, yet in cold (and even slightly damp) weather, they can be surprisingly clear. Streams that flow from glaciers are terrible during the hot summer months, when the heat melts the dirty ice and the water picks up plenty of sediment as it trickles through the fine silicate fields that surround many Western glaciers. In the Cascade Mountains of the Pacific coast, several streams are worthless between April and September, when warm weather causes them to take on the appearance of chocolate milk. However, glacier-fed streams can be surprisingly good when cool weather keeps the water relatively clear. Many anglers ignore them totally because they see them in the summer when they are full of silt. The native trout that inhabit these streams are surprisingly resilient and tolerant of the sediment, and some streams have very good populations that see virtually no pressure from anglers.

Porous rock, especially lava, will absorb a large amount of water and release it throughout the year as springs. Drought conditions that leave most small streams as emaciated trickles rarely are strong enough to affect the flow of water through the springs. Finding these kind of waters is not hard; it requires neither decades of experience nor the laborious calling of dozens of fly shops. All you need is a geological map and a topo map that shows major springs,

and you can often find plenty of water to fish even during the driest summer.

The moral of all this rock talk is to think about how your stream starts. Good trout streams do not appear out of thin air, they appear out of rocks and soil and sky and they take on all the positive or negative qualities that each of these possesses. Because of their size, and the unique geological character of small watersheds, small-stream fisheries can either be made or broken by nothing more than the rocks they flow over.

Small-Stream Hydrology: Structure and Habitat

Besides bad approach techniques, the reason anglers find small streams difficult is due to an inability to read the water. Like many other things in fishing, understanding trout habitat is often ignored and disparaged, while rod choice, fly choice, and casting are trumpeted. But if you have the perfect fly, a $500 rod, and can cast with the accuracy of a smart bomb, it all means nothing if you are throwing it all at water that is barren of trout.

Reading the water on a big stream is a training wheel for reading water on small streams. On big streams, things are hard to miss: pools are the size of baseball fields, riffles are the length of football fields, and Stevie Wonder couldn't miss the runs. In small streams, everything is reduced. Pockets that hold trout are the size of shoeboxes. Everything is so compressed, productive and unproductive water mixing and swirling into each other, it looks like a maelstrom of trout habitat. Because of the compressed and diverse make-up of small streams, spacing between a prime lie and barren water can be as little as six inches. It takes a proficient eye to decipher the collage of small-stream trout habitat.

The experienced small-stream angler can immediately eliminate 80-95% of the water on a small stream. A comparable discriminate angler on a large river probably can only realistically eliminate about 70% of the water. Even with only 30% of the water in play, hundreds of casts are needed to effectively cover a 100-yard run. The small-stream angler can target their 15% of the stream in a handful of casts. This results in a much higher cast-to-hookup ratio for small-stream anglers. The best small-stream anglers can average as high as an 80% cast-to-hookup ratio—four times that of a selective and exceptionally skilled large river angler. This abundance of successful casts is just one reason why small-stream anglers love their trade so much.

Rocks

In Tom Rosenbauer's fine book on trout habitat, *Reading Trout Water*, he astutely writes about rocks in their own chapter, for most other stream features are simply extrapolations on this central theme. On small streams, it is even more important. Knowing how trout hold in relation to rocks in a variety of small-stream conditions will immediately let you catch more, and larger, fish.

To the consternation of students, economics textbooks are obligated to use oversimplified models to describe complex realities. Following that example, in order to describe how to look at rocks, we will look at the case of a single rock in the middle of a constant-velocity run: something that rarely occurs in rivers, but happens all the time in fishing books. But, before we can discuss what the rock does to the water and to the trout, you must find them. Exposed rocks are easy to find, but submerged ones are tough, especially in low light. To spot submerged rocks, I look for three things: the rock itself, a pocket of lighter substrate (this is the finer sand and gravel that can settle in the slower currents behind a rock), or the riffle or "V" on the surface. If you can only see the "V" on the surface, the rock must be further upstream, so try to estimate the current speed and depth of the stream to locate of the rock.

We all know that trout will hold behind rocks, but exactly where is often misunderstood. The rock creates a "teardrop" of reduced current, starting with the round cushion in front of the rock, tapering to a "focal point" downstream of the rock. Despite what many anglers think, there are rarely trout immediately downstream of the rock, because the very slow current offers little access to food. The sides of the rock have an accelerated current, and unless there is a log there or something to break the current, there will be few trout holding there. The sides of the teardrop are much more desirable because they offer slow water for chillin', with close access to swift currents for the grub. Though these areas will hold trout, I usually put them in the back of my mind until I've fished the prime areas, because fish that hold in these lies are generally smaller than the trout in the prime parts of the rock system.

The two prime locations are in the cushion in front of the rock and at the focal point where the two currents converge below the rock. The cushion is nice because it gives fish the first shot at all the food: the other fish in the rock system only eat what the fish upfront misses. This spot also offers excellent current protection because of the little scour hole that occurs in front of most rocks. On the other hand, the focal point is nice because it is where both currents rejoin, offering more food choices than the fish on either side of the teardrop have. But which of the two prime lies is best? This is often debated, and rarely answered. I have always believed that when there is a lack of overhead protection, the cushion in front of rocks is the best spot because the proximity of rock affords the fish a degree of security. On streams with plenty of overhead cover or deep water, making predation less of a worry, the focal point will hold the most, or best, trout.

Classic pocket water is really just an amalgam of single and double-rock situations.

In very fast and very slow streams, trout won't hold immediately behind rocks. In fast streams, the water is too turbulent for trout to comfortably hold—it's like trying to maintain position in a washing machine. The cushion in front of the rock is compressed, and few fish can hold there either. What results is a concentration of trout near the end of the white water behind the rock, where the current rejoins after splitting around the rock.

In slow streams, the current can be slack behind rocks, not fast enough to bring a satisfactory amount of food down to the trout. In this situation, trout can still be found at the cushion in front of the rock, and at the convergence of the currents below the rock. However, the best habitat for trout under these conditions is along the sides of rocks. The current here is compressed and accelerated. And when the current is concentrated and accelerated, so is the food, making this place advantageous when the current is slow enough to be manageable. The rock also offers production, increasing the value of this lie even more.

Pocket water is nothing more than many rocks in the same area. Pocket water is confusing to many beginners, but is excellent trout habitat because it offers depth, overhead protection (thanks to white water, foam pockets, and rocks), food production, current protection (with rocks and debris everywhere, pocket water is rich in dead spots), and oxygenated water. Since many small streams are predominantly pocket water, it is crucial to learn how to fish it if you want to be a consistently successful fish-catching machine.

In pocket water, you should look at each rock individually, as we have discussed earlier in this section. (Pocket water is like the SAT exam: it looks overwhelming in its entirety, but if you attack each problem individually, it is quite simple.) Pocket water fishing is really no different than fishing single rocks, but there are a couple places you should focus on in particular: multiple rocks in the same current lane, and rocks adjacent to the primary current flow.

Each time a rock breaks up the current, the current lane will lose some of its kinetic energy (force). When another large rock is located inside the teardrop of broken current below a rock, the current is reduced even more. If the second rock is located near the focal point of the teardrop, the cushion in front of this second rock will often hold the best fish in the area. It has all the advantage of the focal point behind a single rock, but with even less current to battle (because of the cushion) and it offers the protection of the second rock. Though this spot is widely ignored by other anglers, once you hook some of the fish that use this habitat, you won't repeat their mistake again.

The other place to focus your attention on in pocket water is the rocks adjacent to the main current flow. Not all stretches of pocket water, especially in smaller creeks, have a visible main current channel. But, those that do offer an express food line for the fish, and this makes the protected water on the edges of it desirable locales for trout. Trout will tend to hold on the main current side of the teardrops that form behind rocks. Often, the other side of the teardrop will be totally devoid of trout, and only worth a secondary cast.

Banks

Banks are often described as the most underfished parts of rivers. There are dozens of articles out there about how to fish bank water and why it is so important for trout. In the big rivers of the West, where the middle of the river is deep and swift, this helped me catch innumerable trout. However, when I tried to transfer this success to small streams, I found one major difference. The trout weren't there.

Why would trout be so fond of banks in a 100-foot-wide stream, yet avoid them religiously in one that is 10-feet-wide? The answer is simple—predators. Small-stream trout hanging around the shoreline are an easy snack. There is no shortage of creatures that would love to dine on an eight-inch trout: mergansers, osprey, herons, kingfishers, mink, bears, otters, raccoons, and that runny-nosed kid sitting on his bucket dunking a worm. Banks that do hold trout on small streams offer protection from these marauders. Tree roots, large boulders, logs, undercut banks, and banks with easy access to deep water will hold trout much better than a barren flat on the inside edge of a bend pool.

The best banks for trout occur on streams that flow between steep shorelines rather than those with a flat relief. Flat relief generally means flat sand, gravel, or grass banks, none of which affords the protection essential for trout to survive. Steep banks offer the trout a nice supply of terrestrial insects and close access to deep water. Thanks to the legendary undercut bank, angling credibility has been decimated by decades of tall tales. Everyone who has wet a line has heard stories of big undercut banks with Leviathanesque trout, (tradition dictates that it always be a brown trout), finning in wait for a disorientated minnow, adventurous rodent, or wayward toddler to venture too near to its lair. While undercut banks are often overemphasized by anglers, they can be one of the most important stream features for trout.

I have found out through plenty of fruitless casts that undercut banks, with currents plowing into their banks at ninety-degree angles, aren't nearly as perfect as angling legend makes them out to be. These currents often gouge a deep recess under the bank, and few trout will hold at the lip of the bank, where the force of the current is much more intense. Even those that do, hold there rarely, and will dart forward (out of the bank) to strike your fly, while they could just sit patiently under the protection of the bank and wait for the fly to reach them. The trout could wait forever, but your fly will rarely reach them deep under the bank, for your fly will either snag on the dangling roots, or drag because of the current lanes you must cast through to float it down to this point. This is one of those rare occasions where a small-stream angler will turn to the streamer as a savior, for it offers a hefty morsel to coerce a trout from its lair, and drag on the fly will not effect a trout's motivation to annihilate it.

Undercut banks that have current striking them between a 100- and 135-degree angle are much more hospitable to trout and standard dry-fly and nymphing presentations. Trout hold here closer to the lip of the bank, and will more readily move into the current to take drifting food than their aforementioned brethren will.

Sometimes, undercut banks can hold the only trout in a stream. An early September hike into a remote Wyoming mountain creek revealed a sparse trickle braiding down three pebble-strewn channels, nary two feet across each. When these channels joined each other, the stream was a maximum of three-feet-across and seven-inches-deep, with a wide swath of rocky streambed on either side of the stream—hardly prime trout habitat. Using as much stealth as I could muster, I spent an hour throwing fifty-foot casts from my knees (tougher than it sounds on the softball-sized rocks of the dry streambed), with not a single mercy rise from a small fish. I hiked up and down the stream about two miles trying to salvage something out of this trip that required a five-mile hike, with a 2100' elevation gain. Finally, I stumbled onto a section of stream that ran far back under a willow bank. It was the only place that offered good overhead protection in the whole stream, and if there was a trout missed by the otters and grizzly bears, it would be here. After an inordinate amount of watching and positioning, a long cast produced a ten-inch cutthroat that seemed like a ten-pounder after such a slow day. As I neared the bank to land and release the fish, I noticed a flicker between the roots that extended into the water. I splashed through the pool—the term is used loosely here, it was probably the size of a pool table, including the undercut portion, and probably as deep—just to spook whatever it was back out so I could get a look at it as I was still playing the original fish. Then the pool exploded with over a hundred trout, some as large as fifteen inches, darting every which way to escape the creature that had

discovered their shelter. Almost every trout in that section of stream was holding in there; they wisely figured that overhead security was worth more than competition-free feeding in the exposed riffles and runs.

Occasions like this are few and far between, but they eveal the importance of probing every type of trout habitat when the usual water is not producing fish.

Bedrock

A sure way to get great photo ops and crappy trout fishing is to go to a stream that flows primarily over ledgerock or bedrock. The beautiful cliffs and pools formed by this type of structure are sights to behold, but these streams lack the diversity that life needs to thrive. Insects have few places to avoid the current, as do the trout. A heavy flood will scour out insect life, leaving the stream nearly barren for a year or more.

If you are forced to fish a bedrock stream, look for both trout and insects anywhere cobbles and pebbles collect in the bedrock. Here, the gentle turbulence caused by the uneven bottom creates a hospitable place for trout to live. Another place to look is along a bedrock ledge in slow water. Here, trout will hold along the recesses and irregularities of the rock, darting into the slow run for bites of food. In faster water, these small recesses cannot offer the dead spots trout require for rest. Yet, trout can often be found at the downstream edge of the bedrock ledge, where a large dead spot or eddy is created. This location often holds a few trout of respectable size.

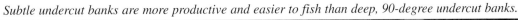

Subtle undercut banks are more productive and easier to fish than deep, 90-degree undercut banks.

While bedrock is poor habitat for trout, it does offer exceptional wading. You may think your felt boots were re-soled with suction cups when you wade through deep, swift waters with ease. For this reason, I like to get out on a bedrock stream, covering several miles of beautiful scenery, while searching for the few precious spots that do hold trout.

Riffles

Riffles are considered the oxygenated food factories of trout streams because they are shallow and light can penetrate them, sparking photosynthesis and all the goodies which that entails. We also know that trout, occasionally large ones, will move into these areas at certain times of the day in order to feed. This is the standard big-stream attitude towards this type of aquatic feature.

Conversely, the small-stream angler knows that because of their shallow depth, aquatic production occurs throughout the small stream: in riffles, runs, eddies, pockets, and any pool of reasonable depth. Riffles in small streams are also so shallow (rarely more than eight-inches deep) that larger trout would be totally exposed to overhead predation whenever they ventured in to feed. Because trout who worked so hard to reach adulthood are rarely willing to die in order to pick up one or two more drifting nymphs, riffles in small streams become primarily a nursery for young trout in the 3-to 5-inch range. Larger fish will rarely leave the security of their prime lies for a couple more morsels of food when they are getting enough food already. For these reasons, the small-stream angler will almost immediately eliminate riffle water from their hit list while fishing.

There are some important exceptions to this rule. One takes place when there is low, warm water of the summer months. During this time, the dissolved oxygen content of the water is so low that trout can only breathe easily in riffle water, where the broken surface helps integrate atmospheric oxygen into the water. I first noticed this phenomenon on the Firehole River in Yellowstone Park, where by July water temps push 80°F and trout start migrating to smaller, cooler tributaries. Most anglers give up on this stream in late June because they think the trout are gone. The assumption that the trout are gone is derived from the lack of trout caught in, and seen rising, in the classic broads (flats) of the Firehole. At this time of year, most of the trout haven't yet left the main river, though they stack up throughout the riffle waters. Even in riffle water that are just deep enough to spill over wading boots, trout will lie fin-to-fin trying to eat as much food as they can before the lack of oxygen drives them out. Here, an angler can land trout after trout until their arm reaches the proverbial soreness that signifies a successful day. I have seen similar behavior on dozens of other small streams during low water, and always start searching the riffles after casts to likely flats and pocket water come up empty.

Another case where trout will feed heavily in riffles is when there is a relatively dense emergence of riffle insects like *Epeorus* or *Cinygmula* mayflies and *Glossosoma* or *Brachycentrus* caddis. Though small-stream trout prefer slower, more protected currents, the need to make the most out of the rare, dense emergence situation will drive trout from their normally prime lies in slower water to feed in riffles. When this happens, and it isn't often, even large trout can be found in shallow water churning up the surface side-by-side with their smaller brethren. Usually this situation doesn't need my reiteration: if you are on the stream, you'll recognize it and react properly. One word though, sometimes these small fish can be surprisingly picky during hatches. Even though this is fast water, standard attractors catch a fraction of the fish that a plausible imitation will. If it's small caddis, go to an X-caddis rather than a Humpy, and you'll be pleasantly surprised.

The final case of when riffles are important is during the spawning season. Most species of salmon, steelhead, trout, and whitefish prefer to spawn over a fine gravel bottom, something found in abundance in deeper riffles and shallow runs. When this happens, the smaller resident fish can almost always be found at the end of the riffle, (or the head of the pool or run below the riffle) packed in, gorging themselves on eggs.

Runs or Flats

When the riffle of a large stream finally runs out of momentum, it usually morphs at some indistinguishable and ever-changing point into a run. Runs are the heart and soul of a large stream, providing living quarters for most adult trout in streams. The same is usually also true for small streams. While pocket water and pools might hold better trout, runs offer currents slow enough for comfort but fast enough to bring food by, and they usually are deep enough that trout can feel safe. This appeals to the majority of fish in any stream.

A small stream with quality flats is one you want to keep to yourself. Pocket water and plunge pools are just fine, but can get monotonous. Flats give you the opportunity to use a variety of techniques to catch fish in a variety of moods. Small streams are notorious for needing only a 3X

When on open flats on small streams, the angler is best off waiting and looking for rises or cruisers.

and a McGinty, but flats and runs can turn this axiom into angling suicide if you follow it religiously.

Small-stream trout in runs often will gravitate to some sort of cover, be it rocks, logs, or overhanging brush. Because the current is slow, trout feel vulnerable to overhead predation, especially if the run is shallow. This is fine for the angler, because these pieces of cover act like a X on a map, showing where the hidden trout lie. Make your first casts in a run towards pieces of overhead cover, and you will likely locate the biggest fish in the area.

Some flats offer little cover, and fish will be cruising for food. Even in streams with dense weed growth, trout will often cruise for food when the current is not swift enough to bring them as much as they would like. Flats conditions are usually the only type of water where fish will cruise while feeding: the current is too great for this behavior in a riffle, and trout hanging out in pools are generally not there for the abundance of food. Fish cruising in this way are difficult to approach and cast to, and extreme care should be taken when working with them. If you are fishing a new stream and approach a long stretch of flat water, don't walk right up to the shoreline to gaze for fish. Cruising fish will scare as soon as a threat shows up on the scene. Get back from the shore, find some cover, and watch fish in their cruising patterns.

In spring creeks, chalkstreams, or tailwaters, the flats sections are areas of dense weed growth and complex currents that anglers both love and loathe. Though the current in these areas is rarely swift, there is enough to put the weeds in motion, which in turn caresses the surface into dozens (or hundreds, or thousands) of vortices and microcurrents that perpetually change as the position of each stalk of weed moves. The result is a puzzle where the pieces change with every glance. Evasive action must be taken by the angler, and long leaders, careful casting, and plenty of observation is needed to have success under these conditions. Fish that dwell in these waters are usually spoiled and have plenty of food to choose from, so they are in no rush to eat your imitation if it is not presented on their terms.

After all these kind words, let's not get too carried away with the positives that flats and runs offer. If a stream is composed primarily of runs, unless it is a rich chalkstream, it usually has a lot less food than a stream with more riffle water. Shallow runs with little cover can easily be barren water if there are good populations of predators. In small, low gradient streams, shallow runs often replace pools as resting places for fish. In these places, fish can be everywhere, but totally unwilling to feed. Finally, fish in shallow, exposed runs may be wary of rising, lest they become easy food for birds of prey, yet they will feed on nymphs. This requires sight nymphing, a technique that can drive many anglers to the nut house. The moral of all this is to look at runs and flats critically before investing all your time into fishing them.

Islands

Islands on large streams are often magnets for anglers. The side channel usually offers slower water with good habitat,

This island splits the creek into two small flows, which are too shallow for substantial trout. The best lie is below the island, where they converge.

and the riffle created where the currents converge on the downstream side of the island is a coveted nymphing area. However, on all but the largest small streams, the small-stream angler should fear islands like the plague.

Islands are a problem for small-stream anglers because they divide an already meager flow. A five-foot-wide stream is already a difficult enough place for trout to survive in, and when that is broken down into a pair of two-foot-wide trickles, you are left with nothing but barren water. A group of four friends and I fished a mile-long section of a four-foot-wide mountain creek one time. Because of the diminutive nature of the stream, we had to split up to fish. I had some phenomenal fishing, landing over 60 fish in the seven- to ten-inch range in a little over an hour. I expected my friends to report similar successes, but when they each reported only two to six fish, we were all shocked. After some quick questioning, I found out they had selected sections of the stream with several small islands that broke up the flow. These guys were throwing perfect casts with the perfect flies, but it didn't matter because the fish simply weren't there.

If you do run into an island on a very small stream, make a cast to the "V" where currents converge behind the island. This is a coveted spot for fish, offering uncontested feeding on all the food from the uninhabited riffles on either side of the island. After casting to this area, omit water on the sides of the island, unless there is some exceptional cover or a plunge pool that looks fish-worthy.

Eddies

Eddies and whirlpools are classic places to look for trout on large, turbulent streams. Eddies offer a slower current and a constant fresh food supply from the nearby faster water, so they are magnets for trout. Eddies occur where a point juts out into a stream or a big rock or log redirects some of the current so that the shoreline portion flows upstream. Almost every eddy also has an eye, where the current is nearly stagnant. Often this area has an eclectic collection of bubbles, foam, insects, and debris that betrays its exact location. Trout will hold in this area as well as along the constant currents at either side of the eddy.

As fabulous as eddies are for trout habitat, they are nightmares for fly casters. Conflicting currents cause flies to go one way and the line to go another, allowing only short drifts before drag sets in. On large streams, this problem is minimized because the current lanes are wider and you can move around to get into better casting position. You can also use big mends of the line to keep your fly drifting drag-free for an extended period of time. With patience and practice, a big-river angler can cope with the problems eddies present.

On small streams, everything is miniaturized. The eddy itself is only three feet across, about the size of a single current lane in a big-river eddy. A tiny six-inch mend is needed in place of that six-foot mend used on the big river, yet it is nearly impossible to pull off without jerking your fly out of the eddy. An eddy on the other side of stream, say behind a semi-submerged stump, is nearly impossible to fish unless you can keep all your line off the water or migrate around the stream so you can present from the same side.

Because eddies gather an inordinate supply of leaf and plant debris, they often harbor the majority of shredder insects like *Paraleptophlebia* mayflies and Limnephilid, *Amiocentrus*, and *Lepidostoma* caddis. During an emergence period, these areas become magnets for trout, and several trout can hold in a relatively small eddy with several more on the downstream edge, all feeding in relative harmony. I guess the abundance of food makes peace more energy efficient than chasing out squatting trout. I have observed three trout in a small eddy feeding heavily on *Amiocentrus* pupae which had a pupation bed of nearly 1000 cocoons in the eye of the eddy. The bugs would pop out of their cases, and though the pupae put up tremendous swimming efforts, few escaped the mouths of the trout holding only a couple inches downstream.

Classic Pools

Describing pools in a book is akin to the textbook habit of using models: reality is never as clean as the description. Every fishing book you read describes a pool with a head, body, and tail, each perfectly formed, symmetrical in shape and girth. However, like snowflakes, each pool is unique, with its own set of problems that confront each angler. Classic pools in small streams are even more variable in their characteristics and no amount of my blabbering will replace experience when it comes to understanding them.

The basic pool structure goes like this: throat (head), tongue, body, and tailout. Of course, each of these main features can be amended with rocks, eddies, seams, and logs, making classic pools extremely diverse habitat structures.

The throat, or head of the pool, is the most variable kind of structure in a pool. If the current is gentle or if there is some additional cover (rocks, logs, etc.), it can be loaded with average-sized trout. During the reduced flows of summertime, throats can be fine places to find them. However, if the current rushes in without obstruction, there will often be no trout at all. White water at the throat of a pool means it should be almost universally ignored.

The tongue of the pool is located in the upper third where the current still is quite noticeable. The seams along each side of the tongue will almost always contain some good trout. An eddy created on the sides of the tongue is also a good bet for better-than-average trout on a small stream. The tongue is usually shallower than the body of the pool, and fish are more receptive to dry flies. Because of the current, upstream orientation of the trout, and broken surface, you can usually approach quite close to the trout.

The body of a pool is more often than not a wasteland for small-stream anglers. If the body is shallow, the fish will position themselves where there is more current and surface turbulence. If the pool is deep, you can rarely coerce a trout to expend the energy to come to the surface for a dry fly. Nymphing will work well if you can reach the bottom, though if you don't get deep enough, few quality fish are naïve enough to strike flies drifting through the middle of the water column. Unless there is some extra cover like a log, stump, or huge rock in the body of the pool, I will usually skip it and look for water where fooling quality trout is easier. Small pools, less than the size of a large pickup truck, should be concentrated on, but the bodies of larger pools can easily be passed over by the discriminate angler.

Tailouts are the money spots of pools, though they are the most difficult for anglers to approach and make presentations to. Most big fish we spot at the bottoms of pools are holding at the tailout before we spook them by walking up. The tailout is where the current accelerates, focusing all the food drifting through the pool on one narrow lane where trout can feast at will. Because of the rapid reduction in depth, there is usually a dead spot in the current, even where there is a clean gravel bottom. It is the perfect spot for a nice trout to set-up shop, and anglers seeking big trout on small streams should begin their search here.

Unfortunately, this perfect habitat is not nearly as heavenly for the angler to fish. Approaching from downstream, you can stay out of view of the trout, but you rarely can prevent your fly from shooting downstream once your line catches the swift water below the pool. Approaching from upstream, you risk spooking the fish while getting in casting position. The casts must be accurate, and you have to fool a fish that is in no rush to decide whether to consume your offering. Assuming you didn't spook the fish with the approach or cast, the same current upwelling that creates a dead spot for trout to hold in also tends to push your nymph up high, away from the trout holding tight to the bottom. For these reasons, I like to make Half-and-Half casts (covered later) from slightly upstream of the trout, remaining away from the bank. If the fish is large, plan out what you will do if the fish races into the swift water below the pool, before your fear becomes reality.

All in all, don't overestimate the value of classic pools as many baitfishermen do. Know where the fish are, know where the quality fish are, and limit your casting so that you target the better fish in the pool first, then worry about the runts if they still are hanging around.

Bend Pools

Bend pools are the lifeblood of small meadow streams and can also be important in suburban environments where bankside improvements have been made. Bend pools almost always follow the same archetype: fast riffle at the head; deep pool, usually with an undercut bank; shallow tailout into another riffle. The great thing about bend pools is they rarely occur in isolation. Meandering meadow streams are usually characterized by a series of bend pools numbering in the dozens for every linear mile of meadow. Bend pools are also one of the special habitats unique to small streams, being far more common on creeks than on larger rivers.

Bend pools, because of the hydrology that creates them, are often the best habitat for large trout in small streams. They offer a riffle above it, churning out trout food 24-hours a day, deep, slow water for protection, and a smooth tailout perfect for feasting on adult insects. This is water that every four-inch fingerling aspires to. On small creeks, many of these pools have only one permanent resident: the alpha trout for that section of stream. The big fish will defend the territory aggressively, chasing out smaller trout trying to squat on their prime lie.

Big fish holes can often be located easily during the unproductive noon hour. Simply let a dry fly drift through the pool. If you get a couple small fish splashing at it, you pretty much know that there is no hog in there to chase them out. If your fly repeatedly drifts through unscathed, take notice and pay a return visit. A seemingly barren bend pool more often than not contains a large fish.

For all the benefits these lies have for fish, the two directions of the current make drag-free drifts made from the inside of the bend quite difficult. If you present from the upstream riffle, you risk spooking the trout. If you present from the downstream riffle without a perfect slack-line presentation, your fly will accelerate from a natural drift. From the outside of the bend, you cannot approach the bank too closely lest you spook the fish through vibrations. As you might have gleaned from my expertise in spooking trout, I have sent my share of bend-pool trout scurrying to safety.

However, I have found that most of the time, a presentation from the outside of the bend pool is best. Use the time of day to dictate your casting priority. During morning, cast to the head (where they feed on drifting nymphs); at noontime cast to the undercut (where the trout are hiding); during evening cast to the tailout (where they can leisurely feed on nymphs or adult insects). If you spot big fish actively rising, cast this theory in the toilet and just catch the freaking fish. Regardless of when you fish them, long tippets will help you maintain a sustained natural drift.

One way to fish this pool from the inside bend is to swing a wet fly or flymph through the undercut. Of course, the same fly can be fished above and below the undercut when trout are feeding on adults and emergers. Streamers fished deep can also be a great way to draw large fish from the security of an undercut.

For all of the bend pools that contain lunker trout, many contain a number of similar-sized average trout. This

The ruffled surface of this bend pool allows
for a careful approach from the inside.

pattern is common where bends are reinforced with riprap, creating a number of small, segregated habitats rather than a prime one for a large fish to guard jealously.

During emergences or low-light periods, smaller trout will hold on the inside seam of a bend pool. Inside seams are more important on larger rivers where depth and cover are more hospitable to fish. This water is quite easy for the angler to fish from the inside of the bend, and certainly should be examined if there are rises, or if you know there are no huge trout that you could incidentally spook.

Confluence Pools

Confluence pools are often where we get our first glance of new small streams. When two streams come together, there is usually a pool. Don't ask me why, it just happens. One of the nice things about growing up in the Pacific Northwest is that there is a lot of water, creating a ton of small streams. A five-mile hike up a large creek will usually bring you to more than a dozen tributary streams. Each one offers a unique and usually productive confluence pool to fish.

This kind of a pool is a good place to fish because it offers twice as many good features that tend to produce trout. There are two tongues, four seams, and usually a couple eddies spinning food around until a trout puts it out if its misery. Usually, one stream is larger than the other, so there is a primary current in the pool, as well as a secondary current of less intense flow. In a big, turbulent pool, the features of the primary current may be too intense, and trout will hold in the gentler currents of the secondary current.

I have an unconfirmed theory that the best trout in a confluence hold near the secondary current of the tributary stream. I think the reason for this is that the secondary current is not as strong and the fish can feed and hold more comfortably than in the force of the main current. The smaller stream also usually offers a different water temperature than the larger stream (slightly warmer when the big stream is very cold, and colder when the big stream is warm). Also, the two streams may carry water with different degrees of turbidity. When one stream is muddy and one is clear, the line between the two is always a productive place for trout to hold and for you to catch them.

Plunge Pools

Few sights get a small-stream angler's blood pumping more than a tiny stream stair-stepping its way down a hillside, with water spilling over the lip of each table-sized pool into another identical basin, ad infinitum. On mountain headwater streams, plunge pools may compose the only type of habitat suitable for trout. They are great habitat because they are relatively deep due to the scouring effect of the mini-falls above it. Because this type of water is usually located in high-gradient settings, there is also no shortage of logs, boulders, and trees to offer shelter and protection to trout.

For the sake of differentiating a plunge pool from a waterfall pool, we will assume that water in a plunge pool falls less than five feet into the head of the pool. A relatively short drop like this keeps the turbulence in the pool confined

to the head, leaving more places for trout to live. A plunge pool is also much more circular than the other types of pools we will discuss. This means there is a less defined current flow, and trout can be almost anywhere in the pool.

Trout holding in plunge pools will usually hold near where the water comes in. This place gives them the first shot at food, and the bubbles overhead make them feel safe from predation. Coastal cutthroat trout are notorious for burying their heads under the foamy heads of pools. This behavior can make it tough to throw a fly to these fish, because your fly can drift unnoticed out of their range in a fraction of a second. For that reason, I usually throw a cast to the calm water to either side of the plunge where trout have plenty of time to see it and pounce on it before it drifts away.

While it is almost guaranteed that you'll find trout in the head of a plunge pool, large fish will also hold near boulders or near the tailout of a plunge pool. While fishing tailouts of pools is notoriously difficult, because of both approaching fish and avoiding drag, plunge pool tailouts are usually easily fished with the pool jumping techniques discussed later.

The biggest drawback to plunge pools is that you can spook larger fish if you hook a smaller fish that thrashes all around the pool. Plunge pools are the trout equivalent of a college dorm, where creatures are compressed into tight, uncomfortable harmony with their peers. If your buddy started tweaking out right in your face, you probably wouldn't be too eager to take a shot of whatever he just drank, and the same goes for trout. If you hook a smaller-than-expected fish, quickly pull it out of the pool to keep commotion to a minimum. Let the pool rest for a couple minutes then try again for the larger fish.

If you fish a likely-looking plunge pool and you catch nothing after a couple well-placed casts, odds are there is a large trout there and you spooked it during your approach. If there are several smaller trout in the pool instead of one large one, it is likely that at least one of them was not put down by you (either because of location or naïveté), and would strike your fly. Because of my Sergeant Doofy-like coordination, I usually spook the trout in a dozen or more of these pools each time I'm on the water. No problem, I will just continue fishing upstream, stopping at all of the pools I spooked on the hike back downstream. This usually gives the pools enough time to rest, enough time for me to reflect on my mistakes, while at the same time allowing me to view the pool from a different perspective when I come back through.

Waterfall Pools

Waterfall pools are much more turbulent and violent than their smaller brethren, and they draw both anglers and sightseers by the dozens. Waterfalls also nurture the rare occasion when tourists are engaged in a more productive endeavor than the angler.

Growing up in Portland, Oregon, I was within thirty miles of over two dozen streams with waterfalls greater than 100 feet, and had plenty of time to glean knowledge from these giants. As a youngster, I quickly learned that fishing below these titans was rarely as productive as the gentler waters downstream. Don't get me wrong; there are trout in that frothing pool, and some nice ones at that. However, waterfalls of this magnitude create pools of violent turbulence, which act both as excellent overhead cover and a barrier that limits trout movement. Trout in these habitats will rarely move more than a few inches for food, and very few trout will risk the energy to travel to the surface in order to obtain a meal.

Waterfalls in the 5- to 25-foot range are usually the optimal height when it comes to the creation of good trout habitat. These create enough turbulence to make fish comfortable, but not so much that trout are confined to feeding in a zone the size of a tea cup. The turbulence is also light enough to let your nymphs make it down to the fish. Why mention nymphs? They are all you should use on waterfall pools; anything else and you are wasting your time. Mature

Pools created by tall waterfalls are often
too turbulent for fly-fishing except near the outlet.

trout are wise enough not to brave the storm of currents to get a tiny morsel on the surface. The tailouts of waterfall pools are unique and are often the most productive places to fish. Because of the great depth of most waterfall pools, the most abundant shallow water in the pool is usually in the tailout. Most of the waterfall pools I have fished tend to drain out of a corner of the pool rather than the symmetrical manner of plunge pools. This allows you to approach from one side, casting across the ground, thus eliminating the drag that comes with a straight-upstream approach.

The best waterfall pools come tumbling down in a cascading manner, rather than in free fall. This allows the energy to be dissipated at each step rather than shooting directly into a churning pool. One time I was being photographed near an 80-foot cascade for an advertisement for my university. Between shots, I flicked a team of nymphs into this clear, deep pool with a marl of logs strewn across the bottom. The photographer, a fellow angler, was surprised at the number of fish I was pulling out of this pool, considering the success he had had below other waterfalls in the area. After about the tenth fish in about twelve casts, I started surprising myself and began to observe the pool more closely. While the waterfall was impressive in height, because of the cascading nature of the feature, the turbulence was largely relegated to the first couple feet of the pool. This allowed the large, woody debris to remain in the pool, rather than being scoured out by a more powerful fall. Thus, the actual physical features of the falls can have a major influence on how it fishes.

Waterfalls with a free fall greater than 10 feet act as a barrier to almost all fish, though many species of salmon and steelhead have been known to pass much taller, cascade-style falls during spawning runs.

A major benefit of waterfall pools is that they are one of the only types of habitat that are given to you on most topographic maps. This can be a great aid in both finding good potential small streams and in deciding how far up or downstream you want to venture looking for good water.

Logs

The fallen log is another commonly misunderstood aquatic feature. Many people seek them out as the Holy Grail of trout fishing, expecting trout to be swarming fin to fin around them. Nevertheless, most anglers spend most of their time on unproductive logs and totally ignore the highly productive ones.

Logs that fall perpendicularly across small streams often hold trout, but not the quantity or quality we expect. The conflicting currents going over and under the log make it an unpredictable and turbulent place to live. Even if trout lived there en masse, it might be advisable to avoid them. It is often difficult to hook fish near this kind of structure because they are usually tucked in very close to the upstream and downstream sides of the log. A downstream presentation that is ignored will inevitably snag up, and an upstream presentation demands a perfect cast with a dry fly, lest you either snag the branches, or drop the fly below the tail of the trout.

If you get lucky and hook the fish, you are rarely in a good position to steer the fish into open water, which must be done quickly, otherwise you are instantly wrapped up in the wood. It is easier to ignore perpendicular logs and devote your time to more practical pursuits on the river.

Logs that fall parallel to streams offer good holding for trout because various branches, knobs, and inconsistencies of the logs offer numerous dead spots for trout to hold, with close access to fast currents carrying food. The log also offers excellent protection, or at least a sense of excellent protection, for trout. In addition to all these glorious benefits, parallel logs are a dream for anglers compared to perpendicular logs. You can make presentations from various angles, and under the right conditions you can even use the log as cover so you can sneak up on the fish and short-line it. Once the fish is hooked, all you have to do is bend your rod to the side to turn the fish's head into the current and steer it into open water.

Stumps, particularly semi-submerged ones, are nice little pieces of trout habitat. There is usually a hole scoured out behind them formed when high water rushes over and around the stump. This is a desirable holding lie for trout. But, the real treasure of stumps is when their large root systems extend perpendicular to the current. Remember how we mentioned that water accelerates around the sides of rocks? Well, as the water accelerates around the stump, the trout can lie under the cushion offered by roots and still have access to all the food compressed into the drift around the sides of the stump. This makes stumps a high priority for anglers.

The downside of logs and stumps is that they can be here one year and gone the next. Large woody debris is much more common in the first five years after a fire or severe flood. But, they are easily moved by the constant force of the current, and only 10% of what initially fell will still be in the stream ten years later. This makes logs an ephemeral resource for anglers.

Logs and large woody debris are much more common in high-gradient, low-order streams than in larger trout streams. Thus, knowing how trout will hold in relation to large woody debris is much more important to the small-stream angler than the average big-river junkie.

Weeds

Weeds are a blessing for small-stream anglers. They are an indicator of, and catalyst for, fertile insect life and large trout. Besides being a salad bar of trout food, weeds offer protection for trout, greatly improving the number and quality of lies. For anglers, weeds can conceal your approach by keeping you out of view. They also act as a buffer, preventing vibrations caused by wading to reach the trout. The combination of these factors, in theory, creates premium habitat for large trout that are relatively easy to approach.

Unfortunately, many anglers, including myself many years ago, see only the frustrations that stream weeds pose

Weeds make small-stream trout fatter and easier to approach.

to anglers. They can cause hundreds of tiny and perpetually changing microcurrents as they massage the surface of the water. They are a nightmare for an indicator-nymphing angler because the weed tops are constantly changing their depth, never allowing you to keep your fly in the proper strike zone. Weeds also occur under relatively flat, gentle water conditions, meaning fish have plenty of time to observe their food before consuming it. Combine this with the fact that weeds grow bugs like crazy, and you have a tough hatch-matching situation. All this makes weeds something to fear for many anglers, even experienced ones.

However, none of these things are anything that a little practice and study cannot quickly solve. By learning about what bugs live there, practicing slack-line casts and approaches, and observing the feeding habits of the trout on that particular stream, you will quickly fall in love with weedy waters.

Bridges

Bridges are the most overrated kind of small-stream trout habitat. They get the most pressure because every Joe Blow that drives over a small stream and decides to wet a line makes his first casts to the light riffle bubbling its way through the shade of a bridge. The discerning small-stream angler will concentrate only on identifying and fishing the most productive bridge situations.

First of all, for a bridge to be considered excellent habitat, the bridge must offer the fish constant overhead protection and shade. This means the bridge must be low and wide. A bridge much higher than twenty feet above the river, unless it is exceptionally wide, cannot offer enough for trout to make it that much better than an overhanging tree. The smart angler will avoid taking automatic casts under high bridges, unless the aquatic habitat looks good in its own right.

Secondly, it must be a bridge, not a full culvert. Many large steel culverts have a bottom of gravel and rocks that entered during flood periods and look to the untrained eye to be a natural substrate. Nice fish will never be found in a culvert because the current velocity (even if there are some rocks in there) is too swift for optimal growth. A few small rings of rising fish may encourage a cast or two, but the result is almost invariably small trout

If you do locate a good-looking bridge, take your time and watch for rises. Since you are usually forced to make straight downstream presentations to fish under the best bridges, you only have one shot at them. Since the best bridges usually hold one of the best trout in a stream, you want to make sure you target that fish with your presentation. Many anglers simply make a cast, catch an average trout, unaware—yet satisfied since they caught a fish—that they spooked the much larger trout on the other side of the bridge. Finding prime locations is difficult because of the shade, and anglers are forced to find lies by the surface characteristics of the water. A tough puzzle to solve.

In addition to the problem of finding the best fish, trout under bridges are also more pressured than fish in other parts

of the stream. Many have been caught several times, and many more have seen poor presentations that have left them more wary of you. Bridge-dwelling fish are easily put down by errant wading or bad casting. In places of extreme pressure, suburban streams or those in Yellowstone, I will often just pass on by bridges, choosing to pursue more cooperative trout in less obvious habitat.

Fortunately, if you don't spook them during your approach, trout under a bridge will rise more freely than trout in other parts of the stream. The fish are comfortable in their überlie, and if you do not spook them with sloppy wading, errant casting, or not-exactly dead-drifting, then you can usually bring them up to any reasonable pattern. I almost always choose a terrestrial pattern in this situation, especially near wooden bridges that may harbor plenty of beetles or termites.

The two keys to fishing near bridges are being discriminating and observant. If you practice those qualities, you will successfully find some of the best small-stream fishing under bridges.

Fences

Fences are one of the only types of trout habitat totally unique to small streams. Large rivers are unwadable to both man and beast, thus effectively acting as a natural barrier to escapes or trespassing. However, small streams can be easily crossed, requiring some sort of fencing. This type of habitat is surprisingly common on small streams in suburban areas, farmlands, and range areas. Like many other things in fly-fishing, we have those nutty Brits to thank for it.

England had few wooden fences until sheep grazing became the major part of their economy in the late sixteenth century. Historians often lament how the practice of enclosure resulted in the eviction of peasants from their lands and the growth of towns, however most of these scholars understandably overlook something very important to modern anglers: Enclosure created a new kind of habitat for trout. Keeping in those wily sheep required fences that spanned all the small streams in the shires. The wood itself, while much more substantial than modern wire fencing, was of little use to anything but small trout. However, these wooden fences were built through rich, fertile chalkstreams, and in time they collected vast mats of weeds. These weeds acted as a pantry for trout food and they also gave some good cover from overhead predators. Anywhere in the world—from Lincoln, England to Lincoln, Pennsylvania— those wooden fences spanning small spring creeks should make anglers take notice.

In the American West, barbed wire is often strung across small streams so that cattle won't wade through the stream and wander off a rancher's property. The scrawny, twisted metal appears to offer nothing to enhance trout habitat, but a closer look reveals something more. Besides cattle, another trademark of the West is highly fluctuating water levels. The seasonal spate flooding that occurs throughout the region washes tons of debris into small streams, and barbed-wire fences act like seines, catching a hodgepodge of grasses, brush, and branches. When the water recedes, these things are left dangling above the stream, enmeshed in fences. The result is the equivalent of a low, overhanging tree branch, which offers shade and overhead protection to trout. In parts of the arid West, this overhead protection is highly coveted by trout and can produce some surprising results.

Small-Stream Trees and Riparian Vegetation

When you turn to trout authorities that are not involved in the flyfishing industry and the potential conflicts of interest that may ensue, there is no debate whether streamside vegetation is important to trout. Trout biologists, stream ecologists, and aquatic entomologists all know that tree structure and composition has a huge influence on all parts of the aquatic world. Simply do a literature search and you can find thousands of scientific articles that discuss the relationships between trees and streams and trout.

Trees affect streams in many ways. They shade the water, keeping it cool and preventing evaporation. Their leaves fall in streams, offering food and cover for various types of aquatic insects. The trees provide home to a variety of terrestrial insects and the adult forms of aquatic insects like caddisflies and stoneflies. Trees control erosion and affect stream sediment load. They also play an important role in picking up nutrients in the soil. When an old tree falls in the river, it breaks up the current and adds more habitat for the trout. Different types of trees will influence streams in different ways, so it is important to be able to identify trees along streams and know how they may affect the fishery.

Trees are important not only for influencing and interceding parts of the ecosystem, but also as indicators of certain climatic conditions. For example, lodgepole pine trees are much more frost-resistant than ponderosa pines. When a stream that normally runs through ponderosas suddenly flows through a grove of lodgepole pines, you've got an indication of a cold air inversion site. In a place like this, cold, moist air often keeps morning-emerging insects on the water longer while they wait for their wings to dry. Knowing information like this can influence how, when, and where you fish, giving you a better chance at catching fish.

Trees, like every other biotic and abiotic factor, are much more influential on small streams than on large streams. As stream size decreases, trees form a more complete canopy, and can be extremely important in affecting stream temperature, algae growth, and insect diversity. On smaller streams, leafy debris and fallen trees can happen anywhere in the stream, unlike a large stream where they often fall only near shore. Also, small streams often have homogeneous tree structures within their watersheds, which results in a habitat and insect populations unique to that watershed. This is different than in large streams where there is a wide variety of trees throughout the drainage basin. This tends to minimize the effects of an individual specie of trees.

There is a line to draw in the importance of riparian vegetation types. As the size of the plant increases, so does its importance. An ancient big-leaf maple provides a great deal of shade, shelter for insects, bank stabilization, and leaf litter inputs, while a bunch of smaller willows clumped together cannot even come close to matching it. Smaller grasses and brush play a supporting role to the big trees, and though anglers would prefer them to be there rather than not, they really don't have as specialized an impact on trout habitat. While streamside wildflowers certainly have specialized impacts on angler habitat and well-being, the trout really couldn't care less about them.

In general, broadleaf trees are much more important to trout streams than conifers. Deciduous trees offer more shade throughout the summer months because of their broader crowns, and they deposit nitrogen-rich leaves into streams in fall. Many genera of stoneflies, mayflies, and midges spend their entire larval stages grazing through leaf packs near shoreline. The best thing that conifers offer is that some tend to branch lower than deciduous trees of similar height. Conifers provide shade close to the water, giving trout a greater sense of security, thus improving the quality of lies. When abundant, this low branching has an insulating effect on streams, keeping them cool in the summer and warmer during the winter.

It is impossible to discuss the importance of every kind of trout-stream riparian tree across the United States, since there are about seventy of importance. I will instead simply mention some of the unique properties of a few trees that are most common in small-stream ecosystems. If this subject piques your interest, please check the bibliography for more texts that go into greater detail about the influence of trees on streams. Your local libraries, county and academic, will be a much greater resource on your local trees than I could ever be. I also will not go into elaborate descriptions identifing the trees, that is something that you can easily get in a regional tree or plant guide. If you don't own one of these books, you may want to pick one up and add it to your angling book collection. It can be a great investment when ascertaining the trout potential of new streams.

Red Alder

Alder is one of the most important riparian plants for several reasons. First of all, it often drops its leaves while still green, increasing the amount of nitrogen returned to streams much more than leaves of other tree species. Alder has a low fiber content, and this, along with its high nitrogen content, facilitates fast decomposition. In a study done by Dr. Norm Anderson, the leaves of the alder tree were consumed by the caddisfly *Lepidostoma quercina* within 30 days. In contrast, it took a similar caddis 300 days before it could begin to consume the fallen needles of the Douglas fir.

To make it just the greatest tree for trout, the red alder is one of few plants capable of nitrogen fixing—taking atmospheric nitrogen and combining it with oxygen and adding a usable form of nitrogen to the soil. The result is increased soil fertility, allowing alders to grow faster, making for more

A rich canopy of red alder over a plunge pool stream is a recipe for well-fed small-stream trout.

undergrowth. The result is better habitat for terrestrial insects, and even more potential leaf litter inputs. Red alders are the überplant on small streams, and should be respected and targeted when selecting potential fisheries.

Vine Maple
The vine maple has one of the fastest decaying leaves in the riparian ecosystem. For insects, this means an excellent food source that can be quickly utilized before the leaves are scoured by winter flooding. To the angler, the vine maple is a curse. Its thick, clingy growth pattern makes for tough bushwhacking and plenty of torn waders.

Willow
Willows serve a number of functions besides concealing anglers from grizzly bears, as they have been known to do in the Northern Rockies. They serve an important function as bank and island stabilizers. Many small streams see radical changes in their riffle/run structure from season to season, islands that are here one year may be gone the next. If there are willows growing on the island, the likelihood of change is greatly reduced.

Willows, and there are over 40 important riparian species across the country, can range from knee-height to shoulder-height, offering variable amounts of shade. Most willows are poor contributors to leaf input, doing little to aid shredder populations. However, because many willows are shade intolerant, they can be indicators of good populations of grazing insects like *Baetis* mayflies and *Glossosoma* caddis.

Willows, like aspen, are a favored tree by beavers, and a willowy meadow stream has the potential to hold a beaver pond or two.

Douglas Fir
The cornerstone of the Northwest economy for the better part of a century, the Douglas fir is a mixed blessing when it comes to small streams. Douglas firs are sunlight hogs, tending to create a thick canopy over a stream, preventing light from reaching the water and sparking photosynthesis. The ominous presence of Douglas firs over a stream restricts the growth of medium-sized deciduous trees (particularly red alder), which are important to shredding insects, and eventually, filtering insects. Douglas firs, however, provide plenty of shade and can keep stream temperatures surprisingly cool, even during a hot, dry summer. This sunlight protection is a negative on high elevation streams, because without the sunlight you don't get a lot of algae growth and pretty poor overall productivity. The thick root systems of Douglas firs also are important in anchoring the soil and preventing erosion. Finally, Douglas firs are high in fiber content (thus slow to break down), and when they fall into a stream, they greatly improve the long-term habitat for trout.

Lodgepole Pine
As I mentioned earlier, the lodgepole is better as an indicator of climate rather than insects or nutrient input. The lodgepole, where it mixes with ponderosa pines, grows in areas of heavy frost and cold-air drainage where the ponderosa cannot survive. Here the lodgepole screams to the angler to fish dries during morning hatches. The cold, moist air that gathers overnight in lodgepole colonies will hinder the drying of insect wings during morning hatches, allowing the angler more opportunities to fish dries in the morning. In places like Yellowstone, where lodgepole forests are the primary ecotype, then the presence of riparian stands means quite little to the angler. Lodgepoles are of little significance when it comes to shade, because they are about as stout as a pencil. They can, however, grow in dense communities posing danger to the eyes and waders of a careless bushwhacker.

Ponderosa Pine
The ponderosa is a big Western tree with rich reddish bark that is more than just eye candy. The bark is rarely well affixed, and tends to harbor a disproportionately large number of beetles and ants. Making it even better, both the bark and large cones will fall off sporadically, depositing the occasional terrestrial on the earth, or even better, the water. The ponderosa rarely forms a thick canopy, allowing plenty of deciduous plant growth (willows, vine maple, etc.) along the banks of the stream. This riparian growth makes for good terrestrial habitat and offers a little leaf input to the stream.

Pacific Yew
This dainty tree, recognizable only to those hardy souls that ply their trade on the small streams of the Pacific coast, is of importance as a bank-stabilizing tree. It probably has the best root system of any small tree in the region. A stream lined with Pacific yews likely would stay clearer following a rainstorm than neighboring streams that lack this little plant. If you can't seem to catch fish, you can also cut one of these trees down and carve out some bows and arrows, which is the primary commercial use of this little conifer.

Aspen

This gorgeous tree is most important to the small-stream angler as an indicator of beaver habitat. If the small stream flows through a relatively flat meadow or valley, and there is an abundance of aspen, keep your eyes out for beaver ponds. Fur trappers used this technique to locate beaver, and it still works today. When you see a stand of aspen, look for chewed up trees (particularly saplings) to indicate recent activity. For all the beauty of their white trunks and golden leaves, the aspen are poor insect food because they take a long time to decay and may not be consumed by shredding insects until all other food is utilized.

Small-Stream Trout

A common malady afflicting many new small-stream anglers is that these fish behave differently than trout in large streams. They spook easier, feed on different foods, take with increased urgency, hold in different water, and are more tolerant of other fish. In fact, the differences between different species on a small stream are far less obvious than the differences between a large-stream and small-stream fish of the same species!

With that said, I will still go into the intricacies of the various species of trout you might encounter on a small stream. I hope these summaries will give you new information that will help you when pursuing them in the stream. For the sake of speeding up my work, I will only mention resident fish and not anadramous fish like salmon or steelhead.

Brook Trout (*Salvelinus fontinalis*)

Some brand names are synonymous with their product. Jell-O™ is used to identify dessert gelatin, Slurpee indicates a sweet frozen beverage, and brook trout mean small streams.

Brook trout were first identified taxonomically by Samuel Latham Mitchell in 1814 through samples taken near New York City. Their natural range is from the Chattahoochee and Catawba rivers in Georgia through the Appalachians, north to the George River in the Ungava region of Quebec. They were also found west, throughout the Great Lakes region, into northeastern Manitoba. Humans have since introduced them throughout North America, and they are now naturalized populations.

Brook trout, as their name indicates, prefer small, cold streams over all others. They can be found in even the smallest spring-fed creeks, as long as there is sufficient cover. Their optimal temperatures are between 55°F and 65°F. As stream temperatures fall below about 43°F (a thermal threshold in early spring and late fall on most small streams), brook trout become more sedated, holding tight to structure and feeding less. Regardless of temperature, brook trout hold in slower currents than most other species of trout. The angler pursuing these fish in a tiny creek should look for them in pools and slower runs rather than swift riffles or pocket water. This habitat preference is reflected in their food choices. Some studies show that brook trout eat more caddis larvae (insects of moderate currents) than did the fast-section-dwelling rainbow.

Brook trout aren't really trout; like bull trout, they are char, a close cousin of the trout. To the angler, char are distinguishable from trout because they have light spots on a dark background while trout have dark spots on a light background. Brook trout have creamy yellow worm-like markings on their backs and crimson spots with periwinkle halos adorning their sides. When spawning, this beautiful pattern is accompanied by fire-red flanks and fins, each boarded with black and white stripes. The result is perhaps the most striking coloration of any species of freshwater fish.

As if their beauty is not enough, the brook trout is considered by many the best tasting trout. Their palatability is a blessing, for brook trout have the annoying habit of overpopulating their aquatic homes. They grow extremely slowly (slower than any of the other small-stream fishes) and can be sexually mature at only four to five inches in length. This means there can be many tiny fish in a stream, and anything over nine inches is a monster. For these reasons it is usually advisable to take home a small-stream brook trout or two for dinner, especially if water conditions are poor for catch-and-release fishing.

Brook trout are regulars in both Western and Eastern small streams, though their tendency to overbreed often results in small, but colorful, adults.

Anglers, if not fisheries managers, have held a soft spot for the gullible brookie because of its free-taking nature. Brook trout are reputed to be the easiest of all trout to catch and they do have a tendency to be free risers. Brook trout are also very territorial, aggressively chasing out similarly-sized fish of other species. In the West, this has been a serious problem, with young native bull trout and cutthroat trout being driven into less suitable areas and experiencing high mortality. Because of the combination of high fish density and their aggressive nature, brook trout are a very exciting fish to pursue on small streams. Brook trout will travel to smash flies at a distance from their lie, hoping to beat the other fish to the meal. They can also be susceptible to wet-fly and sunk-fly presentations in small streams, for they will readily attack a fly that lingers too close, too long.

Brook trout tend to fight in a bulldog manner, rarely leaping like rainbow trout. For this reason, many experienced small-stream anglers fishing multi-species water can predict the species of fish they have on their line before they even get a glimpse of it. This fly angler's party trick is worth learning if you want to look really cool around your friends.

Cutthroat Trout *(Onchorhynchus clarki)*

Cutthroat trout are native to the West, and replace the brook trout as the default small-stream fish of Western America. Cutthroat are some of the most versatile trout, and can be found from the tiniest coastal trickles to large rivers like the Snake and Clark's Fork of the Columbia.

Unlike brook trout, cutthroat trout come in literally dozens of varieties—from the Lahontan cutthroat (*O. henshawi*) of the Great Basin to the Yellowstone cutthroat (*O. bouvieri*). The perpetual aridity of the West has done much to isolate this fish into regional populations, causing the huge variety of color variations and anatomical features. A single description cannot do the species justice; a coastal cutthroat is nearly identical to a coastal rainbow trout (with pinkish sides and abundant spots), while the Yellowstone cutthroat closely resembles a golden trout, with only a handful of spots on the tail and buttery-gold flanks. To complicate matters further, when closely related non-native species are introduced, native cutthroats can interbreed with other species of rainbow and cutthroat trout. All the species and hybrids are beautiful and worthy of a couple photos in your angling scrapbook.

Cutthroats are excellent small-stream fish for several reasons, not the least of which is the tendency for big fish from big waters to migrate into small tributaries to spawn. Lake-dwelling fish that migrate into small streams to spawn can surprise small-stream anglers not expecting them. Tiny streams that drain into Yellowstone Lake can be choked with 20-inch cutthroat in July, providing food for hungry grizzlies and sport for anglers willing to compete with the massive creatures. Rivers like Oregon's Willamette hold five-pound cutthroat that migrate into small coastal creeks to spawn, offering good angling for shockingly obese fish in close quarters. Coastal cutthroat also migrate to the ocean. These sea-run cutthroat act a lot like steelhead, and a small but devout group of fly-anglers pursue them every August and September on the coastal streams of Oregon, Washington, and British Columbia. These 14- to 22-inch harvest trout are some of the most prized small-stream fish in the world. All cutthroat spawn during the early spring (late February to June, depending on elevation) though some species will remain in the spawning tributaries for many weeks before and after spawning.

Cutthroat and rainbows often exist in harmony in small streams, for rainbows take up positions in fast water while the cutthroat hang out in the marginal currents of pools,

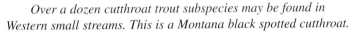

Over a dozen cutthroat trout subspecies may be found in Western small streams. This is a Montana black spotted cutthroat.

eddies, and slower runs. Cutthroat can also rise with infuriating caution, drifting back under your fly for several seconds before finally rising. If you are fortunate enough to get one to rise, they will often take your fly down in their lips rather than in their mouth. Valium is the recommended medication to slow your reaction speed enough to consistently hook these patient fish. Because of their sedated nature, cutthroat are also dominated by other species of trout of the same size.

Many anglers will gripe that cutthroat don't fight, and with many subspecies this seems to be true. With Yellowstone cutthroats you can often get away with light tippets for large fish, because even 20-inch fish will shake their heads once and submit. The most reluctant fighters are the ones often caught in heavily pressured waters, while cutthroat in more remote waters can scrap with the best of them.

Cutthroat rarely grow to enormous size because of a reluctance to turn to cannibalism and a short life span. Few cutthroat in streams will eat other fish, and this limits their size to less than two pounds on fertile streams, and considerably smaller on barren streams. Most cutthroat live between four to five years, so unlike bull trout, they have little time to amass sizeable girth. This is fine with most anglers because a buttery, seven-inch cutthroat is the paragon of beauty.

Rainbow Trout *(Oncorhynchus mykiss)*

The rainbow is the pop star of the trout world: flashy, active, pretty, and easy. The rainbow has leapt, run, and thrashed its way into the hearts of anglers around the world, though this particular trout originated on the Pacific Coast of North America. It shocks most anglers to learn that the rainbow usually is not a small-stream fish. Most rainbows inhabit larger creeks and small rivers, leaving small creeks to cutthroat and brook trout.

The rainbows you encounter on small streams are divided into two different subspecies: the inland redband rainbow *(O. gairdneri)* and the coastal rainbow *(O. irideus)*. The redband rainbow is native to the Northwest east of the Cascade Mountains. It has a much more vibrant color scheme than the coastal strain, with bright pink or crimson flanks and a

*Native rainbow trout inhabit
thousands of Western small streams.*

generous dose of black spots. The coastal fish are muted in color, tending to be more silvery with a faint pink band near their lateral line. The spots disappear and the coloration turns bright chrome when this species migrates to sea and returns as a steelhead. Not all coastal rainbow migrate to the ocean, and many quite happily spend their entire lives in small headwater streams.

Rainbows love swift streams with broken, irregular bottoms. The best rainbow streams, even large ones, have no shortage of boulders, riffles, and pocket water. Because such habitat structures create a limited number of prime lies, rainbow populations tend to be aggressive, chasing out competitors or smaller fish that accidentally hang too close for too long. These aggressive tendencies carry over to their feeding habits and rainbows usually hit flies without much fuss or reflection, making them a favorite among anglers who fish to actually escape stressful lives.

Rainbows have no qualms about cannibalism, and will eat other fish without much thought. While not true piscavores like large brown trout and bull trout, rainbows are opportunistic enough to eat sculpins, dace, chubs, as well as fry and alevins of their own species. However, these fish rarely go Hannibal Lecter in small streams, and most rainbows are quite happy being insectivores. Rainbows fall somewhere between brook trout and brown trout with their affinity to rise.

Rainbows, for their worldwide distribution in a myriad of habitats, can tolerate only a narrow range of water conditions in order to grow and reproduce. They require slightly alkaline water (7.0-8.0 pH) and cannot reproduce in anything with less than a pH value of 6.2. They need swift water with little turbidity, and a temperature regime between 56°F and 67°F for at least six months of the year to grow longer than smelt. For all these finicky biological requirements, the rainbow inexplicably has thrived in Yellowstone's Firehole River with its 80°F+ summer temperatures and water loaded with heavy metals.

The rainbow, while not as common as either brook trout or cutthroat in the smallest streams, are certainly desired by anglers and are worthy of their lofty position in the angling hierarchy.

Brown Trout *(Salmo trutta)*

Large brown trout are often considered the bullies of the aquatic world, and with good reason. They have the temperament, and usually the physique, of an NFL lineman with 'roid rage. They usually reside in the best lies in the river, chasing down any smaller creature that dares to enter their realm. This tendency wins the brown trout few friends among other fish, but many friends of the angling persuasion.

Brown trout are not native to North America, but rather to Europe where they've provided action there for many centuries before their forced immigration to this country. There is a long, labored natural history of brown trout, mostly circulating around taxonomy and nomenclature and numerous alleged subspecies of a fish whose natural range reaches the extremes of foggy Scottish lochs and the dry steppe of the Amu Dar'ya. The result of those 200 years of heated debate was that there was just one species, Salmo trutta—end of discussion. Brown trout are recognized by their buttery yellow or brown flanks, peppered with brown and red spots. Brown trout live for a long time compared to other small-stream fish, often reaching 5 to 10 years of age. In acidic waters, they grow slower and usually live to only 5 years of age, while in harder, more alkaline waters many will grow faster and live up to 12 years.

Brown trout have an affinity for cover that is only matched by largemouth bass. If you are fishing a brown-trout stream, look for undercut banks, stumps, fallen logs, sweepers, and large boulders because they'll harbor browns. Brown trout are also one of the most current-averse species of trout, preferring pools and eddies over riffles and pocket water. Because of their fierce territoriality, brown trout that hold near prime cover are often quite large. In a place that may hold four to five modest brook trout, one brown trout may chase everything away and take up exclusive feeding rights for itself. This character trait, along with a long life and their propensity to consume everything they can fit in their mouths, results in the potential for large fish. Day in and day out, fishing brown-trout waters will give you the best chance to catch large fish in a small stream.

Like cutthroat trout, brown trout offer excellent big-fish-in-a-small-stream potential, because they tend to migrate up from reservoirs and larger streams to spawn. Brown trout will move into spawning tributaries between September and November, though many do not actually spawn until December and January. This offers a wide window (depending on the open season) to small-stream anglers to hook into the fish of a lifetime in a 15-foot-wide stream. Because brown trout spawn weeks or even months after moving into a tributary, many of them take up the best lies where they can rest from their travels. The result is many big brown trout stacking up in pools, especially in swift creeks that require a lot of effort to move upstream. The other result is that the resident fish get forced out of their lies into marginal habitats. During September, when resident fish are still

Brown trout can create big surprises on small streams.

quite active, it is not surprising to pull good resident trout out of lousy water (say a shallow riffle or in the margins of a fast chute), because they were evicted by an aggressive brown trout. In the late season I always make some exploratory casts into water I would never even consider under normal conditions.

Brown trout have legendary appetites, devouring everything from insects and small fish to crayfish and mice to voles and ducklings to cattle and toddlers. They are prone to cause exaggeration in even the most understated angler. Brown trout have offered bored fly tiers the opportunity to experiment with strange materials and sturgeon hooks in order to create the gaudiest fly to fool the lunker brown in the old five-mile hole. For the most part, however, brown trout flies in small streams should reflect their primary diet of insects and small fish (especially sculpins, dace, and sticklebacks). When keying on spawning brown trout, I tend to fish smaller stonefly nymphs and Pupatators rather than convert to huge streamers. The smaller flies—though still hefty size 8s—will aggravate strikes out of the spawners and still fool feeding resident fish.

Nighttime angling on small streams, where legal, is not recommended unless you are a sadist. Though brown trout are renowned for their nighttime feeding, the rough terrain that follows many small streams will make it a suicide mission. If you do choose to pursue brown trout in darkness, do it on a section of stream you are familiar with in daylight. There is nothing like discovering a sharp stick in the dark. Also, put red plastic wrap over your lights. It is less spooky to fish and doesn't attract as many bugs. Finally, concentrate your efforts on nights with a full moon, and use large dry flies that can be skittered on the surface. They are usually visible in moonlight, and you don't have to worry as much about snags and detecting strikes.

The brown trout is one of the greatest testaments to the theory of natural selection. After being angled over for over 2000 years, and the last 1000 quite intensively, all the stupid fish died long ago. What is left are the fish that eluded the net, dodged the spear, ignored the bait, evaded the weir, and snubbed the fly. Remember this next time you blindly wander up to a brown trout creek with all the stealth of Barney the Dinosaur. Brown trout, even on small streams—especially on small streams—require respect and care if you seek consistent success.

Bull Trout *(Salvelinus confluentus)*

For many anglers, searching for bull trout is like searching for Sasquatch. These sometimes enormous fish can be found in large lakes and rivers throughout the inland Pacific Northwest and Northern Rocky Mountain states. However, small-stream anglers in tiny, remote headwaters can be shocked by ten-pound bull trout dragging their nymphs (and leader, line, and rod) downstream.

Bull trout are born in small streams. While many go off to spend their formative years in big rivers, lakes, and reservoirs, they all eventually return to spawn in smaller headwaters. Even the largest bull trout returns to tiny second- or third-order streams to spawn. Their dependence on the tiniest of streams, unparalleled by other trout and char, has been the cause of their demise. These are the waters most dramatically effected by clear-cut logging, bad mining practices, and poor road construction. All have hurt bull trout populations, leading to their federal listing as a threatened species under the Endangered Species Act. Bull trout are particularly susceptible to sedimentation because their young remain in the gravel for several months after hatching. A small stream with an abundance of sediment will suffocate these little guys before they can move out and fend for themselves.

During most of the past decade, the terms "bull trout" and "Dolly Varden" were thrown out interchangeably for the native char of the Pacific Northwest. In 1978, taxonomists distinguished between the two: the name Dolly Varden (*S. malma*) is being reserved for the ocean-going native char of the Northwest. That leads us to the fact that bull trout are not trout, but rather char-like brook trout. These fish actually look eerily similar to brook trout in their younger stages. However, bull trout lack the worm-like vermiculations on their back and dorsal fins. It is important to learn the differences between these fish, as in many places the introduction of brook trout threatens bull trout. Brook trout have a reproductive advantage over the bull trout because they require less specific conditions for optimal spawning. Brook trout also will interbreed with the bull trout, which as char are close relatives, which can eventually breed out the native species. Where both species exist, regulations often encourage keeping brook trout, and it is important that anglers can distinguish between them so as not to do more harm than good by keeping the wrong species.

Bull trout that choose to remain in their native spawning streams tend to feed on whatever sparse insect populations that exist in these usually infertile streams. These fish remain small, in the 6- to 9-inch range at maturity. However, many (if not most) bull trout migrate to larger waters, like big lakes and broad rivers, and grow to massive sizes. Bull trout have an appetite that is rivaled only by large brown trout. Large bull trout feed almost exclusively on other fish, including mountain whitefish, sculpins, dace, chub, and even stocked rainbow trout. Bull trout that live in lakes with abundant kokanee populations (a landlocked strain of sockeye salmon often introduced to deep Western lakes and reservoirs) can easily grow to over twenty pounds. Since all these fish are wild and bound to a natural urge to reproduce, they will all move into tiny streams to spawn. Now that I am talking about it, do you wonder why you might not have heard about this? How many anglers do you know that would want to divulge the location where they hunt salmon-sized trout in a stream as wide as a pool table?

Large bull trout in smaller streams remain close to the bottom of pools under almost all conditions. Only when spawning or during the occasional feeding run will they be found in riffles or shallow runs. The smaller bull trout can be found in normal trout habitat throughout small streams. Spawning occurs from late August through late October in most waters. Migrating fish will just rush through the riffles, pausing to rest in pools. Many bull trout will remain in their natal streams for several weeks prior to actually spawning, and though they aren't actively feeding, they can be persuaded to strike with large saltwater streamers and baitfish imitations. When I say large, I mean large: 6- to 8-inch flies are not out of the question. In a larger spring creek in Oregon, before the stocking program was ceased, one of the favorite patterns used to be an 8-inch imitation of a stocked rainbow trout!

Pursuing these spawning fish, where legal, is an ethical issue for many anglers. If you choose to fish for them, use great care to play them quickly and give them plenty of time to recover. Never pursue a fish that is on the redd or immediately after the spawn is finished. Many people wonder why I even bother talking about the rare bull trout, but once you hook a ten-pounder, a rare feat for any fly-angler, you will be a bull trout advocate for life. And they need all the friends they can get.

Golden Trout *(Oncorhynchus aguabonita)*

The golden trout originated in a very small region of the upper Kern River in California's Sierra Nevada Mountains. They are divided into two strains: the Volcano Creek golden trout (*Oncorhynchus aguabonita aguabonita*) with its large spots that are confined to the tail of the fish, and the more heavily spotted Little Kern River golden trout (*Oncorhynchus aguabonita whitei*). Both species have golden-yellow sides, purplish parr marks, and a copper or red stripe down their flanks and over the gill plates. It is widely considered the most beautiful trout, and though I love the brook trout, it is hard to muster an argument against this gem of a fish.

While the golden trout is native only to a small area of the Sierra Nevada that was segregated during the glaciation of the Pleistocene epoch, it has been widely stocked in alpine lakes and small streams of the West. Where it does occur it is neither prolific or a large fish because of the infertile waters it inhabits. Anything over 12 inches is a large golden trout. They will migrate to the outlet streams of mountain lakes to spawn in the alpine spring from May to early July. Some fish may remain in the outlet streams for several weeks following spawning, offering a chance for anglers to land a larger-than-average golden.

The ease of catching golden trout has been well documented, and there is no shortage of accounts from the late-nineteenth and early-twentieth centuries attesting to huge stringers of admittedly small golden trout. Their eagerness to take, among other environmental factors, has left the golden trout as a federally listed threatened species under the ESA. It is up to all of us small-stream aficionados to stand up for this rare fish, one of the gems exclusively available to the small-stream and alpine angler.

Montana Grayling *(Thymallus articus montanus)*

The queen of small streams, the Montana grayling is the Rocky Mountain equivalent of the golden trout of California. The grayling is one of the most beautiful, rare, and sought-after game fish in the United States. It is another treasure only available to the small-stream and alpine anglers of America, something big-river addicts can only dream of.

The Montana Grayling was once native to all the tributaries of the upper Missouri drainage, but because of irrigation, poor ranching practices, and an assortment of management mistakes over the past century, it is now relegated to about 8% of its historical range. The Montana grayling now mostly inhabits pristine small streams and high lakes in Yellowstone, Glacier National Park, and Southwest Montana, with the notable exception of the Big Hole River.

The Montana grayling looks like a cross between a whitefish, sailfish, and trout. It has the body and forked tail of a whitefish, the large dorsal fin of a sailfish, and the mouth of a trout. It inhabits a similar area to the mountain whitefish, moderately deep runs with a decent current. Like the whitefish, it holds and feeds close to the bottom, though it is renowned for its willingness to rise to a small dry fly during hatch periods. In my own experience, I have caught most of my grayling on a large beetle pattern. This shows absolutely no consistency with what I mentioned earlier in this paragraph, so I guess I have been lucky enough to find some opportunistic grayling.

Only found in Montana, Wyoming, Canada and Alaska, the grayling is one of the most prized small-stream fish in North America

Because of the infertile waters this fish inhabits, grayling rarely grow to a large size. I was fortunate enough to land a 15-inch grayling in Yellowstone back in 1999, a feat I doubt I will ever repeat. All the other grayling I have caught, seen caught, or heard alleged accounts of being caught, have been under 11 inches in length. Yet, if we small-stream anglers associated beauty with length, we would all be dredging the Great Lakes with huge Rapalas. Every angler should have the experience of holding a little eight-inch grayling in their hand, lifting its large dorsal with their other hand to reveal its purple shroud with pink and blue highlights. Like golden trout, the petite grayling stands as a living example of the delicacy and fragility of its existence.

Mountain Whitefish *(Prosopium williamsoni)*

I am often teased by fellow anglers for continuing to fish whitefish water, even though I have little chance to hook trout. I am part of a growing group of fly-anglers that tolerates, even enjoys, catching whitefish on the fly rod.

The whitefish is extremely common in Western rivers, though they are more prevalent in larger streams than in small creeks. In *Yellowstone Fishes*, John Varley and Paul Schullery note that for a small stream to support mountain whitefish, the stream must have "an adequate number of pools at least 16 feet long and 3-4 feet deep (summer flows) in order to support whitefish." If the small stream you are fishing is a direct tributary of a larger stream, then you should expect whitefish to be present in the slower runs and pools in the lower sections of the small stream. Contrary to the opinion of most anglers, the whitefish does not compete for resources with trout. Nature doesn't allow pure competitors to evolve; each species finds a niche and adapts to it.

The whitefish has evolved primarily into a bottom feeder with a small, underslung mouth, focusing primarily on Diptera larvae, caddis larvae, and small stonefly nymphs. This small mouth means that flies for whitefish should be kept small and a hemostat should be carried to dig out the hooks. Besides the mouth, the whitefish has larger scales and a more deeply forked tail than a trout, and it lacks spots. Whitefish tend to have white or coppery sides and a dark-olive to purplish back. An experienced angler can also distinguish a whitefish from a trout when he spots it in the water, for whitefish appear to be more broad in the shoulders and less streamlined than a trout.

I welcome the presence of whitefish on small streams. They provide an excellent way to get people to practice their deep nymphing on small streams. Catching a number of fish out of a deep pool will give people both positive reinforcement and oust the mindset that indicator nymphing is only a technique for large rivers. Whitefish are also a schooling fish, and where you catch one fish, you can usually locate others. Plus, whitefish can often grow much larger than trout inhabiting the same water. The chance for a 20-inch whitefish can be a welcome respite from 10-inch cutthroat.

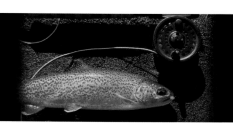

Chapter 4
Small-Stream Entomology and Fly Patterns

Few things in fly-fishing are more important than knowing about what trout eat. Perfect casting, rods, reels, waders, approaches, fancy leader materials, aluminum fly boxes, or three-dollar fly patterns mean nothing if trout don't want to eat what we present. The true essence of fly-fishing is to fool a fish into putting something into its mouth, and the best way to achieve that is to understand what normally goes into a fish's mouth.

Many big-stream anglers that I know think that they know more than enough about entomology, and that small-stream entomology will be a basic review. Many are shocked to learn that the larger, alkaline streams that sustain most of our trout fishing are at the simple end of the entomological scale. Streams like the Deschutes, Bighorn, or the Battenkill may be loaded with bugs, but the populations are extremely homogeneous, with ten or fifteen species composing over 85% of the insect biomass. When you move to a small stream you will find a cornucopia of insects, many of which are foreign to the large streams we are used to fishing. The green drakes, salmonflies, and Hydropsychidae caddis so prevalent in our big waters are replaced in our small streams by *Cinygmula*, *Paraleptophlebia*, and *Epeorus* mayflies, *Alloperla* stoneflies, and *Glossosoma* caddis. All these insects are footnotes in most angling entomology texts, ignored by even the small population of Latin-language freaks (of which I am a card-carrying member) that pepper our sport. Yet, knowing these insects can open the vault of angling entomology, helping you to solve what is going on in the small stream, letting you discover the identity of those mystery hatches on big rivers.

One major reason for the difference in the makeup of insects in a small stream is food availability. Insects in small streams, those that are second through fourth order, find a major portion of their food in the form of terrestrial inputs: leaves, woody debris, pine cones, nuts, fruits, and grasses. These things are called "coarse particulate organic matter" (CPOM), and this food material is used by a particularly functional group called shredders. Some examples of shredders are *Paraleptophlebia*, *Alloperla*, and *Limnephilidae* caddis. Many anglers know what behavior type (e.g. *Ephemera* mayflies are burrowers and *Siphlonurus* are swimmers) certain insects are, but often neglect to learn what they eat. Often this factor is as important as what type of water the insects inhabit.

Most blue-ribbon streams are fifth- through seventh-order streams, with open canopies and a complex web of life. On these streams the amount of terrestrial litter input is far lower, and most new food in the stream is generated through photosynthesis (i.e. algae). Shredders are nearly absent (except those that feed on dead weeds), and grazers start to appear in large numbers. Grazers include the salmonflies and *Baetis* mayflies. Between the grazers and collectors, plenty of food material is kicked and chopped up into what is known as "fine particulate organic matter" (FPOM). The FPOM serves as food for a whole other group of insects: the collectors. Collectors include *Brachycentrus* and *Hydropsyche* caddis, several species of stoneflies, simullid larvae, and a few mayflies. Collectors are not as common in small streams, because the processes needed to generate FPOM takes a long time. However, in some tailwater and spring creek situations, collectors can be locally important.

Another factor in the differences of aquatic insect populations is sunlight penetration, or insolation. Light is necessary for photosynthesis, which is in turn necessary for algae and plant growth to take off. Many small streams never see direct sunlight and others only get an hour or two of direct sunlight. This results in few grazing insects and a less complex web of life. However, the exception to this is the open meadow stream. On this type of water, there is little canopy, plenty of sunlight penetration, and more grazing insects than shredders.

Finally, the physical structure of small streams influences the types of insects that inhabit them. Many small streams are swift, boulder-strewn waters, where only aquatic insects that are well adapted to clinging and crawling can

Peering into slow margins can reveal an array of important caddis and mayfly species, which we would miss if we only "kicked riffles" during sampling.

comfortably inhabit. Aquatic insects that rely on swimming (*Siphlonurus*) only end up washing downstream and eventually exit most small-stream habitats. Burrowing insects (brown drakes and *Hexagenia*) rarely find the soft, fine substrate needed to dig their homes in, and they are extremely rare in small-stream environments.

What is important to remember with small-stream insects is that their presence is due to a number of factors, not just one. One time I fished with a group of experienced guides who expected a certain stretch of a famous river to be loaded with salmonflies. The upper river was loaded with the insects, and the lower water appeared similar with fast runs and boulders. They were looking for a large population while I quickly deciphered that the population was marginal at best. Why? Because there was much more silt in the lower river, which covered the plant debris typically eaten by salmonfly nymphs. Simply knowing the diet of the insect gave me the insight that would take weeks of fishing or several hours of sampling to find out.

In addition to the differences in aquatic insect populations, small-stream fish rely much more on terrestrial food sources. During the summer months, terrestrial food sources often contribute well over half of the caloric intake of small-stream fish. The reason for this is simple: as stream width decreases, the shoreline-surface area ratio increases. The fish are closer to the candy jar, and thus get to revel in the spoils more often. Large-stream fish may only respond to terrestrials within a couple feet of shore, but since the entirety of a small stream is within a few feet of shore, trout see and rise to terrestrials freely.

When the word terrestrials is mentioned in fly-fishing circles, most minds (including my own) immediately associate it with dry flies. This is not always the case. A smorgasbord of terrestrial insects find their way onto the water, and most of them sink either because of their body structure or their attempts to escape. Alderflies, black flies, crane flies, inchworms, crickets, most ants and some beetles all sink relatively quickly under fast water conditions. It is important to remember that with the swift and broken currents found in many small streams, the descent of these insects into the watery abyss is often accelerated. A submerged driftnet set up throughout a summer day will often reveal a surprising number and variety of drowned terrestrials. Don't be so quick to omit oft-forgotten patterns like hard-shelled ants, weighted inchworms, and bead-head cranefly adults from your fly box.

Important Small-Stream Insects and Their Imitations

This section is devoted to particularly important small-stream insects, especially those that tend to be overlooked by most books and magazine articles dealing with aquatic entomology. Most of the information contained herein is derived from personal experience and from scientific journals and entomological texts, so hopefully it can provide some new information that you may not have heard before.

The insects will be discussed in their order of importance to small-stream trout, as dictated by the average of forty-seven published stomach samplings taken by entomologists and fisheries biologists. In this ordering, I am considering foods as a part of total nutritional or caloric volume, not necessarily quantity, for then we would be mired in a swamp of tiny chironomids, black flies, and *Baetis* nymphs. Within each family group of food, the various genera will be ordered in their importance to trout in small streams throughout the United States, with a particular emphasis on the West.

This ordering may appear to be far different than what you may have heard in other books or experienced on your own waters, but remember, we are dealing with a whole different type of ecosystem. Many angler samples, besides being gathered with less-than-accurate methods, are done on larger trout streams. Since this is a nationwide average, there will also likely be vast discrepancies with your local streams. In a Pacific coastal stream, cranefly larvae may rank much higher, while on a Pennsylvanian spring creek, scuds and sowbugs/cressbugs are the most important foods for trout.

I apologize for using extensive Latin when discussing insects. It causes no shortage of teasing and goading from friends and fellow anglers, who prefer to just call a bug whatever everyone else does. The only problem is, nobody really knows what they are talking about when they say Blue Dun, Pink Bodied Yellow Quill, or Yellow Sally. Sure, they know what they are talking about, but someone from another state or region might have a totally different insect that they call by that name. A perfect example is the March brown mayfly: an angler on the McKenzie gives the name to mayflies of the *Rhithrogena* genus, while an angler on the Battenkill applies the name to a *Stenonema* mayfly, while a British angler uses the name for an *Ephemera* mayfly. Though many in the fly-fishing world strive to resist accuracy for the sake of ease, this was the reason old Charles Linnaeus developed the binomial nomenclature system 300 years ago. Seriously, how can it be harder to learn the name *Epeorus* (a name that distinguishes a genera of insects from all others) instead of Pink Bodied Yellow Quill, a moniker that bears little resemblance to the insect which it is intended to name?

Following a summary of the insect, I will provide a couple fly patterns used to imitate that insect. Since there is no shortage of sources for attractor patterns, I won't list them here. I will list some unique nondescript patterns, along with recipes and summaries that may be useful on some small streams.

After we discuss the important small-stream insects, I will include a shorter section on the marginally important small-stream insects. These insects receive a lot of publicity in other areas, and since they are rarely crucial food sources on most small streams, I won't waste your time with them here. The fly patterns for these insects will be omitted as well. The bibliography also lists the important angling entomology texts, and you can locate more information on these insects there.

Trichoptera: Caddisflies

Family: Glossosomatidae
Genus: *Glossosoma*

Glossosoma caddis are the Rodney Dangerfield of the caddis world: no respect. Even the great Ernest Schwiebert only devoted 1/2 page to this insect in his classic book *Nymphs*! This second-class status has to be attributed to their diminutive size (generally 3-10 mm long), for they occur in almost every stream in the country, and often in dense numbers. These caddis are important everywhere in the West, and according to Robert Usinger Jr. in his book *Aquatic Insects of California*, "All but 2 of the 21 species described in the genus are found in the western United States and Canada." On many small streams without dense overhead canopies, they are often the most common aquatic insect, save the midge, which is always king. The *Glossosoma* genus is very diverse, with various species emerging throughout the angling season, from February through November. They can be found from the tiniest headwater streams to the broadest valley rivers, wherever there is algae for the larvae to feed on. Some related genera (like *Anagapetus*) inhabit exclusively cold-water springs, making them important to trout on some spring creeks.

These caddis create small dome-like cases and scoot around like snails on rocks as they graze on algae and diatoms. Their small size, and relative abundance, immediately warrants comparison to their Ephemeropteran equivalent, the *Baetis*. Like *Baetis*, trout will focus their feeding on *Glossosoma* caddis when there are larger insects available.

Glossosomatid larvae often inhabit the top surface of rocks, where algae and diatom growth is at its maximum. Their rocky cases are a great defense mechanism, and protect them from all but the most persistent antagonist (such as an insect-collecting fly-fisherman). The rocks that form their cases are immense relative to their body size, the equivalent of us moving desk-sized boulders! Their cases are open at the head and tail end, and from the rear end of the case the anal hooks at the end of a Glossosomatid's abdomen help anchor it to the substrate. If you ever try to pry one of these off their rocky perch, it is easy to appreciate the strength and tenacity of these insects. This strong anal hook is necessary to anchor these insects in their often-precarious residences. Glossosomatids often hold in the most exposed currents; glossosomatids were the only insect group in a British study in which over 45% of the individuals were found in exposed locations.

When these small, tan, 3-10 mm larvae grow, they abandon their old cases and build new ones from scratch. However, Glossosomatids are more willing to abandon their cases in times of stress than most other case-building caddis. At these times they are quite vulnerable to trout. As they amble naked along the bottom they often lose their grip and end up drifting downstream. Tan, uncased larvae imitations can be deadly at these times.

The pupae mature in a cocoon attached to rocks in the same moderate currents that the larvae inhabit (unlike many other types of caddis that migrate into relatively slower water before beginning the pupal phase). Though they stay in the same section of the river, studies have shown that *Glossosoma* will migrate to the less intense currents behind rocks when preparing to pupate. The pupae are about the same length as the larvae, and have a tannish-cream abdomen and a dark-brown thorax. As the pupae begin to emerge, many crawl towards shore rather than swim to the surface.

In Oregon, Glossosomatids emerge almost exclusively between May and August, with the notable exception of *G. pyroxum*, which can come off in good, fishable numbers on the upper Willamette in November and December. Similar emergence periods of May through September hold for Glossosomatids in most other western states. Adults are between 4-10 mm long with dark-olive or dark-brown bodies and dark, speckled wings. The adults are only briefly available during emergence, but are especially targeted by trout when they dive underwater to lay eggs on the substrate. This is the most important stage of the life cycle for fishermen. About three hours before I wrote this piece, I had over 50 *Glossosoma* females crawling down my legs into the water attempting to lay eggs on my boots while fishing on the Yellowstone River! I know I made many trout happy every time I moved my feet! A study by Howard University biologist Dr. Rick Duffield et. al. revealed that brook trout in a small Wyoming stream consumed three times more female *G. verdona* adults than male *G. verdona* adults. This is a likely result of the underwater ovipositing of the females. Fishing a tiny diving caddis or a small, sunken Elk Hair Caddis is strongly advised when egg-laying behavior is observed.

Glossosomatids are often the most numerous caddis on our smaller western streams. And though they are amongst the smallest caddis, the angler should pay attention and take note of their presence.

Glossossoma Caddis are the Baetis *of the caddis world their imitations are essential for small-stream aficionados.*

Cased Glossosoma Caddis

   Hook: Dai Riki 305, #18-22
 Underbody: Tan sparkle dubbing
   Head: Brown sparkle dubbing
   Case: Fine gravel from stream you are fishing, super glued to top
       of body

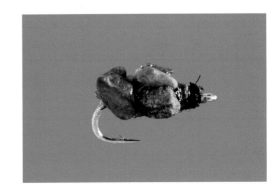

This version of a cased caddis is a dead ringer for the natural, and the construction of the case is similar for other stone- or gravel-case makers: use similarly proportioned stones for Limnephilidae and *Dicosmoecus*, and use coarse sand for Lepidostomidae. The key to forming the body is to give two base layers of super glue, then gently mold several pebbles to the shape of the body, then add two more layers of super glue. This fly should be fished at dusk and sunrise when caddis larvae are most likely to freely drift near the bottom as they migrate to greener pastures.

Uncased Glossosoma Caddis

   Hook: Dai Riki 305, #16-20
   Body: Tan sparkle dubbing
  Ribbing: Fine copper wire
   Head: Brown sparkle dubbing

Caddis are most likely to encounter *Glossosoma* larvae when the larvae flee their cases during times of stress. These little unprotected bugs look like tiny trout Twinkies. Besides *Glossosoma*, this pattern imitates a myriad of other immature caddis larvae that trout feed on heavily during the summer and fall.

Diving Glossosoma Caddis

   Hook: Dai Riki 310
   Butt: Insect-green dubbing
   Body: Dark-brown caddis emerger Hareline Dubbin'
  Ribbing: Fine gold wire
  Thorax: Gold bead
 Underwing: 4 strands of black or peacock Krystal Flash
   Wing: Dark partridge feathers
 Antennae: Brown-dyed pheasant-tail fibers or Krystal Flash

This is a simple pattern to imitate one of the more common insects on our small streams. It has the flash and silhouette to imitate a diving caddis, and fish will hit it on the dead-drift or the swing. Many people try to use soft hackles to imitate diving caddis, but most of these lack the flash to really imitate the natural.

X-Caddis

   Hook: Dai Riki 305, #16-20
   Tail: Brown Antron
   Body: Dark-brown dubbing
  Wing: Dark deer hair

CDC Caddis
Hook: Dai Riki 305, #16-20
Body: Black or dark brown dubbing
Wing: 2 black or dark dun CDC feathers
Legs: CDC fibers
Head: Dubbing to match body

Genus: *Rhyacophila* (Green Rockworm)

Because the *Rhyacophila* has no case, anglers automatically think they are the most desirable caddis for trout. This is not always the case. The *Rhyac* is common in fast small streams, and anglers on large and small streams should carry plenty of imitations of the larvae and adult stages.

The larvae of this insect are predatory in nature, so they do plenty of crawling around on rocks with the help of strong anal hooks. The larvae are concentrated in swift riffle water, making them critical to small-stream anglers. The bright green larvae are about 9-18 mm in length, though the larvae are always smaller in the drift (when they are curled and scrunched up) than when they are in your hand crawling around. However, when tying your own patterns, be sure to keep them thin; avoid unnaturally thick bead-bodied imitations. They look good in the shop bins and sell well, but more emaciated imitations fish much better.

One common vice among anglers is to call all green caddis larvae Green Rockworms. Considering that several species of hydropsychids and limnephilids, as well as the widespread genera *Brachycentrus* and *Amiocentrus*, all have green-hued larvae, this minor mistake can lead to bad fly choice, mistaken hatch periods, and poor choices of where to fish imitations. Of course, they will still catch fish, but not as easily or plentifully as if the accurate insect had been identified.

Because the pupae emerge in swift water and rise quickly, they are of less importance to the angler. Some people do well (frustratingly well) by swinging soft hackles and pupae patterns prior to this hatch. Sometimes this technique is deadly in small streams where you can swing a fly under branches that prohibit a standard presentation.

The adult *Rhyacophila* usually have a green body and a soft gray wing, and range from 8-14 mm in length. Compared to the more stout Spotted Sedge or Grannom, this insect seems like a frail little bug. Like most caddis, the adults live in the streamside foliage for a couple weeks after hatching, swarming over the stream during periods of low light. Some people think this caddis lays its eggs under water, while others think it drops them on the surface. I think I have seen both occur. Just be observant and open to different techniques when the females are laying eggs.

Green Rockworm Larvae
Hook: Dai Riki 135, #10-16
Body: Insect-green sparkle dubbing
Back: Mottled oak Thinskin
Ribbing: 6X mono
Head: Golden brown squirrel fur
This is my fallback rockworm larvae pattern, though you will find many people packing bead-bodied patterns these days. The problem with those patterns is that they are simply too thick, especially in their smaller sizes. This pattern should be tied quite thin, and can be churned out of the vise at an incredible rate.

EZ Rockworm

    Hook: Dai Riki 135, #10-12
    Weight: (optional) 5 wraps .010 lead wire
    Body: Olive Estaz, clipped short
    Head: Golden brown Arizona synthetic Peacock Dubbing

This simple pattern can be whipped out in no time at all, and thus can be quickly added as a dropper to almost any pattern. I find that it is a little chunky for a rockworm larvae, but works splendidly as an olive Hydropsychid imitation. Like many other quick-to-tie patterns in my arsenal, this one came from guide Gary Muck.

Deer Hair Pupa

    Hook: Dai Riki 135, #12-16
    Body: Olive caddis emerger Hareline Dubbin'
    Ribbing: Fine gold wire
    Thorax: Brown or olive deer hair, dubbed onto a base of olive or brown sparkle dubbing (clipped top and sides)
    Head: Brass bead

This pattern works well in fast-water situations. If you look at a lot of natural caddis pupae, you'll notice the abdomen is one color, while the head, legs, and wingpads are often a slightly different shade. The imitation of that color differential is one of the keys to this pattern. If you apply paste floatant (or permanent floatant) to the thorax, it can capture some mean air-bubbles, like a naturally rising pupae. The colors in this pattern can also be altered to imitate nearly any caddis larvae.

X-Caddis

    Hook: Dai Riki 305, #12-18
    Tail: Brown/olive Antron
    Body: Olive sparkle dubbing
    Wing: Dun deer hair

CDC Caddis

    Hook: Dai Riki 305, #12-18
    Body: Green sparkle dubbing
    Wing: 2 dun CDC feathers
    Legs: CDC fibers
    Head: Dubbing to match body

Family: Limnephilidae

The Limnephilidae family is vast and complex, and it is tricky to assign importance to particular insects without descending into more painful details. The fall caddis (*Dicosmoecus spp.*) can be extremely important in Western small streams. These big grazing larvae (25-45 mm in length) are easily spotted crawling on the rocks in the marginal water near shorelines. Don't worry too much about the larvae because their hefty cases sink them back down if they are dislodged. However, any sightings should be catalogued in memory, and you should return to the stream in September for some special action.

The majority of pupae will crawl out, but a few swim and a few are dislodged, and trout are not blind to Tootsie-Roll-sized orange bugs drifting by their noses. The pupae are poor crawlers and lack the anal hooks which allow larvae to remain grounded. Pupae imitations can bring wicked strikes, and many trout hook themselves when taking them. It is hard to miss a size 8 orange bug. The pupae will emerge in late evening, and I rarely use a pupae imitation until 5:00 PM.

The adults will be sporadically available, and trout can be eager to consume their last large meals of the season. The adult can range from 20-35 mm in length, with an orange or rusty brown body and a brownish wing. The females have an awkward way of plopping on the surface and squirming to release their eggs. For this reason, a skittering retrieve can attract V wakes from several yards away. However, on many streams, for some unknown reason, the trout will not touch adult October caddis.

The various species of Limnephilidae are known as summer fliers, though they emerge in the spring through the fall. There is a wide range of larval sizes, colors, case styles to cover, and depending on your region, I have to leave it to you to learn more about this bug. (In Oregon alone, there are over eighty species in this family of caddis!) Many of your mystery hatches are composed of either members of this family of caddis or its close cousin Lepidostomidae. The Lepidostomids are easily distinguished from the Limnephilids because their larvae lack the dorsal hump on their first abdominal segment.

Cased Limnephilid Caddis

    Hook: Mustad 9671, #8-16

Underbody: Dubbing, any color

    Case: Fine gravel from the stream you are fishing, pine needles, or fine natural woody debris

    Head: Brown or black sparkle dubbing

You can never have too many caddis imitations on small streams, and this is another one I like. Limnephilid caddis are one of the largest caddis families, and the larvae use a variety of materials to build their cases. Collect some naturals from nearby streams to see your local preferred case style. My favorite style to fish with is the one with fine gravel epoxied and super glued to the body, mostly because of the weight this style gives the pattern.

Desolation Caddis

    Hook: Dai Riki, #4-12

    Body: Dubbed deer hair (dark brown is my favorite)

    Wing: Brown raffia (Swiss straw), treated with two coatings of Flexament

    Head: Dubbed deer hair to match body

This is a European pattern used in Austria and Scandinavia, and it has proven itself successful in America as well. There likely is no material that is as hard to dub as deer hair, so have patience when tying it. It may help to use a lot of dubbing wax or to dub a base of fur before applying the deer hair. The deer hair helps it float, though it actually rides in the surface film. A scraggly fly is OK, even preferable, because it imitates a stillborn caddis, with wings, legs, and pupal shuck all askew. The color of the deer hair and the raffia can be changed to imitate any kind of caddis.

October Caddis Adult

Hook: Dai Riki 270, #8-12
Body: 50% orange Scintilla and 50% orange/yellow
      Scintilla Dubbing
Hackle: Brown, palmered and clipped
Underwing: Root Beer Krystal Splash
Overwing: Dark deer hair or elk hair
Head: Brownish-orange deer hair, bullet-head style

This is a pattern to satisfy the desires of anglers rather than fish. Fish rarely take adult October caddis, but occasionally, these patterns mysteriously catch a bunch of fish. This pattern is primarily used as a strike indicator for large October caddis pupae imitations or smaller nymphs.

October Caddis Pupae

Hook: Dai Riki 270, #10-12
Body: 50% orange Scintilla and 50% orange/yellow Scintilla
      Dubbing
Ribbing: Small pearl Mylar tinsel
Thorax: Tungsten bead
Wingpads: Duck quill or raffia
Legs: Dark Hungarian partridge
Antennae: 2 orange pheasant tail fibers

By the time September and October roll around, most of the food sources in small streams are very small. At this time of the year, the big October caddis pupae get ready to emerge and offer trout a meal that is more nutrient-dense than 100 *Baetis* nymphs! Trout will be on alert in case one of these big orange bugs loses its grip during its migration to the shoreline. During the fall, this nymph replaces the Pupatator as my point fly in my standard nymphing setup.

Genus: *Brachycentrus*
Species: *Brachycentrus americanus, Brachycentrus occidentalis*

Brachycentrus is America's caddisfly. The species *B. americanus* is present all over the country, providing excellent spring emergences on large and small streams alike. The other important species, *B. occidentalis,* is restricted to waters west of the Rocky Mountain region. Its nickname, the Grannom, is adopted from the English form of this insect. While the Grannom larvae are filter feeders, a functional group uncommon in small streams, they are the most common filter feeder there and thus deserve some attention from anglers.

The larvae of this insect attaches their cases to the tops of rocks in precariously fast currents, where they have plenty of water to filter their food. They also can be found attached to weeds in slower water. Though their cases are solidly attached, they can be dislodged by wading anglers and end up in the gullet of a hungry trout. The larvae build a brown-colored chimney case out of plant material, which has four distinct sides. The larvae are generally 6-12 mm in length, and bright neon green in color. These caddis are also the most heavily preyed upon kind of cased caddis, likely because of the digestibility of their cases.

Pupae can be important to the angler, and many anglers ignore the adults totally and focus on the green and black, 8-10 mm long pupae. However, pupae imitations should be used only during the pre-emergence period, for the Grannom has a concentrated emergence with few stragglers.

Swarms of adults are what one expects on the big rivers when fishing the Mother's Day Caddis emergence, though more sporadic emergences are the norm on small streams. Grannoms emerge in the mid-spring (April-May), but an emergence of smaller *Brachycentrus* comes off in midsummer. Some people call it a second generation emergence, but this is unlikely since *Brachycentrus* are univoltine. The adults are about 8-12 mm long, with a dark olive body and even darker, almost black, wings. During the cooler spring months, Grannom emerge during the warmer afternoon hours, but during the summer, they delay their emergence until evening.

Cased Brachycentrus

      Hook: Mustad 9671, #12-18
Underbody: .015 lead wire
  Abdomen: Brown pheasant tail, or 3 dark moose mane fibers wrapped around the body
     Collar: Insect-green sparkle dubbing
       Legs: Dark partridge
     Head: Black bead

The Cased Brachycentrus is a very realistic imitation of one of the most common caddis in our streams which is often available to trout due to Brachycentrid's dangerous affinity for fast currents. *Brachycentrus* are the most common cased-caddis larvae eaten by trout. With the lead wraps and the bead head, it can get deep fast and can be a killer fly on both creeks and larger rivers throughout the country.

Grannom Soft Hackle

      Hook: Dai Riki 300, #12-14
Abdomen: Peacock herl
 Ribbing: Fine silver tinsel
  Hackle: Black CDC over gray partridge
    Head: Black or dark dun ostrich herl

Everyone knows that I am not the most enthusiastic fan of using soft hackles, but the success that many anglers have with soft-hackled imitations cannot be denied. This fly is best fished on the swing when fish are seen boiling just below the surface during a thick *Brachycentrus* hatch.

X-Caddis

      Hook: Dai Riki 305, #12-14
      Tail: Olive Antron
    Body: Olive/green or black sparkle dubbing
    Wing: Dark-dun deer hair, or dyed-black deer hair

CDC Caddis (Dark Brown or Black, size 16-20)
  Hook: Dai Riki 305, #12-14
  Body: Insect-green sparkle dubbing
  Wing: 2 black CDC feathers
  Legs: CDC fibers
  Head: Black dubbing
  Antennae: 2 black stripped-hackle stems

Genus: *Amiocentrus*
Species: *Amiocentrus aspilus*

   Amiocentrus aspilus is an elongated Brachycentrid, which borders on marginal importance to most Western anglers. They are only located in some Western localities, preferring slower water with a higher degree of decaying vegetative matter than their cousins, *Brachycentrus americanus*. This habitat requirement relegates *A. aspilus* to plunge-pool streams west of the Cascade Mountains, as well as spring creeks and macrophyte-rich freestone streams throughout the West. Fortunately, for the angler, where they do occur, they occur in sufficient densities so as to make them important to the trout. In one stream in the northern Oregon Cascade Mountains, I located over 200 mature larvae (IV and V instar) per square foot of bottom in a leaf-strewn side eddy. Dr. N.H. Anderson, emeritus professor of aquatic entomology at Oregon State, once located over 700 larvae per square foot on the Metolius River in Oregon. When insects of their size are this dense, trout take notice.

   The *A. aspilus* larva is a thin insect, with a wiry chimney case of wood or plant material. It resembles a stretched-out Grannom larva, though the Grannom case has four distinct sides, while the *A. aspilus* case is shaped like a cone. A mature larva usually tops off between 8-10 mm in length. As mentioned before, *A. aspilus* larvae prefer water with plenty of decaying vegetative matter, and when present, can often be found crawling around on the shallow margins of pools and eddies where leaf matter is most abundant. The slow-water preference of this larvae minimizes its importance to small-stream trout. Though when they are caught in the drift, it takes a long time for their light plant material case to sink to the bottom.

   For anglers, the most important stage of this insect is the pupal stage. Since the pupae congregate in slow-water eddies and pools, they create large pupation beds. The pupation tubes point straight up, so the angler can clearly see if the bugs have popped out or not, without going through the trouble of searching or screening the bottom. With the local densities in which these insects occur, trout downstream of these beds are suckers for pupae imitations. With the local abundance of this food source, they can also be damnably picky for small-stream fish. The pupae of this species are often 7-11 mm in length, with green abdomens and darker thoraxes.

   Adults of this species are rather ephemeral for Trichoptera, and will rarely live longer than several days. These insects are often a grayish-brown in color and range in size from 7-11 mm. They generally emerge in midsummer. Though the larvae are quite recognizable, I have not been able to distinguish a natural *A. aspilus* adult in the field.

Cased Amiocentrus
Hook: Dai Riki 700, #14-16
Abdomen: Brown pheasant tail, or 3 dark moose mane fibers wrapped around the body
Collar: Insect-green sparkle dubbing
Legs: Dark partridge
Head: Dark brown sparkle dubbing

You'll notice that this pattern differs little from the Cased Brachycentrus at first glance. The big difference is that this fly is unweighted. The bead head and lead wire would cause the fly to sink too rapidly in the slow waters that the natural calls home. This fly should be fished in marginal seams along eddies, as well as immediately downstream of eddies.

X-Caddis
Hook: Dai Riki 305, #14-16
Tail: Brown Antron
Body: Olive sparkle dubbing
Wing: Dun deer hair

CDC Caddis
Hook: Dai Riki 305, #14-16
Body: Olive sparkle dubbing
Wing: 2 dark dun CDC feathers
Legs: CDC fibers
Head: Dubbing to match body
Antennae: Stripped dun hackle stems

Family: *Hydroptilidae*

The microcaddis is truly deserving of its moniker: most are so small that they drift undetected right through most anglers' (and entomologists') seines. At only 1-6 mm in length, the importance of these insects to small-stream trout can easily be debated. The larvae of this caddis are free living, though they create a tiny, laterally flattened purse case out of silk and sand for their final instar. The IV and V instar larvae also have an abnormally bloated abdomen, which makes them easily distinguishable from other free-living larvae. These caddis can appear in very dense numbers in certain areas, and this is probably the only time they should be imitated.

The microcaddis is an enigma to most anglers. Many anglers confuse the true microcaddis with the smaller members of the Glossosomatid family. Since even entomologists with Ph.Ds in aquatic entomology can't distinguish adult caddis species without a microscope and wing venation key, it is safe to say that most anglers who run into an emergence of infuriatingly small Glossosomatids likely found the name microcaddis more fitting. This has resulted in a number of articles and columns that are misdirected. Because of this misperception, and the fact that most entomologists and fisheries biologists don't consider the microcaddis to be a significant part of the trout's diet (less than 0.2% in terms of biomass is a conservative estimate), I tend to disregard their importance to trout. Microcaddis, like midges, should only be imitated when trout are visibly feeding on them and no other bugs are out, lest you go postal on a bunch of naïve fingerlings.

Microcaddis Larvae

Hook: Dai Riki, #20-22
Dubbing: Black sparkle dubbing
Ribbing: Fine gold wire

This tiny nymph has become one of my favorites for both microcaddis larvae and black fly larvae. It may be small, but is not difficult to tie; you can tie a year's supply in less than an hour. Be careful when using small flies like this on small streams so you aren't constantly hooking tiny trout.

CDC Microcaddis Adult

Hook: Dai Riki 300, #20-22
Body: Dark brown dubbing
Wing: Dark dun CDC

This fly is really easy to tie, but difficult to fish because of its size and dark color. I only use tiny patterns like this one when I see that naturals and fish are refusing larger patterns. After the fish soak this pattern and it slowly sinks, keep on using it! It fishes great as an impromptu wet fly.

Ephemeroptera: *Mayflies*
Genus: *Baetis*

The queen of American mayflies must top the list of small-stream mayflies simply because of the diversity of habitats you'll find them in. From tiny alpine trickles to the broad Missouri River, as long as there is algae to graze on, there will be *Baetis*. They have also adapted to a variety of bottom conditions, from slow weedy waters to massive boulder fields. For all their eclectic habitat choices, *Baetis* are most common in broad shallow riffles and runs where ample sunlight is available to nurture a good crop of algae.

The *Baetis* nymph is a staple of the trout diet. If I had to choose one fly to fish on any stream in the country, during the course of an entire season, an imitation of the *Baetis* nymph would be my first choice. The *Baetis* nymph can range from olive to dark-brown in color, and 3-10 mm in length. *Baetis* nymphs are excellent swimming nymphs, though most spend their time crawling around grazing on the thin layer of algae and diatoms coating the rocks and plant stalks. Because they can swim well they tend to undergo a much higher rate of diurnal drift than other aquatic insects. The wingpads on the *Baetis* turn dark prior to emergence, and this is a good way to predict an upcoming emergence of these insects.

As the *Baetis* emerges, it rises to the surface, where trout intercept many of them before they can emerge. A floating nymph or a nymph imitation just under the surface can be more effective than dun imitations during the hatch. Most species of *Baetis* emerge February-April and September-November, though in low elevations the emergence will continue throughout the winter. In high elevation streams, adults will come off even in the warm August months. *Baetis* emergences occur most often on cool, damp days and prolonged sunny stretches during the prime emergence season, often producing a super hatch on the first rainy day. The adults molt into spinners within hours of emergence, and females return to lay eggs the next day. Many females crawl underwater to lay eggs on submerged eggs or rocks. During this journey many are dislodged, and trout are known to feed heavily on these drowned adults. On small streams, where exposed rocks and logs are much more common than in broad rivers, nearly all females lay their eggs this way, making a sunk female imitation indispensable.

Mr. Jones' Baetis Nymph
    Hook: Dai Riki 310 or 305, #16-22
    Tail: Olive pheasant tail fibers
    Ribbing: Fine gold wire
    Thorax: Olive or golden Arizona synthetic Peacock Dubbing
    Wingcase: Pheasant tail fibers
    Legs: Peacock Krystal Flash

This is an absolutely killer fly and one I use throughout the season. It bears a close resemblance to a standard Pheasant Tail, but by adding dubbing instead of peacock herl for the thorax, you can keep the thorax more proportional. The Krystal Flash legs offer a little flash that seals the deal for many trout. Fish this one on streams of all sizes.

Baetis Killer
    Hook: Dai Riki 310 or 305, #16-22
    Tail: Olive Hungarian partridge fibers
    Thorax: Olive rabbit dubbing
    Ribbing: Fine gold wire
    Thorax: Olive rabbit dubbing
    Wingcase: Black ostrich herl or black marabou, clipped short

This is another nymph that fishes well anywhere there are *Baetis* nymphs. This fly is particularly effective just prior to an emergence, as the black herl wingcase matches the dark case of the naturals.

Baetis CDC Dun
    Hook: Dai Riki 310 or 305, #16-22
    Tails: Dun Micro Fibetts
    Body: Olive dubbing or olive turkey biot
    Underwing: 3 strands gray Krystal Flash
    Overwing: Dun CDC

A perfect fly to imitate *Baetis* duns, this pattern is simple to tie, an excellent floater, and it has a superb impression on the surface. I use this pattern on streams of all sizes, throughout the entire season. This fly is so easy to tie and so realistic, why waste time tying anything else?

Diving Baetis Spinner
    Hook: Dai Riki 310 or 305, #16-22
    Tails: Dun Micro Fibetts
    Egg Sac: Bright yellow dubbing
    Body: Olive/brown turkey biot or olive brown dubbing
    Wing: Z-wing or tan raffia, tied back and clipped to shape
    Hackle: Starling, 1 1/2 wraps

When *Baetis* spinners lay eggs, many dive under water to do so. This fly imitates those spinners, and fishes well when you see lots of adults flying around but you can't seem to pull up any fish with dun imitations. I often fish this fly dead drift under an indicator like a nymph. If you want, you can add a pearl bead in the thorax.

Genus: *Cinygmula*
Genus: *Cinygma*

What is this bug doing so high? Where are the imitations in the fly shops? Where are the articles in the magazines? You probably will be shocked when I tell you that *Cinygmula* would have been the number one small-stream mayfly if it weren't restricted to the Western states! According to Hafele and Hughes, eight of the nine *Cinygmula* and all four species of *Cinygma* are found in the West.

One reason that you may not recognize the name of this insect is because the Latin name of the insect is rarely discussed. The wise world of angling has instead opted for several different confusing aliases like Blue Winged Red Quill, Red Quill, and Blue Quill. Considering that various species of *Rhithrogena, Ephemerella, Heptagenia,* and *Paraleptophlebia* all share the red quill moniker, you'll see why I use Latin almost exclusively when discussing insects.

Cinygmula and *Cinygma* predominate in the small, higher-elevation streams from Arizona to Glacier National Park. These insects, who have a very similar physical appearance, inhabit a wide variety of waters. In a study by J.V. Ward, these critters were the only insect that inhabited all elevations of John Gierach's favorite small stream, the St. Vrain River in Colorado. These insects can be found in small numbers on many of our large streams, but they are often overshadowed by other, more numerous species. There is also the problem that most adults are virtually identical to a Pale Evening Dun, which results in mass confusion even when *Cinygmula* are present.

Cinygmula nymphs are not huge, and at a modest 7-12 mm, trout will not move a great distance to pick one off. These nymphs are often colored various shades of brown, and this may be to camouflage them amongst the wood and leaves that they feed on. Like other Heptegeniids, they are very fond of fast water. Their affinity is probably related to the fact that their bodies are quite adapted to inhabit swift currents. Their bodies have a very dorsal-ventrally flattened shape, and their heads are unusually large relative to the size of their bodies. This head shape lets them face into the current, allowing water to flow around the body in a teardrop shape. Though flattened like all Heptegeniids, they often are found in the slowest parts of fast water: under rocks and in crevices between boulders. When they wander out to feed, the swift water occasionally dislodges them and makes them available to trout. *Cinygma* is the only Ephemeropteran found by Dudley and Anderson to feed on wood. Other mayfly nymphs will feed on the algae that grows on it, but won't consume the wood itself. This is an important detail to the small-stream angler, and automatically places *Cinygmula* high on the list of insects important to headwater trout.

Cinygmula nymphs are more susceptible to dislodging following spate conditions than other Heptegeniids, and thus must be considered more important than their cousins *Rhithrogena, Heptagenia,* and *Epeorus.* Larger *Cinygmula* nymphs tend to follow a nightly drift pattern (like many other aquatic insects), though they drift best on moonless nights. *Cinygmula* will also take to drift upon the immediate start of high-sediment periods, thus being a good nymph to imitate at the start of spate flooding. Considering the high-elevation habitats they love so much are susceptible to numerous summer thunderstorms, there are abundant possibilities to imitate this nymph. With all this time drifting, it is no surprise that these nymphs are quite commonly fed upon by small-stream fish. Several stomach pumpings I have done on trout in the Oregon Cascades confirmed this. Most anglers have a phobia of fishing nymphs on small streams, and I hope that this information on *Cinygmula* can coax some anglers into exploring this technique.

The literature on *Cinygma* and *Cinygmula* is so sparse that no one really knows their exact life cycle and emergence habits. For the sake of discussion, let us assume that these insects emerge by swimming to the surface like other Heptegeniids. I have never seen fish feeding selectively on emergers, but considering the swift waters these bugs inhabit, many rise below the surface swirls and go undetected.

The adult emergence of *Cinygmula* peaks in the early summer, May-June, and the adults are brownish-olive in color. Since hatches of *Cinygmula* are almost always sparse and occur over a several month period, trout are used to seeing them and are rarely selective toward them. This fact makes them an excellent insect to imitate. Hafele and Hughes mention that the adults almost perfectly match those of *Heptagenia* (the Pale Evening Dun), and from what I have seen on the water, this is a pretty safe generalization. The scientific world has not really come to a conclusion as to how long *Cinygmula* live or their egg-laying habits, though that detail hasn't prevented several angling writers from speculating. I have not experienced a thick emergence or spinner fall of these insects, but they can be seen almost every day of the early summer flying around a small creek near you.

There are two important species of *Cinygmula* in the West:

Cinygmula ramaleyi: According to Schwiebert, the "taxonometric genotype of the *Cinygmula* flies," this emerges in June at 8,000 feet in Colorado. It is usually 3/8" in length, while the nymph is a dark mottled grayish-brown, and the duns are olive-gray. *Cinygmula mimus* is a similar insect that also emerges in the Rocky Mountain states.

Heptegeniid Nymph

>   *Hook:* Dai Riki 305, #12-16
>   *Tails:* 3 olive or brown pheasant tail fibers
> *Abdomen:* Chocolate Hareline caddis and emerger Dubbin'
> *Ribbing:* Olive Flexi-Floss
> *Wingcase:* Olive or brown pheasant tail fibers
> *Thorax:* Chocolate Hareline caddis and emerger Dubbin'
>   *Legs:* Olive or brown pheasant tail fibers, 2 to each side
>   *Head:* Black nickel bead

This patterns is great for many species of the Heptegeniidae mayfly family: *Epeorus, Cinygmula, Heptagenia,* and *Stenonema.* The mottled coloration of this pattern is much more realistic than the standard Hare's Ear, and it takes only a couple seconds longer to tie. You can spice this pattern up with Krystal Flash if you like.

Parachute Cinygmula

>   *Hook:* Dai Riki 305, #12-16
>   *Tails:* Dun saddle fibers
>   *Body:* Blend of pale yellow and light brown sparkle dubbing
>   *Wing:* Dun Antron yarn
> *Hackle:* Light dun hackle

Parachute patterns are excellent for *Cinygmula* imitations because they are visible and decent floaters, yet they offer fish a vastly superior imitation than the standard imitations. Because the *Cin* is a swift-water insect, I like to tie this fly with a couple extra wraps of hackle to keep it floating high.

Genus: *Paraleptophlebia* (Mahogany Dun)

The mahogany dun is another insect that is quite prevalent on small streams. These insects are one of the most well known of the small-stream insects because they also appear on large weedy rivers like the Henry's Fork. If you learn about one mayfly in this book, this should be it for several reasons: they emerge in dense numbers, they inhabit slower waters where an accurate imitation is necessary, and they are small (and small is always tough). *Paraleptophlebia* nymphs are generally 6-9 mm in length. The nymphs are dark brown in color, have three tails, and are readily distinguishable from other mayfly nymphs by their Y-shaped, tuning fork gills along their abdomen. *Paraleptophlebia* are crawler nymphs, though they are not very good at it, and they get caught in the drift quite often. The nymphs prefer slow currents with abundant organic litter, making plunge pools and slow eddies perfect habitat for these creatures. In moderately paced streams with thick deciduous canopies, mahogany duns are often the most common mayfly nymph. Trout that live in swift water near slower runs see plenty of nymphs that amble into fast water and are caught up in the drift, and are extremely vulnerable to nymph imitations. Mahogany dun nymphs are also very active in the hour or so prior to emergence, and many species will migrate to shoreline areas to emerge, providing the anticipating angler excellent results with small nymphs.

One reason for the underestimation of mahogany duns by anglers is their tendency to live in marginal shoreline habitats. Anglers tend to either screen riffles (where these insects are absent) or pick up and look at rocks (few mahoganies can hang on when pulled through the full current); either way, they miss the insects. Professional entomologists will screen the same area, and by using proper sampling methods, will find that mahoganies are the most common mayfly in the stream!

Mahogany duns are brown; shocking, I know. They also have a dun-gray wing, three tails, and are 7-9 mm in length. They float an inordinate amount of time before flying away, making them important to trout during emergence. They also tend to emerge sporadically over a long period, giving the angler time to adjust to his or her tactics. Because these insects emerge in slow water and take their time, trout can be picky. This is one of a handful of small-stream emergences where normally uninhibited trout will become selective. A couple different patterns, especially some flat-water flies, will prove surprisingly valuable.

There are two species of mahoganies that you should particularly concern yourself with. The Slate-Winged Mahogany Dun, *P. adoptiva*, (common in the East and Midwest) is an early emerger in eastern waters. It prefers slightly faster and pebble-bottomed streams than most kinds of mahogany duns. They emerge best on cloudy and cold days in May, from 11 AM to about 5 PM. The other is the Large Slate-Winged Mahogany Dun (*P. bicornuta*) that occurs in the West and is the largest mahogany dun in North American waters. It tends to be an early fall emerger in most streams, from late August through late October.

Gilled Mahogany Dun Nymph

> *Hook:* Dai Riki 305, #14-18
> *Tails:* 3 brown pheasant tail fibers
> *Abdomen:* Brown ostrich herl
> *Ribbing:* Copper wire
> *Thorax:* Brown sparkle dubbing
> *Wingcase:* Lacquered dark partridge
> *Legs:* Dark partridge fibers

Mahogany dun nymphs are extremely common in small streams with lots of leafy deposits or weed growth. Imitations of the critter should be fished along the edges of slower waters where they are most common. While a simple dark brown Hare's Ear can be an excellent mahogany dun nymph imitation, this pattern is just a joy to tie.

Mahogany Dun Comparadun

Hook: Dai Riki 300, #14-18
Tails: Dun Micro Fibetts, split
Body: Brown sparkle dubbing
Wing: Deer hair

Simple yet deadly, the Comparadun is one of the best patterns to fool fish during mahogany dun hatches. When tied properly—with wide, long tails and splayed deer-hair wing—this pattern can be a good floater and excellent to fool slow-water fish.

Mahogany Dun Spinner

Hook: Dai Riki 305, #14-18
Tail: Dun Micro Fibetts
Body: Blend of brown and rusty-brown sparkle dubbing, or brown turkey biot
Wing: Gray Antron or dun hen feathers

I usually eschew spinner patterns for small-stream fishing, simply because there are few places where spinners are selectively fed on. This insect is a candidate for spinner imitation because the spinners come down in slow water, where fish have the luxury of ignoring anything but accurate patterns. The rusty-brown colored spinner also will imitate other small spinners (PED, *Cinygma*, PMD) and is a good choice when fish are sipping small things in the surface film in the evening.

Family: *Heptageniidae*
Genus: *Epeorus* (Little Yellow May, Pink Lady)

The *Epeorus* mayfly is a significant insect on many streams throughout the country. While there are many other obscure mayflies that live in fast waters, Epeorus' unique method of emergence makes them the most misunderstood mayfly in the angling world.

Not a fashionable insect with prolific hatches on flat water, *Epeorus* are sparsely distributed throughout most swift streams, and most trout see them enough to recognize them as food. Many people mistake *Epeorus* and nymphs with another Heptageniid, *Heptegenia*, the pale evening dun. My theory is that this confusion arises from the fact that the later has a fly named after it while the former lacks that honor. This confusion is easily resolved: simply looking at the tails of the nymph (two on the *Epeorus*) will resolve any uncertainties.

Their need for oxygen-rich and pollution-free waters restricts them to pristine, small-stream environments all over the montaine West and Appalachian East. These insects are rarely found in the Midwest or other areas that lack rapid currents. This insect is also uncommon in temporary streams or trout streams that see drastically reduced flows during certain seasons (like Pacific coastal streams).

The nymphs are dark-hued clingers and are easily distinguished by their two tails, a physical characteristic shared by no other mayfly nymph. *Epeorus* nymphs, like all Heptageniids, are well adapted to their fast-water environs. Their body, head, and legs are all dorsally flattened to give them a Spider Man-like grip on rocks. Often I will pull rocks out of fast water and the only mayflies that survive the quick trip through the fast current are *Epeorus*. Because of this adaptation, *Epeorus* rarely lose their grasp on the substrate. However, they are terrible swimmers (perhaps the worst, considering they don't even migrate or rise prior to emergence), and if dislodged can drift long distances before regaining contact with the bottom. Despite their pitiful swimming skills, they rarely lose their grip, and thus they are rarely available to trout abundantly.

When preparing to emerge, *Epeorus* will migrate to the bottoms of rocks, where current is at its calmest, split from its nymphal shuck on the bottom, and then it is buoyed to the surface by self-generated gases enveloped under the wings and legs. This shimmering, bright yellow insect, rising quickly to the water's surface, like the trout equivalent of a butterscotch disk, is too loud for trout not to take notice. It is safe to say that trout focus most of their feeding on *Epeorus* during this short ascension period of the dun. Because of this unique emerging style, there are very few (none, that I have seen) emerging nymphs and stillborn duns that make it to the surface.

The adults rarely stay on the surface for a long time like other mayflies (PMDs in particular), but trout will feed on them when they are available. The adult is a usually a true yellow hue, though there can be some variation in color between a light brown and a light tan, though *E. albertae* (the Pink Lady) can carry a pinkish hue among the females. I have never seen, nor heard of, a very good *Epeorus* spinner fall, and considering the types of water they inhabit, imitations of this stage would be quite difficult.

Heptegeniid Nymph

       Hook: Dai Riki 305, #12-16
        Tails: 3 olive or brown pheasant tail fibers
  Abdomen: Chocolate Hareline caddis and emerger Dubbin'
    Ribbing: Olive Flexi-Floss
Wingcase: Olive or brown pheasant tail fibers
   Thorax: Chocolate Hareline caddis and emerger Dubbin'
      Legs: Olive or brown pheasant tail fibers, 2 to each side
     Head: Black nickel bead

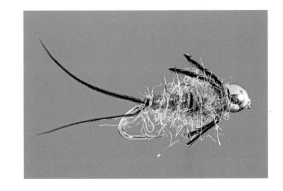

Rising Epeorus Dun

       Hook: Dai Riki 300, #12-16
        Tail: 2 split dun Micro Fibetts
      Body: Yellow sparkle dubbing
   Thorax: Pearl, medium glass bead
Underwing: Gray CDC
  Overwing: Gray raffia, trimmed into wing shape
     Head: Yellow sparkle dubbing

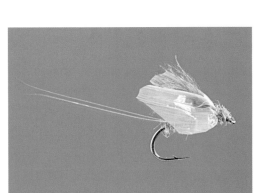

Epeorus duns emerge in a very unique way: they molt into duns on the bottom of the stream and rise to the surface with the aid of trapped gasses. The result is a bright yellow, shimmering bug that must look like a shiny butterscotch candy disk to the trout. The CDC, bead, and sparkle dubbing combine to make this pattern very realistic. The dun of this insect doesn't float on the surface long, so if you see the duns fluttering around, give this pattern a try. You can fish it with an indicator or without, just make sure you impart some false rises to make it look like the insect is moving towards the surface.

Genus: *Ameletus*

This stout insect is perhaps the heftiest mayfly common in western small streams. It is often mistaken as a Gray Drake or March brown by anglers accustomed to fishing larger streams. The prolonged emergence season, large size, and active nature of the nymphs makes this an insect that small-stream anglers keep in the fore of their mind.

Often reaching 12-14 mm in length, the *Ameletus* nymph is a swimmer of Olympic stature. Its powerful thrusts can propel the insect upstream in the disrupted currents of the bottom. This insect prefers swift mountain streams, but doesn't live in the riffles. *Ameletus* prefers the marginal water of eddies, pools, and shoreline slack water where it can graze on plant matter. Because the nymphs can swim well, imitations are rarely dead drifted. Fish them with short strips, coming out of side eddies, and marginal water, and into good trout-holding water. You will be surprised by the aggressive takes you receive.

The addictive nature of fishing nymph imitations of this insect can cause you to try it everywhere, but nymphs occur sporadically across the West. It is important to make sure there is a population of this insect, or else trout will only give your rapidly swimming nymph a passing glance. Because nymphs live in the margins, simply picking up rocks or kick netting through a riffle will reveal nothing. I have found that simply pausing and peering into margin waters will reveal the presence of *Ameletus*. If you can't see well, then run your net through the marginal water. You will likely find *Ameletus* along with *Paraleptophlebia*, *Amiocentrus*, and various other critters that you omit when simply sampling riffle water.

Because this insect crawls out to emerge, like a stonefly, the emerging period is of little importance to the angler. While there is still much debate over how many adults are available to the trout as well as how the females deposit their eggs, I can say with confidence that if you see the adults fluttering around, an imitation will produce fish. The large size is too much for small-stream fish to ignore, even if the naturals land on the surface only occasionally.

Ameletus Nymph

> *Hook:* Dai Riki 300, #10-12
> *Tails:* 3 short, gray ostrich herl tips
> *Abdomen:* Dark gray sparkle dubbing
> *Ribbing:* Fine silver tinsel
> *Wingcase:* Dark partridge, epoxied
> *Thorax:* Dark gray sparkle dubbing
> *Legs:* Dark partridge fibers

The only real powerful swimmer in small streams is the *Ameletus*, and it can cut through the water like Ian Thorpe. I fish this nymph with rapid, short strips. The nymph is weighted with a couple wraps of thread, so it sinks when it isn't moving like the natural. You can get a more active nymph by tying it with an extended body of gray superfloss, but in swift water where this insect is common, fish don't have the luxury of being too picky.

Ameletus Hairwing Dun

> *Hook:* Dai Riki 305, #10-14
> *Tails:* Moose hairs, sparse
> *Body:* Dark gray dubbing
> *Ribbing:* Iron Gray 6/0 UNI-Thread
> *Hackle:* Grizzly
> *Wing:* Dark gray deer hair

The *Ameletus* can be a rather stout insect, and this chunky pattern creates a great silhouette for picky fish. As soon as I see a couple of the naturals flying around, I am sure to tie on this large pattern because of its visibility and capacity to pull fish up from unlikely depths.

Genus: *Stenonema*
Species: *Stenonema vicarium, S. canadense, S. fuscum*

While the Western angler has never heard of these insects, the Heptegeniids are as important to smaller Eastern trout streams as any other genera of mayfly. This genus contains three critically important species, both to trout and angling lore: *Stenonema vicarium* (American March brown), *S. canadense* (light cahill), and *S. fuscum* (gray fox).

Like other Heptegeniids, *Stenonema* nymphs have large heads, flat bodies, and a mottled olive-brown body. They love swift, rocky water, making them important to small-stream fish throughout the East. Like stoneflies, they migrate to shallower riffles and edgewater prior to emergence. Also like stoneflies, trout follow them, gobbling them up before and during emergence. Nymph imitations of this insect should be fished dead drift in unusually swift water. You will be surprised where trout take them.

Schwiebert, in his masterpiece *Trout*, mentions the laborious hatching behavior of *Stenonema* mayflies. These struggles can keep the nymph and dun on the surface for a combined drift of 80-100 feet before emerging. This means dun and emerger patterns should be deadly during hatches. The duns of this mayfly genera seem to grow lighter as the season progresses. The darker March browns (size 10-14) emerge in late spring, then the gray foxes (size 12), then the light cahills (size 14) arrive in August.

The spinner falls of these insects, unlike those of the Western Heptegiiniids, can offer excellent fishing. Trout will focus on the egg-laying females, so be prepared for picky trout in slow runs and flat pools when the spinners are on the water.

Heptegeniid Nymph

      Hook: Dai Riki 305, #12-16
      Tails: 3 olive or brown pheasant tail fibers
  Abdomen: Chocolate Hareline caddis and emerger Dubbin'
    Ribbing: Olive Flexi-Floss
  Wingcase: Olive or brown pheasant tail fibers
    Thorax: Chocolate Hareline caddis and emerger Dubbin'
      Legs: Olive or brown pheasant tail fibers, 2 to each side
      Head: Black nickel bead

Simply change the colors and size, and you can imitate any of the species in the *Stenonema* genus. On slower waters, the metal bead head can be substituted with a multi-colored glass bead to get a slower sink rate and less flash. This still gives you the large head and taper that distinguishes Heptegeniid mayflies from all others.

Genus: *Heptagenia* (Pale Evening Dun)

The *Heptagenia* genus is a mayfly that is prolific in the West, common in the East, and nowhere to be found in the Midwest. Like all the other insects of this family, the *Heptagenia* can be important to small-stream trout.

However, the *Heptagenia* is not as important as its cousins for a couple reasons. First of all, it tends to be a big-stream insect, preferring the broad riffles of the Big Hole, Snake, upper Colorado, and the Deschutes. Secondly, this insect is often given credit during emergences of other insects. If most anglers see a yellow mayfly emerging in the late afternoon, they call it, naturally, a pale evening dun. It was just as likely a *Cinygmula* or an *Epeorus*, but because of its common name, *Heptagenia* steals the credit for the hatch and subsequent fishing.

Like all the other nymphs in the family, *Heptagenia* nymphs live in swift riffle water, their flat bodies conforming to the rocks to improve their hydraulics. Their similarity to *Cinygmula* is striking, and even Schwiebert discusses both insects in the same breath in *Trout*. They both have abnormally large heads, flat bodies, and strong legs. Jim Schollmeyer mentions that *Heptagenia* are good swimmers, though this is not a characteristic of most Heptageniids. The nymphs will migrate to shallower, slower water prior to their emergence and trout will follow the migration, feeding on them en route.

The adults of the pale evening dun are, surprise, pale yellow. However, some can be bright yellow, and others, even a pale olive (like the Eastern species, *H. pulla*). The adults are fed on heavily by trout, often in moderate-paced runs and current edges, where emergences are most common.

Heptagenia Nymph

> *Hook:* Dai Riki, #14-16
> *Tail:* Dark partridge fibers
> *Abdomen:* Brown fox squirrel dubbing
> *Ribbing:* Small oval gold tinsel
> *Wingcase:* Lacquered turkey quill
> *Thorax:* Ginger and brown ostrich herl
> *Head:* Black-nickel bead or black or brown-glass bead (optional)
> *Legs:* Dark partridge (optional)

The *Heptagenia* nymph is more active than its cousins, and can be found in the drift and in stomach samples in surprising numbers for a Heptageniid. This pattern is a little different from others, but it produces fish. You can add a bead if you like, but it seems to fish better without one.

Heptagenia CDC Flash Dun

> *Hook:* Dai Riki #16-20
> *Tail:* Split gray Micro Fibetts
> *Body:* Pale yellow or light brown/yellow sparkle dubbing
> *Underwing:* 3-4 strands pearl or gray Krystal Flash
> *Overwing:* 4 Dun CDC feathers

This style can be used to imitate any mayfly dun, and is useful when trout are taking duns that just emerged. When the mayfly emerges, their wet wings can set off some flash, and the Krystal Flash imitates this well. This is a superb floater in the fast waters that the pale evening duns emerge from.

Genus: *Rhithrogena* (Western March Brown)

The Western March brown is one of the most highly touted insects in the West, probably because of the time of the year that they emerge. March browns are the first large insect to emerge on most streams early in the season, and this may make anglers a little overly enthusiastic when it arrives. Kind of like Chicago Cub fans who are pumped up about their team next season, but quickly return to reality after the first shut out (a.k.a. their first game) of the year. Needless, to say, like the Cubs, the March browns are overrated most every season.

This is especially true on small streams, where March browns are often only the third or fourth most common of the Heptageniid family. Even where there are good populations of *Rhithrogena*, the nymphs are some of the best clingers around, and are rarely knocked into the drift. With the aid of a suction disk (caused by the location of the gills) on their belly, these insects stick to the substrate like Gary Payton's defense. The logical result of these things would be to focus on other insects, but instead, we anglers have decided to devote dozens of patterns and plenty of magazine articles to this insect.

Maybe the cause of the attention is their slow emergence. Since March browns emerge in cool, damp spring weather, they take a much longer time than other mayflies to dry their wings and fly away. This allows plenty of time for trout to pick off the duns, and anglers can in turn happily use their dry flies longer.

Regardless of its importance, the March brown nymph is about 8-12 mm long, with three tails, and generally a mottled brown or gray in color. Like other Heptageniids, they have a very flat body and a large head. As I mentioned earlier, these insects are tenacious clingers, which is important, as they really love fast riffles and runs. I have found that when you rub rocks off in fast water during a stream insect sample, there are often a few March brown nymphs still clinging to the rocks. The nymphs are most available to trout when they move to the tops of rocks to feed on algae or when they migrate towards slower water in the weeks prior to their emergence.

The adults are a little larger than the nymphs, usually between 8-15 mm in length. The adults have only two tails and a mottled brown wing. Many anglers who tie imitations of these insects, imitate the reddish-brown back of the insect, however, they would be far better off imitating the lighter tan underbelly. I made this mistake for a long time, and only in the past couple seasons found improved angling with the latter coloration. The adult March browns emerge in slightly slower water than the nymphs prefer, and often there are plenty of trout picking off these insects in the current seams between fast and slow water.

Heptageniid Nymph

     Hook: Dai Riki 305, #12-16
     Tails: 3 olive or brown pheasant tail fibers
  Abdomen: Chocolate Hareline caddis and emerger Dubbin'
     Ribbing: Olive Flexi-Floss
Wingcase: Olive or brown pheasant tail fibers
    Thorax: Chocolate Hareline caddis and emerger Dubbin'
      Legs: Olive or brown pheasant tail fibers, 2 to each side
     Head: Black nickel bead

The March brown nymph is initially what I tied this fly to imitate, but I found it most effective on streams that didn't even hold March browns! This fly should taper strongly towards the rear of the fly, and the bead head should be the largest part of the fly. The big bead head is used to imitate the large heads of the Heptageniid family. If you have the desire, you can tie this pattern on a flat hook (or with flattened lead wire) to create a more realistic pattern. However, because this insect dwells in fast water, trout don't really have a long time to look critically at your fly.

March Brown Flymph

     Hook: Dai Riki 305, #10-14
      Tail: Brown hackle fibers, sparse
     Body: Tan or March Brown Hare-Tron dubbing
  Hackle: Brown dyed grizzly, 3 wraps
     Head: Red thread

When trout are rising to nymphs and emergers just under the surface, few things can be as deadly as soft hackles and flymphs. A friend of mine, Jack Lynch, made me a convert to these flies after I couldn't get trout to rise to my parachute patterns. The ability to swing this fly under the surface and draw trout out from thick cover makes it an effective small-stream fly.

Parachute March Brown

Hook: Dai Riki 270, #10-14
Tail: Brown hackle fibers, sparse
Body: Tan rabbit or sparkle dubbing
Wing: Olive-dun Antron yarn
Hackle: Brown dyed grizzly, parachute style

I have always thought this color pattern outfished the standard Parachute Adams during the March brown hatch, and I use this pattern in smaller sizes as a searching pattern throughout the summer. A couple strands of dun or root beer Krystal Flash can be added to the wing for a little extra flash.

Low-light Spinner

Hook: Dai Riki 305, #10-18
Tail: Split Micro Fibetts
Body: Fine synthetic dubbing
Wing: Clear Antron
Wingcase: Yellow, pink, or white craft foam

There are few occasions where small-stream trout get picky, but when they do, few things can beat a spent mayfly pattern. There are dozens of spinner patterns out there, but most are too delicate, too sinkable, and too hard to see to be productive on most small streams. This fly is extremely durable, and the foam post aids greatly in visibility. You can also easily adjust the color of the dubbing to match the natural insects by dubbing them with white fur, then coloring it at the stream with a waterproof marking pen.

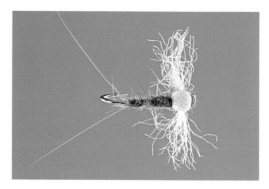

Plecoptera: Stoneflies
Family: Chloroperlidae
Genus: *Alloperla* (Little Green Stoneflies)

Chloroperlids are some of the more diminutive members of the Plecopteran order, only maxing out at 1/2" in length, though it may make up for it in its generous distribution. The over twenty species of the *Alloperla* genus can be found from the Pacific to the Rockies, and from small to large streams. The concentrations of *Alloperla* seem to be densest in medium-sized streams with good deciduous foliage in the riparian area. Hafele and Hughes mention the best habitat being small Pacific Coast streams, where dense alder stands provide plenty of organic matter for the nymphs to hide in and consume. I have also seen good populations on small Cascades streams with a mixed maple-alder canopy, as well as in Rocky Mountain streams that harbor beautiful aspen groves.

Alloperla nymphs are generally 1/8-1/2" in length, and colors range from tan to brown, though approximately four species wear a gaudy bright-green color during their nymph stage. The nymphs prefer sheltered currents in the vicinity of swift water. Unlike many stonefly nymphs, you can't check for the presence of *Alloperla* by simply picking up rocks in riffles. These nymphs are often found in the slower water of eddies or at the heads and tailouts of pools, crawling under their blanket of leafy debris. The nymph stage generally lasts about a year, though the nymphs are only in an imitatable size after December.

Alloperla nymphs are sensitive to sand and other suspended sediments (the pounding of which on insects is tantamount to us being bombarded with golf-ball-sized stones), and often will freely drift after a high-sediment spate in order to seek out less abrasive confines. Imitations of drifting nymphs can be quite effective at these times.

The nymphs of these insects do not undergo a large, shoreward migration like golden stoneflies or salmonflies. Many opt for the exposed rocks in their home riffles, and emerge there. In the small-stream habitat of *Alloperla*, these protruding rocks are quite common, and often littered with the shucks of previously emerged insects. Thus, the pre-emergence nymphing period for these insects is marginal at best.

Alloperla is a summer emerger, with adults ranging from 3/8"-1/2" in length, and a either yellowish-gray or green color. The adults live awhile after emerging, and according to many fishing texts they are not very active in the daytime. Despite this lack of activity, enough flutter around that trout will eagerly take an imitation. I have found several adults in the sample of a trout taken at 4 PM, several hours before the mating swarms comes off the shoreline brush. Some studies have shown peak feeding on *Alloperla* occurring between 2-4 PM.

The egg laying of *Alloperla* can be rather impressive, and some of the best small-stream fly-fishing I have experienced has been during these evening swarms. Like most stoneflies, *Alloperla* females lay eggs by dropping down and touching the tip of their abdomen to the water's surface. In this process of regeneration, many females meet their end by becoming stuck in the water and, subsequently, devoured by trout. The females tend to have a red tip at the end of their abdomen, and it can be very productive to imitate this feature when tying an imitation. Trout have been known to key in on females Chloroperlids. In one study by Richard Duffield, adult female were consumed at a rate of 10 to 1 over adult males. Because of this evidence, I feel it is essential to imitate the red egg sac of the female.

Some important species of Alloperla include:

A. borealis: predominates in Montana and Wyoming. This stonefly is about 1/2" in length, and almost the shade of a chartreuse highlighter. It emerges in the evenings in July and early August, though it can often be found flying around rivers throughout the day.

A. pacifica: This insect is more common west of the Cascades in Oregon and Washington. It is a tad larger (5/8" long) and more yellow than A. borealis. It emerges between late June and early July.

Sweltsa lamba: Common in the Rockies and sporadically common in other places throughout the West. An afternoon flier, the adult females are particularly important to dry-fly anglers.

Alloperla Nymph
   Hook: Dai Riki 300, #12-14
   Tails: Chartreuse monofilament or micro-rubber legs
   Body: Bright green dubbing
   Ribbing: 4X monofilament
   Thorax: Bright green dubbing
Wingcases: Light Green Wapsi Thinskin
Antennae: Same as tails

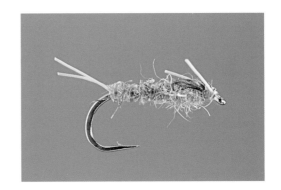

This nymph is gaudy, but when the bright-colored nymphs are present it can be deadly. The *Alloperla* nymphs are sensitive to sediment and flooding and like to migrate during these times, combine this with their bright color, they are an obvious choice for trout to feed on. Always tie up some in tan or brown to imitate the standard nymphs as well. The standard colors also double as imitations of *Isoperla* and juvenile *Hesperoperla* stonefly nymphs too.

CDC Alloperla

      Hook: Dai Riki 300, #12-14
      Butt: Red dubbing
      Body: Pale yellow/yellow sparkle dubbing
      Wing: Pale yellow CDC

The *Alloperla*, or little yellow Sally, is one of the most important insects in Western small streams. The nymphs graze in the leaf packs that gather at the heads of riffles, while the adults flutter about the streamside trees. This pattern floats well and is quick to tie. The red butt seems to be essential because it imitates the egg sac of the female, which are much more commonly consumed than the female.

Family: Perlodidae
Genus: *Isoperla* (Little Yellow Stonefly)

    The stoneflies of the *Isoperla* genus look quite similar to those of the golden stones. The visual and behavioral similarities are no doubt due to their close relation, both being members of the Perlid family of stoneflies. The *Isoperla* stonefly is most important on small streams, though it can be a significant contributor to the diets of large-stream trout.

    The *Isoperla* nymph runs about 7-16 mm in length, and has the yellow and black coloration of a golden stonefly nymph, though the *Isoperla* has dark stripes running the length of its abdomen. This nymph is an aggressive predator, and combining this with the fact that they live in swift, turbulent currents, they can easily be dislodged into the drift. It is one of the only small stonefly nymphs that I imitate on a regular basis.

    The adult *Isoperla* is yellow or brown in color, and 8-18 mm in length. Like the nymph, it looks a lot like a smaller clone of a golden stone. They are less active during the day than Chloroperlids, and more active in the evenings when they often swarm over the water. Unfortunately for many big-stream anglers, most species of *Isoperla* come off during the late spring-early summer season when a myriad of other large insects (golden stones, salmonflies, green drakes, Grannom, and brown drakes) are emerging. The result is that many anglers overlook the hatches, and fish can be gorged and reluctant to feed even when the insects are common. On small streams, however, the *Isoperla* can be one of the most common emerging insects during this season and fish will respond much more eagerly to imitations. Finally, don't let the fact that many anglers call these insects yellow Sallies confuse you. These are not as yellow (or chartreuse) as the true yellow Sallies (the Chloroperlids), whose coloration is different and their adult activity often occurs at different time.

Isoperla Nymph

      Hook: Dai Riki 270, #10-14
      Tails: Golden goose biots
  Underbody: Light yellow dubbing
    Overbody: Black or dark brown Body Stretch
     Ribbing: 4X monofilament
  Wingcases: Same as overbody, with painted-yellow markings
   Antennae: Golden goose biots

This pattern is not nearly as hard to tie as it looks. This is one of the few really realistic patterns that I tie, but it catches plenty of fish, and few other patterns have produced as well. Considering how long it takes to tie large patterns like the Kaufmann's Stone, this one is a quickie. You can add lead wire or a bead in the thorax to weight the pattern. A black bead head can also look good on this pattern.

BH Hare's Ear

Hook: Dai Riki 300, #8-12
Tail: Brown Hungarian partridge or English grouse fibers
Thorax: Dark hare's ear blend dubbing
Ribbing: Small oval gold tinsel
Thorax: Dark hare's ear blend dubbing
Wingcase: Lacquered turkey feather
Head: Gold or copper bead head

A classic that belongs in every fly box, the Hare's Ear should be weighted to keep it near the bottom. I don't use the Hare's Ear as much as most people, but when I am stumped, I fall back on it and it rarely fails to produce at least a couple fish. If you are using this pattern to imitate the *Isoperla* nymph, it works best after December, when the nymphs approach the length of a size 12 hook.

CDC Isoperla

Hook: Dai Riki 270, #10-14
Body: Golden yellow/yellow-brown sparkle dubbing
Wing: Golden yellow CDC
Underwing: Golden stone Krystal Splash
Overwing: Shimizaki Fly Wing
Legs: Golden yellow CDC

This is a cool pattern to tie and fish with, and I really enjoy sitting down at the vise to whip out a bunch. It is not difficult or tedious to tie, so you can stock up with a ton in your box. This insect can be important on larger streams during the glamour hatches, so make sure to pack a couple everywhere you fish during early and mid-summer.

Family: Nemouridae

The little brown stonefly is a rarely encountered critter on big streams but is abundant in small- to medium-sized streams. Stoneflies of all families are most common on cold, swift, and clean waters, making them important on small streams. Smaller stoneflies like Nemouridae, *Alloperla*, and *Isoperla* often are three or four times more important to the diets of small-stream fish. For all of the press received by golden stones and salmonflies, the Nemouridae are the most common stonefly in the Rocky Mountains.

The nymphs of the Nemourid family are medium sized, ranging from about 1/2 to 3/4 inch in length, though some species (and similar-looking relatives from other genera) can reach one inch in length. The nymphs graze in the detritus and leaf packs, which fortunately for the bugs are most abundant in the six months prior to emergence. Because they don't always inhabit clean riffles, many anglers miss them when taking aquatic samples.

The adults of the Nemouridae family emerge in the early spring, and along with March browns, are the first big insects to emerge each season. Prior to emergence, the nymphs migrate to slow water where they crawl out and split their shuck. The adults are poor fliers, but usually take to the wing during warm, sunny days in the spring. This is the time when most females return to deposit eggs, and when adult imitations are most effective. While most adults are brown, I have found some to be an almost olive color.

Nemourid Nymph

Hook: Dai Riki 270, #10-16
Tails: Tan or brown micro-rubber legs
Body: Dark rabbit dubbing
Ribbing: Small oval gold tinsel
Legs: Tan or brown micro-rubber legs
Thorax: 1 or 2 copper beads
Wingcase: Lacquered turkey
Antennae: Tan or brown micro-rubber legs

This nymph is closely related to a BH Hare's Ear, but with some significant changes. The bead in the thorax has a more subdued flash than a standard bead-head pattern, and the micro-rubber legs have much more motion than chunky medium-sized rubber offers. Keep it slim!

Nemourid Adult

Hook: Dai Riki 270, #10-16
Body: Brown sparkle dubbing
Underwing: Root beer Krystal Flash
Wing: Shimizaki Fly Wing
Overwing: Brown CDC
Head: Brown sparkle dubbing
Legs: Brown CDC

This is my imitation for the adult on slower pools and flat sections. This fly is realistic and works well on tough fish, but it isn't nearly as durable as the Stimulator imitation.

Brown Stimulator

Hook: Dai Riki 270, #10-16
Tail: Dark elk, sparse
Abdomen: Brown dubbing
Hackle: Brown palmered
Underwing: Root beer Krystal Flash
Wing: Dark deer or elk hair
Thorax: Peacock herl or peacock Arizona Dubbing
Hackle: Grizzly

This is the fast-water fly I like to use to imitate the spring Nemourid hatches. I will also tie it with a dark olive abdomen and thorax to imitate the olive relatives to the Nemourid stoneflies. Fish can be reluctant to rise during these early hatches, so I love to use this pattern with a small dropper nymph.

Family: Capniidae

In the cold days of January, few things can bring a smile to a nymph-weary angler's frozen face. The Capniid is one of them. These tiny, 3-6 mm long, black stoneflies will emerge between mid-December and early March. They are a welcome sight to a shivering angler who is cursing the snow and brain-dead from roll casting a set of nymphs through every slow run.

The nymphs of this insect are small, dark, and slender, and many lack wingpads. They are of minimal importance to fish, because they tend to dwell in the organic debris at the edges of riffles in back eddies. Their shoreward migrations rarely bring them into the drift. Combine this with their small size (which reduces a trout's incentive to move far for one), and they rarely raise the interest of the small-stream angler.

The adults of this insect are the real draw. They can be found crawling around the snow along streams, and some will fly onto the water's surface. I say some, because many Capniids emerge with micro-wings or no wings at all. I assume these are males, or else the species would need a little egg-howitzer to get their eggs back into the water. The adults live quite a long time, as far as aquatic insects go, because they feed on surface algae and hide in little caverns in the snow. When you see these bugs crawling on the snow and fish are rising, then try to imitate them. If one, but not the other, is occurring, then you could be wasting your time throwing Capniid imitations. I have found that the best time to imitate these insects is on slower limestone creeks and on small tailwaters. These fish seem to be more receptive to everything during the cold winter months.

CDC Cap Daddy

Hook: Dai Riki 300, #6-20
Body: Black Antron yarn tied extended
Wing: Gray CDC
Thorax: Black sparkle dubbing
Legs: Black Antron fibers

The winter stonefly is small, and a simple imitation is the best way to fool small-stream fish. Make sure to tie this fly long and skinny, as the adult has little bulk. Look for the adults crawling on snow or rocks before tying on this fly because it is rather difficult to see and thus a poor choice for searching water.

Genera: *Acroneuria, Calineuria, and Hesperoperla* (Golden Stoneflies)

The golden stone is the one big stonefly that can claim at least a minor role in the diet of small-stream trout. The giant salmonfly (*Pteronarcys californica, P. princeps*) receives the majority of print devoted to stoneflies, though they are also the most limited in habitat, preferring only large, swift, and well-oxygenated rivers. Golden stones are not snobby in their habitat preferences, and can be found anywhere from mega-rivers like the Yellowstone to mountain trickles that you can almost straddle. They do prefer streams in the 15- to 35-foot-wide range though, about the size of our larger small streams.

Golden stonefly nymphs are a substantial meal for small-stream trout because of their immense size (most run 25-40 mm long). The nymphs are generally mottled dark brown and yellow, with a lighter underbelly. The nymphs are most available to trout during their pre-emergence migration. This migration coincides with the high-water period on many western streams. This large insect becomes a staple for the trout during the high-water periods because of their visibility and nutritional value. The nymphs can be found in riffles and pocket water, though imitations of them are extremely effective when fished deep in pools.

Golden stoneflies are predators. Most anglers could give a wooden nickel when it comes to what a freaking bug eats, but it is more important than you would think. Because golden stones spend all day crawling around rocks searching for Chironomid larvae and mayfly nymphs to grub on, they are exposed to the currents regularly, and are frequently knocked off. Compare this to the other large stonefly, the salmonfly, which spends its daylight hours hidden under rocks eating dead plant material. The result is that this insect is rarely in the drift until it migrates (or undergoes behavioral, diurnal drift) at night. Thus you are much more likely to catch fish on a golden stone nymph during the daytime, simply because you know what it eats.

Golden stoneflies emerge between early May and mid-July on most small streams. Because of water temperature differences, the emergence period on small streams may be radically different than the well-known hatch times on nearby large streams. So be prepared to explore, scout streams, and take notes as to when the adults are about. There is no doubt when they are around, they will be fluttering around with the grace of a drunk frat boy between the trees on either side of the stream. The adults are a golden-brown in color and large, 35-45 mm in length.

Like crane flies, golden stoneflies are a great insect to imitate on small streams, because their size is a magnet for nice fish and a repellent to tiny fingerlings. When imitating these big insects, it is tempting to tie on a size 6 or even a size 4, because many of the adults fluttering over the stream are about this size. This is wrong! The really big patterns will draw strikes, but the ten-inch small-stream trout just can't squeeze the large, stiff patterns into their mouths. You'll see no shortage of splashy rises but feel nothing but slack line when you try to set the hook. Instead, keep your patterns in the size 8-10 range unless the fish only want something huge.

The People's Stonefly

Hook: Dai Riki 700B, #4-10
Tails: Golden goose biots, tied in V-shape
Thorax: Golden stonefly blend dubbing
Back: Brown or black raffia
Ribbing: Small copper wire
Thorax: Golden stonefly blend dubbing
Legs: Grizzly Spirit River rubber legs
Wingcase: Brown lacquered raffia
Antennae: Golden goose biots
Head: Gold or copper bead
Note: Can tie underbody with flattened lead

This is the big nymph that I use on most small streams. The golden stonefly is quite important on many larger small streams, and such a big morsel is almost impossible for spring trout to ignore. This pattern can be tied on a flattened lead underbody to make the fly more flat. It does make the fly more realistic, but I'm not sure it catches that many more fish to be worth the trouble of tying it.

My MacStone

Hook: Dai Riki 270, #4-8
Thread: Chartreuse 6/0 UNI-Thread
Body: Yellow macramé yarn—burnt at end, sides colored with golden and orange model paint pen
Underwing: Golden stone Krystal Splash
Overwing: Dark elk hair
Head: Deer hair, tied bullet-style
Legs: Grizzly Spirit River Sparkle Legs

This pattern evolved from Al Troth's MacSalmon pattern. I've always thought that the colors macramé yarn comes in were not even close to the shade of the naturals. I started painting the sides and bottom of the yarn and have finally become comfortable with the hue. You can also paint a black butt on the fly to imitate the egg sac of a returning female. Because of the bulk of the yarn, this pattern style is only appropriate for larger stonefly imitations.

Chironomidae: Midges

Like everywhere, midges play a central role for trout feeding on small streams. However, because of the many complications discussed in the following lines, their importance to the angler is decidedly less pronounced.

It is a common cliché to say that midges come in every color and size imaginable. On small streams, with their bewildering ecological diversity, even this cliché seems a little understated. For the sake of our mutual sanity, let's just have a basic discussion. Midges go through a complete metamorphosis: with larvae, pupae, and adult life stages. The larvae look like tiny, thin worms, with no appendages to challenge fly tiers. This stage is the longest stage, lasting a few weeks to a few years, and the larvae spend almost all their time under the substrate. The larvae will then pupate, capture a thin layer of gas under the pupal skin, then rise to the surface with the aid of this natural floatie. It is during this glistening, flashing stage that the midge is most susceptible to predation by trout. The adult then emerges at the surface, quickly flying away from the water and trout. The adults of most midges will later return to the water's surface to lay eggs. Midges live in any kind of aquatic habitat, even temporary streams, but they are most common in parts of streams with soft sediment that allows the larvae to dig out little tunnels to live in.

Midges that are practical for small-stream trout range from about size 12 to 24. (Notice that there are midges bigger than size 18, which runs contrary to the common angler word association between midge and minute.) Some of the best midge fishing I have had on streams was with midge pupae in the size 14 range.

When debating the merits of imitating midges, I first look at the speed of the stream. In fast small streams, small midges (under size 16) rarely come out of my fly box. In this water, a small midge must literally tap the trout on the nose or else the trout expends more energy to obtain the fly than it receives from eating it. In a slow stream, where both you and the fish can spend far too long observing your respective quarry, midges will prove a good pattern to fool picky trout. Also, slower streams have an abundance of the silt/mud substrate that midges love so much. I will also choose smaller midges because trout expend less energy to eat them in slower currents.

Of course, in small streams loaded with small trout, midges and other small flies must be used sparingly, lest you hook fingerling after fingerling. Besides being terribly annoying, hooking and handling these tiny trout will do much more harm than it does to normal trout. In an afternoon of indiscriminate fishing with a small midge, an angler could hook (and probably kill) a 103-inch trout. That is why small flies, especially small midges, should be reserved for targeting larger fish or those feeding on indiscernible things in the surface film.

CDC BH Brassie

Hook: Dai-Riki 135, #12-18
Abdomen: Copper wire (or green, red, or black)
Wing: Gray CDC feather, cut short
Thorax: Peacock herl
Head: Copper, gold, black brass bead

If you are looking for a near-perfect nymph (realistic, heavy, flashy, subtle) this is it. The CDC BH Brassie is dense enough to fish as a dropper behind a relatively small dry fly, or it can be used as a dropper off a larger nymph. The CDC wing is key since it gathers a bubble of air, imitating the thorax of an ascending chironomid. Since chironomids are basically emerging everywhere, all the time, it is tough to fish this pattern at the wrong time!

Hern Worm

Hook: Dai Riki 135, #10-14
Tail: Olive pheasant tail
Ribbing: Fine gold wire
Thorax: Olive caddis emerger Hareline Dubbin'
Head: Dinsmore No. 6 Tin Shot
Note: You can add .010 lead wire to increase the weight of the fly In Oregon, our fly-fishing-only waters prohibit any added weight to your fly line. Without shot, the only way to get tiny flies deep is with a big stonefly nymph or Woolly Bugger. Unfortunately, these large flies tend to spook fish focused on tiny larvae and pupae. This small, dense pattern is the perfect solution to the problem—a subtle, dense escort for the tiny nymphs—and it catches no shortage of trout on its own.

CDC Adult Midge

Hook: Dai Riki 310, #16-22
Abdomen: Sparse dubbing (black, brown, dark gray)
Ribbing: Iron Gray 8/0 UNI-Thread
Wing: Dun CDC feather tip

This is about as easy as a small fly gets. When there are small midges on the water, as long as you can approximate the size and color, you should get some action. These flies should be kept skinny to imitate the naturals. This fly can also imitate small caddis and stoneflies, so it is an essential for any angler's box.

Hymenoptera: Ants, Bees and Wasps

Ants

Ants are social creatures, occurring in abundance almost everywhere there are trout. In fact, in most studies done by fish biologists and entomologists, ants are the most common terrestrial insect ingested by trout.

While everyone is familiar with ants, it hasn't stopped many people from asking, "What is the difference between an ant, a flying ant, a carpenter ant, and a termite?" First of all, ants are ants, and there are thousands of species throughout the world. Flying ants are simply ants with wings. A flying ant has four wings (two pairs of different sizes). What kind of ant (worker, soldier, queen; male or female) depends on the species, so the term flying ant really gives you no idea what the ant actually looks like. A carpenter ant is an ant that lives in trees, and it may or may not have wings. Finally, the termite lives in wood and may (or may not) have wings. They are distinguished from regular ants because they have two similarly sized wings (when they have wings), straight antennae (ants have bent antennae), and no pinch in their waist.

Carpenter ants are the most important group of ants for anglers to focus on because of their size and abundance around riparian areas. These insects don't live in just any old tree, rather, they prefer deadwood with enough moisture for decay to set in. Where is dead, wet wood common? That's right, near streams. Anytime there is dead wood around streams, you can bet ants are well recognized by the trout. Carpenter ants are large enough to imitate with easy-to-see flies (size 8-16 hooks), and many have wings. Winged carpenter ants will also undergo large migrations (usually in late spring), so they can be important even where resident ants aren't all that common.

Field ants are the ones we see with the large mounds in grassy meadows or patchy woodlands. These ants are much smaller than carpenter ants (about size 16-24), and can vary in color from black to red to multicolored. Field ants are easy to locate if you sit down next to a stream to tie up a leader or to rest a pool. They usually find you without any problem, crawling on your arms and legs like you are a big jungle gym. Since these ants rarely have any reason to get near the water, they are rarely found in the densities that carpenter ants do. However, they are sporadically available to trout, and trout will seldom pass up such an easy meal. In fall, some adult males and females will sprout wings and take to the air to find places to start new colonies. This is the best time of the year to imitate these smaller ants.

We all know what ants look like: thick abdomen, skinny thorax, thick head, six legs. That's it, right? Imitations are a snap then, right? Well, not quite. One thing that is often ignored are the wings on many species of ants. These wings are the vehicles that propel most ants into the water, so in order to give trout something similar to the natural, imitations should be winged. Secondly, ants have an exoskeleton and many tiny hairs on their abdomen. The resulting effect is a glistening, wet look akin to jelled hair. Keep these things in mind when sculpting your imitations.

Bees (*Apis*) and **Wasps** (*Vespia*)
Like the grasshopper, honeybees and bumblebees are insects we encounter in our yards and parks everyday. Many people immediately associate the abundance in their yards with abundance in trout stomachs. The result of this has been flies like the McGinty and other similar black and yellow-banded patterns. Bees and wasps are rarely as important as many anglers think, but knowing where and when these insects are abundant can give you an additional option during summer months.

Honey bees (*Apis melifera*) can be extremely abundant in select locations. On creeks flowing through farmlands, orchards, or near plant nurseries, keep your eyes open for large boxes stacked up near each other. Often, these are bees brought in to pollinate the plants. On streams like this, bees can make up 5-10% of the terrestrial diet. Honey bees and bumblebees can also be present in large numbers near pasturelands with plenty of clover and suburban areas with flower gardens. These areas are the only places I will fish bee patterns.

The most important wasp to anglers on small streams (and everywhere else) is the mud dauber. These wasps will fly down to the water's edge to collect mud to build their nests. These insects occasionally get into the water, and trout will recognize them and rise to imitations. Mud daubers have an extremely fragile-looking body, with a large head, thorax, and abdomen, all connected by a thin section of exoskeleton. Most mud daubers are black or metallic blue, about the shade of a bottle fly. Like bees, these insects are most common during hot summer months, June-September. I only choose to imitate them where they should be most common, near moist, muddy banks, otherwise I keep my Mud Daubers in my box.

Two-Tone CDC Ant
    Hook: Dai Riki 300, #10-12
 Abdomen: Black Hare-Tron Dubbing
   Hackle: Black, sparse
  Thorax: Black Hare-Tron Dubbing
     Wing: 2 dun CDC feathers, 1 white CDC feather, all tied down over the thorax

Ant patterns should overflow your small-stream box during the summer months. This is a good one because of the realistic imprint it leaves on the surface, and the visibility afforded by the white CDC wing. As with all CDC patterns make sure you carry a powder desiccant and floatant that will not hamper the floatability of the CDC. On small streams, this can save you from having to put on a new fly every five minutes.

Blacktail Ant
Hook: Dai Riki 305, #12-16
Abdomen: Maroon/dark red dubbing
Wings: Cream raffia
Hackle: Black, sparse
Thorax: Black dubbing

This simple pattern works well for heavily-pressured fish. The raffia wing, though fragile, has the perfect translucency when wet. When dry, the abdomen can look gaudy, but water reduces the color and it looks quite realistic.

Royal CDC
Hook: Dai Riki 305, #12-18
Tail: (Optional) A few moose mane fibers, splayed
Body: Peacock herl, red floss, peacock herl
Wing: 2 white CDC feathers tied down-wing style

This pattern is the other member of the royal family that I fish, and I think trout hit it as an ant pattern, especially when the tail is omitted. This fly works best in smaller sizes and cast to spotted, rising trout.

Cascade Flying Ant
Hook: Dai Riki 305, #6-20
Abdomen: Black Hare-Tron Dubbing
Wings: Grizzly hackle, clipped to shape
Hackle: Brown
Thorax: Black Hare-Tron Dubbing

Few fly patterns can achieve visibility under all light and water conditions, but this fly pulls it off well. People thought I named the fly because it caught fish throughout Oregon's Cascade Range, but the fly earned its name because it could be seen on all the diverse waters of the region. This fly has become my fallback searching pattern when nothing else seems to bring fish up.

Coleoptera: Beetles
Since there are more species of beetles on Earth than any other order of life—25% of all extant animal or insect species on the planet are beetles—you would immediately think anglers would have books full of imitations as a resource base for new ideas. No. At least they'd have a couple hundred. Not exactly. Well, for sure they would have a dozen, right? No, the beetle is often included as an afterthought in most writings on terrestrials, after all grasshoppers and ants received their necessary worship.

Beetles are amazingly diverse, making up some of the largest and some of the smallest insects in the world. The 60,000 species of the family Curculionidae alone dwarf both the number of mammals (4,500) as well as the total number of vertebrates (40,000). They take on numerous body shapes, case colors, and wing positions, making imitation of individual species a maddeningly precise task. The various species of beetles also feed on different things, making some more important to trout than others. To make it even more complicated, many species of beetle are aquatic or semi-aquatic, making larval stages relevant to trout as well.

Fortunately for anglers, most beetles look the same from underneath: black with legs. Sure, the body size and general silhouette may vary drastically between species, but you don't need to carry a huge variety of patterns and colors. A wide range of sizes, however, is critical. I usually carry beetle patterns ranging from size 6 to size 24, in shades of black, brown, peacock, and occasionally green or tan. Ever wonder why you have never seen a size 6 beetle in a fly shop? Tie one up and you'll understand. Despite anglers' aesthetic hang-ups, large beetle patterns can shock up some large, picky trout during the hatchless days of late summer. Some patterns have a nearly circular shape, while others are as slim as a caddis larvae pattern. None, however, take more than three minutes to tie or are adorned with intricate color patterns. Many anglers like to add an orange tuft of yarn on the back of the fly to improve visibility. I do not do this because the natural rarely sports an orange mohawk on its back, and because I can usually approximate the location of the fly if I lose sight of it during the drift. Beetles are so diverse that trout are usually forgiving when it comes to exact imitations, though there are enough exceptions to warrant a good variety of patterns.

Since beetles are modestly important to trout everywhere, let's look at some places where beetles are particularly abundant. First of all, herbivorous beetles are most common in conifer stands and near flowering plants. Surprisingly, conifers are a better food source for beetles than deciduous trees, and many species of the family Scolytinae live in or just under the bark of many trees. In stands of ponderosa pines, where chunks of bark regularly falls off the trees, these beetles can be sent drifting into the trout's world. In suburban or civilized streams, ladybugs and Japanese beetles can all be important to trout. I have always had success with ladybug imitations in these places, and they are often the first pattern I try when exploring the water. Besides food preferences, season and temperature can be important in regulating beetle availability to trout. Most North American terrestrial beetles are most active between April and October, giving them one of the longest seasons of any terrestrial important to trout. Most beetles in our part of the world also have a preferred temperature range of 15-23°C. When the temperature gets too hot or too cold (above 28°C or under 8°C), their activity levels and availability to trout is significantly reduced. This is why a beetle pattern is generally not the best choice on a frosty September morning.

As I mentioned earlier, the study of beetles is complicated by the exploits of aquatic beetles. While they are modestly significant (1-2% of the diet) on lakes and larger streams, their importance in small streams is limited. Many aquatic or semi-aquatic beetles in small streams are borers, which burrow through woody debris. Because these insects neither drift regularly nor are susceptible to flooding, they should be ignored by all but the most curious anglers.

The importance of all this beetle babble is to expound on the important role beetles play for the angler. While they only compose 3-5% of the diet of the small-stream trout, their variety means that the angler is much more likely to fool a trout with a beetle imitation than with an imitation of another insect. Medium-sized beetle patterns are great attractors, while large and small patterns are excellent ways to fool trout that have seen everything before.

BA Beetle

Hook: Dai Riki 300, #8-22
Body: Peacock herl or Black Hare-Tron Dubbing
Legs: Black palmered hackle, clipped on the bottom (for size 16 and larger); deer-hair fibers (for size 18 and smaller)
Back: Black craft foam strip, tied off and leaving a small butt for head

This is my standard beetle pattern, and all sizes work well. For pressured fish, I tend to turn to this fly in extreme sizes (size 8 or 20) to draw strikes. This fly, when tied right, can be extremely durable and last through more than two dozen fish. You could add some bright yarn on the back or a drop of pink or orange fingernail polish if you have trouble seeing the fly in the water.

Ladybug Beetle

Hook: Dai Riki 310, #18-22
Body: Black Hare-Tron Dubbing
Back: Red closed-cell foam, (orange is optional)
Legs: 3 black deer hairs, or 3 pieces of Black Krystal Flash, tied across and cut short
Head: 2 turns of Black Hare-Tron Dubbing
Spots: Black ultra-fine permanent marker

This is a fly that dupes more anglers (especially their non-angling spouses) than trout, but its toll on trout still has been quite respectable. If you fish anywhere near an urban area with cultivated gardens, ladybird beetles are common insects, which could wind up drifting down a stream. The spots on the back are just frosting, because trout never see them, but I like fishing the pattern much more when I feel it "looks natural." Around my native Portland, Oregon, where roses and aphids are plentiful, a ladybug pattern is equally effective on small-stream trout and small-pond bluegill.

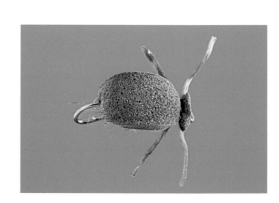

Brown Rubber Leg Beetle

Hook: Dai Riki 305, #10-18
Body: Golden Arizona synthetic Peacock Dubbing
Back: Brown craft foam
Legs: Grizzly Spirit River sparkle legs

This is a simple beetle pattern to tie, and quite effective for trout living in arid parts of the West. The few anglers who do use beetle patterns tend to always use black patterns, and this is a great alternative for pressured fish. You'll notice I don't add the bright orange piece of yarn on the back. If you have trouble seeing the fly, use a drop of orange or white fingernail polish on the back of the fly.

Tipulidae: Crane Flies

Commonly called daddy-long legs, mosquito eaters, or mosquito killers, few of us have given much thought to the importance of these insects to trout. There are only a few species of truly aquatic Tipulids, but even the terrestrial larvae are fond of moist soil near streams. The damp loam, which coats the floors of the western Cascade rainforests, is perfect habitat for crane flies. Many of the riparian zones in that area are virtually teeming with crane fly larvae, which are unleashed to waiting trout by the runoff of one of the common Northwest rainstorms. These insects are very versatile, and adapted to live in the harsher conditions that exist in the Great Basin and Rocky Mountains. They are also common in the South, the Midwest, and in New England. Anywhere you fish for trout, you can be pretty sure that there are crane fly larvae in, under, or very near the water.

Most people will recognize the adult crane fly: fairly skinny body, very long and frail legs, and long wings which usually lie over the back. However, the larvae of these insects are probably foreign to anyone who has not actively pursued them. The larvae resemble thick worms: with an usually cylindrical, occasionally flattened, body that is somewhat blunt at the head and slightly tapered at the rear. Colors are often drab, with grays, light olives, and light tans being most common. They are easily distinguished from other large aquatic grubs because of their retracted head. Many of these insects are herbivores, though some are aggressive predators that actively seek out midge and mosquito larvae meals. However, the feeding habits of most genera are subterranean. This means that they become available to trout only when flooded out by a spate, not because of particular feeding habits. When they are washed into a stream, they are very much sought after by trout. The larvae have no swimming ability whatsoever, and once they are caught up in the drift, they are goners. With these larvae commonly reaching one to two inches in length, and some pushing three inches, you can be sure that trout never ignore such a large morsel.

Most Tipulid larvae are terrestrial, which means they make their home in the soil near, but not under, streams. There are some aquatic tipulids, and these larvae are most common in mossy bottoms or in areas where the riparian soil is often too dry or rocky to allow good burrowing (like in the Great Basin or the Southwest). When searching for either of these insects, it is important to remember to stir up the substrate several inches deep. Many anglers never find them in their samples because they neglect this tactic. On many streams, especially small streams that you suspect of harboring good crane fly populations, it is wise to carry a small hand trowel. You can use this to dig to look for terrestrial Tipulids. It is wise to concentrate your search to only the top 6 inches of soil and within 10 feet of the stream, for this is where terrestrial Tipulids are most vulnerable to spate flooding.

The pupal stage is largely unimportant to anglers. Almost all Tipulid larvae, terrestrial and aquatic, migrate to stable ground near streams to pupate. They pupate under the soil (or leaves and logs, if the soil is unsuitable), for one to two months. Because crane fly emergence is spread throughout the spring, summer, and early fall, and since pupation is done on land, the exact emergence period is of no significance to the angler.

The adults of both aquatic and terrestrial crane flies start to emerge during April in the lower elevation and late May in the higher elevations of the West, and they continue to emerge throughout summertime. Adult numbers wane slightly in midsummer, but increase as September rolls around. Adults prefer the shady and cool riparian zone during the summer, and can be found hanging around ferns, rootwads of fallen trees, as well as streamside rocks and brush. The best indicator that you have found perfect adult crane fly habitat is entering a stream corridor that is 20° cooler than it is outside the corridor. Adults are clumsy fliers, so they are sporadically available to trout.

Perhaps the reason we don't see imitations of crane fly larvae or adults in our local fly shops is that they are overshadowed on many of our glamour streams. Rivers like the Deschutes, Yellowstone, and Henry's Fork have moderate populations of tipulids, but they also have many other insects that draw our attention away. But the value of crane flies to a lover of the smaller stream cannot be disputed. Like with terrestrial insects, the smaller the stream, the greater the shoreline to surface area ratio, ergo, there is a greater likelihood of Tipulids entering the streamflow. They are a food source that is easily recognized by the trout, and are quickly pounced upon.

Cranefly Larvae #1

Hook: Dai Riki 270, #4-12
Underbody: 0.025" lead wire
Body: Gray cranefly mix: 50% olive/gray hare's club,
20% dark olive caddis emerger
Dub: 15% gray Scintilla, 15% olive Scintilla
Ribbing: Fine silver oval tinsel
Head: 80% black Hare-Tron, 20% peacock Arizona synthetic
Peacock Dubbing

Fly-tying experts always advocate erring on the sparse side when tying flies. Forget that with crane fly larvae. If you find a natural, you will see that it is a chunky-looking grub, and segmented bulk is a trigger for trout. Another common problem shared by most crane fly larvae imitations, is that they make the head far too large. If you find a natural, you can see how the head is very small and can retract into the body. When tying this fly make the head tiny: less than 10% of the length of the body.

Z-lon Crane Fly Adult

Hook: Dai Riki 270, #8-12
Body: Brown or tan Z-lon, twisted and doubled back on itself
Legs: 6 knotted pheasant tail fibers
Wings: Brown-dyed grizzly hackle tips
Hackle: Brown-dyed grizzly

Few flies can compare with adult crane fly imitations when it comes to a perfect small-stream fly. They are big, so they stay out of the mouths of small fish, they float well, and they are rather visible. They also imitate an insect that small-stream trout probably recognize. This pattern is more durable than the deer-hair version and quicker to tie. This pattern is also my general crane fly attractor.

Deer Hair Crane Fly

Hook: Dai Riki 270, #8-12
Body: Brown or natural deer hair, tied extended body
Legs: 6 knotted pheasant tail fibers
Wings: Shimazaki Fly Wing, cut to shape
Hackle: Grizzly

This is my favorite crane fly because of its floatability and very realistic appearance. It is a good skater as well, as the deer hair enhances the buoyancy. This fly is not very durable, even with the deer hair, so I try to save them for when I am targeting a particularly large fish.

Who's Your Daddy

Hook: Dai Riki 270, #8-12
Body: Tan, cream, or gray vernille, with the butt-tip burned
Legs: 6 knotted pheasant tail fibers
Wings: Gray or cream raffia
Hackle: Brown, sparse, and tied back
Head: Black, copper, or gold bead

I first saw this one in a book by Bob Church, and never thought that a bead-head crane fly adult would work. Boy, was I wrong. Many adult crane flies get enmeshed in the surface film, and in rough water, they drown. The bead head really does nothing but get the fly down deep and gives that all-important flash. This can be a very good fly on swift streams because it is a big morsel for trout.

Orthoptera: Grasshoppers and Crickets

I can hear the death threats pouring in from all the hopper fanatics across America. How can hoppers be rated so low? Everyone has a ton of hopper imitations in their fly boxes, and every year they never fail to hook plenty of trout. For most anglers, the word "terrestrial" is synonymous with "hopper." I hope this little ditty will hammer that relationship from your mind forever.

Hoppers are the sexy pattern to use in fly-fishing. They're big, visible to both anglers and trout, and they make trout go postal. Novice anglers and even non-anglers can walk into a shop and easily recognize hopper patterns, while other patterns simply bring confused looks. When no insects are emerging, and every step along a summertime shoreline brings a flurry of hoppers into the air, they seem a logical fly selection. Hoppers are also easy to fish, and often catch enough fish to cause anglers to continue to use them. The reality that has eluded anglers for decades is that hoppers simply are not the optimal choice in most terrestrial situations.

Don't get me wrong, I love to fish hoppers. They are easy flies to fish, and the strikes are often aggressive enough to keep me using them when I know they aren't the best choice. Hopper flies are fun to tie well, allowing the tier vast creative freedoms. I often spend rainy winter days at the vise dreaming of sweltering August afternoons, while whipping out a batch of hoppers flies. When I meet young anglers I hand them out like candy, because I know they are the perfect flies for the beginning angler.

However, average and advanced anglers often retain their use long after they are essential. Certainly, anglers can catch fish with grasshopper flies, but rarely as many as if they used beetles, ants, or other terrestrial patterns. The biggest problem with hoppers is that they are just effective enough that anglers don't notice that they are not maximizing their success.

The basic fact is that trout simply do not eat hoppers! At least, not in the quantities we think they do. Anglers have always seen the trout world through terrestrial eyes; we look at insect colors from the top, we often use adult imitations of insects while trout feed on the easier-to-eat pupae, and we choose our terrestrials by what we see jumping around when we walk from our car to the stream. I think anglers like the idea of trout eating hoppers more than trout actually enjoy eating them.

After years of suspecting that hoppers were not high on the trout palate, I figured I would sample the stomachs of some trout that lived in prime hopper habitat, Yellowstone National Park. Taking samples of 50 trout caught on dry flies in several different streams (Gibbon River, Slough Creek, Yellowstone River, Madison River, Blacktail Deer Creek, Fan Creek, and Glen Creek), even I was surprised by how few hoppers were consumed by trout in the Park. However, this surprise was amplified by the abundance of their imitations found in local fly shops.

I have also found that the rise to hoppers seems instinctual rather than by choice. Have you ever noticed how most fish rise to a hopper right after it plops in the water? After catching 60 fish on hopper patterns on small streams in Yellowstone, I found that over 70% of rises occurred within two seconds of the fly hitting the surface. This is not the picky rise of a selective fish, this is instinct. When a big piece of food hits the water, the trout doesn't even think, it eats. This instinctual reaction probably accounts for most fish we catch on hopper imitations. Compare this rise speed to trout that came up for ant and beetle patterns. With another group of 60 fish hooked on ant and beetle patterns, less than 40% of rises came within 2 seconds of the fly hitting the surface. There is still an instinctual reaction, but it is much less pronounced than with the hopper patterns.

All that being said, hoppers, like all other terrestrials, are more important on small streams than on big streams. Due to their large size, they make good flies for keeping small fish off your hook. They are also great late in the season, when you want to fish a dry, but also want a nymph to catch those fish reluctant to rise. Hopper flies also are good choices on small streams with deep pocket water and flat pools. Fish won't rush to the surface for a little ant, but they will hit a juicy hopper without a second thought.

The moral of all this is not to get you to dump all the hoppers from your box, rather to consider when and why you are using them. It took me a lot of time and studying to shed the dark cloak of hopper dependency, but it has certainly has paid off.

Jungle Hopper

Hook: Dai Riki 270, #4-14
Tail: Red hackle fibers
Body: Antron bright green, yellow, or cream
Ribbing: Brown hackle, palmered and clipped
Legs: Knotted dyed grizzly hackles, clipped short
Wing: Turkey quill
Head: Deer hair, tied bullet style

This is my favorite hopper pattern. It is the best for flat-water situations, especially on lakes, because of a very realistic profile. Floats well all the time, but even better when coated with floatant. Pressured fish that refuse standard patterns that everyone fishes (Joe's Hopper, Parachute Hopper) are more willing to take this realistic fly.

Improved Madame X

Hook: Dai Riki 270, #10-14
Tail: Light elk hair
Body: Yellow craft foam
Underwing: Root beer Krystal Flash
Wing: Light elk hair
Legs: Chartreuse Spirit River Grizzly Legs
Head: Elk hair, tied bullet-head style

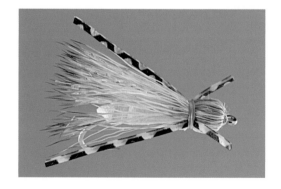

This is a great easy hopper imitation for fish that aren't too picky. I became disenfranchised with the original Madame X when it only took a few fish to render it ragged and unfloatable. Is unfloatable a word? Anyway, this pattern is a superb small-stream fly because it offers great visibility, floatability, durability, flash, and it is a snap to tie.

HoHopper

Hook: Dai-Riki, 270 #4-12
Body: Yellow or cream deer hair, doubled over itself
Ribbing: Yellow thread
Wing: Yellow or tan synthetic winging material
Legs: Knotted grizzly hackle stems, dyed yellow
Head: Deer hair tied bullet-head style

OK, maybe three hopper patterns is overkill, but everyone else likes to fish them, so I might as well throw out some cool-looking patterns, right? This one is a super floater because of all the deer hair. It is important to cover the deer hair with Flexament, or else your fly will be shredded beyond recognition after only a couple fish.

Foam Cricket
Hook: Dai Riki 270, #8-14
Body: Black cylindrical foam
Hackle: Black palmered
Underwing: Black or peacock Krystal Flash
Overwing: Black deer hair
Head: Black deer hair

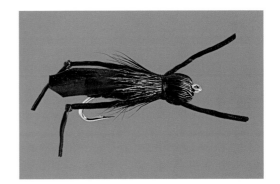

I hate using cylindrical foam material, and this is the only pattern I really use it on. To form the body, you must slice it with a razor, fill the notch with super glue, and then slip the notch onto the hook and hold in place. This is a great floater and a great fish catcher, but because it is much more laborious to tie than the Letort Cricket, I try to use it only under tough conditions with particular trout.

Letort Cricket
Hook: Dai Riki 270, #8-16
Body: Black sparkle dubbing
Underwing: Black lacquered turkey
Overwing: Black deer hair
Head: Black deer hair, spun and clipped

A simple pattern that is perfect for small creeks, the Letort Cricket originated on the spring creeks of Pennsylvania. I really like the ease with which this pattern is tied, and it is simple enough to not look odd in small sizes. Incidentally, the small sizes of this pattern double as excellent black caddis (particularly *Brachycentrus*) imitations.

Simuliidae: Black Flies

Black flies, like mosquitoes, are often more renowned for what they do to fishermen than what they do to fish. However, unlike mosquitoes, which prefer stagnant, shallow water to breed in, black flies are very eclectic in their habitat choices: chalk streams, tiny alpine pools, and vast rainforest rivers all make suitable homes for black flies.

There may be an angler bias towards the larvae of these insects, them being maggots and all. Maggots are a far cry from the elegance of the mayfly family, and not exactly what a lot of people want to recreate at the vise. Besides their unsavory reputation, many anglers simply discount them because they don't show up in many stream samples. Anglers have a tendency to take samples only from the most perfect calf-deep riffle water they can find. This is where most insects lie, but not all. Simuliids will occasionally inhabit riffle water, but many like the slightly slower runs and the marginal water of eddies.

Black flies are not the most important food source for small-stream trout, usually composing .5-4% of a trout's diet, but in some places they play a more significant role. While big, broad rivers is often the first thing to come to mind when black fly habitat is mentioned, you should also associate black flies with fast water, because that is where they are by far the most common. Most black fly larvae are filter feeders, so if you find them in small streams, it will often be rich water: tailwaters, spring creeks, or streams with geothermal inputs have the best populations.

The black fly larvae range between 4-13 mm in length, and are usually cylindrical in shape. Near the head the larvae have feathery fans that are used to filter their food through the current. These critters typically have pale hues, ranging from pale yellow to pale gray, though some are totally black. For years I never knew what the black ones were, and I mistook them for microcaddis or various other critters. All I knew was the patterns I tied up to imitate them caught plenty of fish.

Adults black flies are very recognizable, and many of us get up-close glimpses as they are biting our arms, necks, or any other exposed flesh. Like mosquitoes, only female black flies take blood meals. However, I look at these occasional blood-letting sessions as informative: they let me know when the adults are abundant. There are usually 2-5 generations per year of black flies in lower-elevation waters, and only 1-2 generations in alpine or arctic streams. This means that the adults are much more common throughout the summer in lower elevation streams. Adult black flies are not the most common thing in trout stomachs, but they show up with enough frequency among high-elevation and slow-water fish to warrant an imitation or two.

Yellowstone's Slough Creek maybe the perfect stream to imitate adult black flies on. Slough Creek is surrounded by broad meadows and has a large number of semi-stagnant backwaters that are rich in black fly larvae. These insects emerge after ice-out and choke the air, buzzing everywhere and biting anything that moves. I have a personal policy of not fishing this stream before late July, simply in order to avoid the hypodermic swarms. The few times I hiked up into this stream, I regretted it: the bites, but not the fishing. For awhile I thought that fish were taking my black beetle for what I intended, a black beetle. But after a couple stomach pumpings and patient observation—very patient considering the bites you sustain while standing still—I came to a different conclusion. I saw fish rising to black flies and the larger horseflies with surprising regularity, and stomach samples backed up this visual evidence. I smashed three horseflies and threw them in the water, only one made it through a small pool of feeding fish. Then an epiphany: with all the anglers slapping bugs all day long, there had to be a bunch of flies falling onto the water. Hence, an artificial spinner fall of dead or dying bugs. I went back to camp and tied up a half dozen black fly patterns. I had no idea what I was doing, but with a foam body, fly-film wings, deer-hair legs, and little dabs of red paint for eyes, it looked close enough for me. Fortunately, the normally finicky trout of Slough Creek thought so too.

Beadhead Maggot
    Hook: Dai Riki 135, #12-16
    Butt: 7-10 wraps of fine silver tinsel
    Body: Gray, white, or cream dubbing
    Ribbing: Fine oval silver tinsel
    Head: 1/8" or 3/32" black metal bead
    Gills: White Antron or CDC

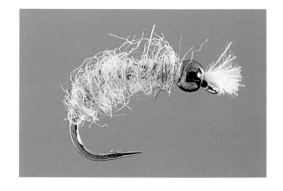

The name maggot is a sure way to keep this pattern out of the fly bins at the local shop, but that is the purpose. Few fish see black fly imitations, but those of us who use these patterns are quickly giving them an education. The gills on the front of this fly seem to make a difference, but keep them short.

Plastic Maggot
    Hook: Dai Riki 135, #12-16
    Body: White, cream, or gray Antron dubbing
    Ribbing: Clear Larvae Lace or Swannudaze
    Head: Brown sparkle rabbit dubbing
    Legs: Brown Antron fibers

The difference between black fly larvae imitations and chironomid imitations is that black fly larvae are chunkier at the bottom end and taper down to a smaller head. This means you should forget about the taper that you tie every other pattern with. The legs on this pattern can either be tied out in front of the head or perpendicular to the body behind the head. The clear ribbing makes the fly pretty bulky, so keep your dubbing thin.

Adult Black Fly

Hook: Dai Riki 305, #12-16
Body: Dark Blue metallic Flashabou, over rabbit dubbing
Wings: Zing Wing
Legs: Black elk or deer hair
Head: Black sparkle dubbing

Black fly adults are typically ignored by anglers, but not by trout. In the stomach samples I researched for this book, trout ate more black flies (both adults and larvae) than grasshoppers in 55% of the studies. This is shocking considering the number of hopper imitations out there. Even the most naïve angler should carry at least one black fly pattern for every four hoppers.

Maxie's Marauder

Hook: Dai Riki 305, #8-10
Body: Black foam strip
Ribbing: Several sparse wraps of bronze dubbing
Wings: Tan or gray raffia
Legs: Black elk or deer hair, even thin strips of black super floss
Head: Black sparkle dubbing
Eyes: Red monofilament, burned-red ultra chenille or painted red spots

This fly was created after I was nearly sucked dry by the enormous horse-flies up on Slough Creek in Yellowstone. I whacked a natural that was feeding on my arm into the water, and within about thirty seconds a big cutthroat swam by and gobbled up its mangled corpse. If I was really bright, I could come up with a crushed horsefly pattern. The red eyes on this pattern match the prominent eyes on many species of the natural. This pattern is best on small streams that flow through marshy meadows and bottomlands.

Amniphoda: Scuds

No experienced angler needs a lesson on the importance of scuds to trout. The presence of scuds in a small stream gives the stream the Midas touch, almost always signifiying large or plentiful trout. Where scuds are present, they are extremely important to trout, composing up to 40% of their diet. Large scud populations are found in spring creeks, tailwaters, and freestone streams with geothermal inputs. Weeds, especially water-cress, are almost always associated with scuds. Scuds are rarely found in sparse populations; if there is one, there are a thousand.

Scuds, also known as freshwater shrimp, have a smooth shellback, are laterally flattened, and have seven pairs of legs, with the first pair adapted for grasping onto vegetation. Scuds propel themselves by wiggling their little legs as fast as possible while thrusting their bodies—the latter reserved for short bursts only. It is widely assumed in the angling world that scuds swim on their backs, and I made this mistake until I was chided by a professor of aquatic entomology. Scuds actually swim on their sides, with their bodies elongated so their legs can catch as much water as possible. Most scuds are between 4-18 mm in length, and they come in shades of tan, gray, and olive. When scuds die or are mating, they can turn shades of pink, orange, and yellow. Juvenile scuds are visually identical to their fully-grown brethren, and can often greatly outnumber the larger adults.

Scuds are probably the most active drifters of all aquatic trout foods, and this is likely related to their excellent swimming ability. Their active drifting and abundance through all months of the year makes them extremely important to trout. However, in the overall scope of small streams, scuds are a less important food source because the conditions in which they thrive are only found occasionally in small streams.

Tiny Tan Scud

Hook: Dai Riki 135, #20-22
Tail: Brown Hungarian partridge fibers
Body: Tan Hare-Tron dubbing
Shellback: Pearl flash material
Ribbing: Fine copper wire

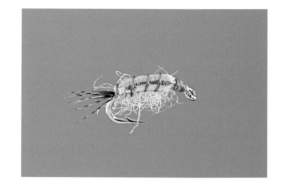

When late-summer trout get picky, I turn to this little nymph. It works well even on streams with no scud or sowbug population. It is very inconspicuous, buggy, non-threatening, and I will bet my life that fish have not been caught on this pattern. Think, the last time you were in a fly shop, how many #22 scud patterns did you see? None. This fly can be fished on 7X fluorocarbon tippet and can catch even the most heavily-pressured spring-creek trout.

Swiss Scud

Hook: Dai Riki 135, #12-16
Body: Olive/gray sparkle dubbing
Shellback: Olive raffia (Flexament the back to make it shinier and more durable)
Ribbing: Small copper wire

This is a great pattern with more subtlety than scud imitations with its bright shellback materials. This fly should be lightly weighted for sight nymphing, or so you can drop the fly on the bottom when fish are cruising and picking scuds up. This pattern is essential for any lake or stream that have scud populations.

Crooked River Scud

Hook: Dai Riki 135 #12-14
Body: Orange, pink, or pale olive Estaz, clipped top and sides

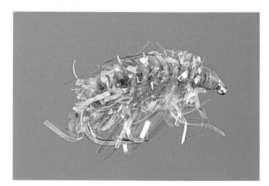

This must be one of the easiest-to-tie patterns that I have ever seen, created by Crooked River guide Bill Meyers. One can easily whip out a year's supply in the matter of an hour. It offers a lot of sparkle and can be awesome in the café-latte-colored water of Oregon's Crooked River. The olive version can also be useful in lakes and rivers when fish want something a little flashier than normal.

Oligochates: Aquatic and Terrestrial Worms

No food source for trout has been so widely disparaged as the poor aquatic worm. Even some of the best and most learned fly-anglers turn up their noses at the suggestion of fishing an imitation of a worm. The anglers' association of worms and bait-fishing is the obvious source of this bitter stance. However, trout don't care what bait-anglers should imitate and what fly-anglers should imitate, they just eat what is in the river.

Aquatic worms should never be ignored by anglers, and can compose between 2-7% of a trout's caloric intake during the course of a year. On small streams, where the banks (the pantry where this morsel is stored) are much closer to the trout, worms can be even more important. Because of their size, nutrient value, and vulnerability, these critters have earned a high place on the trout's menu.

Aquatic worms are most common in the silty bottoms of spring creeks and tailwater streams, though some can be found in any freestone stream that doesn't see huge fluctuations in its flow. These are actual aquatic worms, that live in burrows in the soft mud and silt-bottomed sections of creeks and rivers. Most of these creatures are small, ranging from 1/2-2 inches in length, and can vary in color from reds and maroons to yellowish-tans and browns. These worms will squirm rapidly when dislodged, and flies tied on curved-shank hooks or tied extended-body style imitate their appearance well. The fully aquatic worms are most available to trout in places of high angler traffic. Often, fishing well below a wading angler with imitations of worms (or crane fly larvae, fish eggs, sowbugs, or any other food source that lies buried or half-buried in the substrate) can be extremely productive. Trout are always down for making a meal out of these large, calorie-rich critters.

In addition to the fully aquatic worms, the moist banks of most trout streams are rich in small terrestrial worms. During periods of high water and flooding, these worms get washed into the stream, quickly drown, and drift freely until eaten by trout. This is by far the most common situation where trout eat worms, for only a small number of streams fit the conditions needed for fully aquatic worms to thrive. The terrestrial worms are usually the same color and size as their fully aquatic cousins, with trained taxonomists being the only people who can differentiate the two. With their size and color, worm imitations make great patterns to sight-nymph in slow runs when they get a little clouded up by a storm.

San Juan Worm

    Hook: Dai-Riki 135, #10-14

    Body: Red, wine, or brown ultra-chenille

Truly one of the most underrated patterns, the San Juan Worm has been a great nymph throughout the season since the Yellowstone Fires of 1988. The increased susceptibility of Yellowstone streams to erosion (because of the reduction of terrestrial flora) made these riparian-dwelling angleworms more common in the streamflow. Following one of the common summer thunderstorms, few flies can compete with the San Juan Worm. Since they are easy to tie and cheap, no angler has an excuse to be on the river without a dozen.

Isopoda: Sowbugs

Considering the lofty position that scuds hold in most angler's minds, it is amazing how underrated sowbugs are. Where found, sowbugs (a.k.a. cress bugs) can be a critically important component of a trout's diet. Sowbugs are most common near cold springs where there is an abundance of weed growth. In many of the spring creeks of the East, sowbugs are very important to trout. Unfortunately, outside of Big Spring Creek and the Letort, sowbugs often scuttle around with anglers taking little notice.

One reason that sowbugs are overlooked is that at a quick glance, they appear similar to scuds. Many anglers just think they are a different kind of scud. However, a closer inspection will reveal that sowbugs are dorsal-ventrally (top to bottom) flattened, while scuds are laterally flattened. Sowbugs also have legs that protrude more to the sides than do scuds. Their length is usually between 5-18 mm, and sowbugs are generally a smoky-gray color. For the most part, they are identical in appearance to the sowbugs we find in our gardens at home. Unlike scuds, which are active swimmers and drifters, sowbugs have the swimming ability of a quadriplegic horse, and will drift out of control until a trout gobbles them up.

Another reason anglers overlook sowbugs is that many live deep in the rootwads of watercress and other aquatic plants. The simple kicking of a riffle may not reveal sowbugs that live part of their lives under the substrate. Sowbugs inhabit most streams where scuds are common, and can be a good food to imitate when fishing over heavily-pressured trout. In the West, few anglers carry sowbug imitations when fishing in scud rivers, and this is a big mistake. I have occasionally found sowbugs of terrestrial origin in the stomachs of small-stream trout, but not enough to make me want to try to imitate them.

Shaver's Sowbug

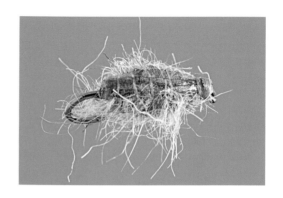

   Hook: Mustad 9671, #12-16
 Underbody: Two layers of .020 lead, crimped flat with pliers, then super glued
   Body: Gray dubbing, picked out on sides
   Back: Clear Body Stretch
  Ribbing: Clear 6-pound monofilament

 Far too few anglers imitate sowbugs, especially in the West. Most streams that harbor a scud population sustain sowbugs as well. Sometimes the sowbugs are living in the root systems of aquatic plants, so they go unnoticed by casual observers. Also, many anglers mistake sowbugs for scuds. The smart angler will take advantage of these mistakes and use a sowbug pattern to catch those experienced trout that have seen (and been caught on) every scud pattern ever devised. A sowbug pattern is not used everyday, but can really be an ace-in-the-hole pattern when nothing seems to bring fish.

Homoptera: Cicadas

Cicadas were always a mythical food source for trout, so I thought. During a float down the Deschutes during the peak of the June salmonfly hatch, I rolled out my blanket to camp under a group of trees. In the morning, I awoke to a clicking sound near my head. I thought it was just a cricket and batted it away. I was shocked to feel a great buzzing on my hand and immediately jumped to do battle with whatever stick I could find. Looking around, I found no sticks, but instead was greeted by an army of hundreds of adult cicadas that covered my blankets, fishing gear, and coolers. After I packed all my gear into the boat, conceding the grove to the Huns, I thought to myself "maybe the trout noticed this too." Of course, I never thought of imitating these gargantuan creatures on this or any other float trip, but I did have a big black Chernobyl Ant in my box that probably could pass for a cicada. I still don't know why I had that ugly fly in my box, as there are few patterns I loathe more than that monstrosity! After two casts, I was sure it could pass for a cicada. Unfortunately, after a couple fish, I lost the fly and had to return to "just" throwing adult salmonfly imitations. Poor me. Since then, I have always carried two or three adult cicada imitations in my fly box. Though I have only had a handful of encounters with the adults, because of their size and population densities they instantly become a desired food source for trout.

Killer Cicada

   Hook: Dai Riki 270, #10-4
   Body: Black foam
  Hackle: Black palmered, trimmed short
   Legs: Black round rubber
 Underwing: Pearl Krystal Flash
   Wing: Black elk hair
 Overwing: White calf tail or poly-yarn

This pattern is one of those to be tucked into your "just in case" box, because you never know when you will encounter them. I know people who use this as a scouting and searching pattern, but I have never had a ton of success with it when the naturals aren't present

Megaloptera: Alderflies and Dobsonflies

There are two major groups of Megaloptera that are important to the trout: alderflies (genus *Sialis*) and dobsonflies (family Corydalidae). Of the two families, alderflies are more important because their habitat extends across the United States, while dobsonflies are largely confined to the eastern states.

Alderfly larvae are generally between 15-25 mm in length, with six legs and several segmented lateral filaments along their abdomens, and a long, single caudal filament. At first glance, this can look a lot like a *Paraleptophlebia* (mahogany dun) nymph, but the alderfly larvae only has one tail. Like mahogany dun nymphs, alderfly larvae prefer the silty and detritus-strewn confines of eddies and pools. The larvae spend one to two years crawling among the substrate eating other invertebrates and small crustaceans before crawling out of the stream to pupate on the shore. The adults emerge throughout late spring and into the summer months and are active throughout the day. Adult alderflies look like stout, dark-bodied caddisflies, and range from 15-20 mm in length. Most alderflies prefer to run around like stoneflies, because their flying skills are rather embarrassing. The adults lay their eggs on riparian rocks, logs, and leaves. With their bad coordination, they will occasionally find themselves on the water. The adults sink upon contact with the water, thus sunken adult imitations are the preferred method. Alderflies are sporadically distributed throughout the United States, though they can often have dense, localized populations.

Dobsonfly larvae are often called Hellgrammites by anglers, and they are often called the "big bastard that eats us" by other aquatic invertebrates. At a whopping 35-70 mm, these monsters can eat almost every kind of aquatic insect that shares their riffle habitats. The larvae of the dobsonfly looks a lot like the alderfly larvae, but it is much larger. The life cycle of the dobsonfly is rather slow, and the larvae will live 2-5 years under water. These bugs will crawl out of the water to pupate in the riparian soil during spring and early summer. Though large, the adults are of minimal importance because they are nocturnal. The dobsonflies are even more restricted in their distribution, and they are much more common in the East than in the West.

Alder Fly

> *Hook:* Dai Riki 300, #12-14
> *Body:* Peacock herl
> *Wing:* Dark turkey quill
> *Hackle:* Black hen

Hey, a wet fly! This fly should be plunked down on the surface so it sinks quickly like the natural. To expedite this descent, coat the fly with Xink or add a small black bead head. Adding lead under the herl will cause the fly to spin or ride upside down. Cast this fly to an overhanging branch, where a rising fish has been spotted. It will often produce a savage strike within a second or two of touching down on the surface.

Creepy Crawler

> *Hook:* Dai Riki 700B, #2-8
> *Underbody:* 20 wraps of .020 lead wire
> *Tail:* Black or dark gray goose biots, tied in "v" shape
> *Body:* Mixed black and brown Hare-Tron
> *Ribbing:* Black V-Rib
> *Legs:* Black micro rubber
> *Thorax:* Same as abdomen
> *Antennae:* Black or dark gray goose biots, tied in "v" shape

This is a serviceable hellgrammite imitation, along with Dave Whitlock's Hellgrammite, though this is slightly quicker to tie. My experience with these big nymphs is obviously less thorough than a native Easterner, though I know they can be effective in the high, cold waters of spring.

Lepidoptera: Caterpillars

These little tan and bright green creatures we know as inchworms are members of the moth family. Most of the ones we see near our trout streams are of the family Geometridae. They usually spend their larval period among the leaves and needles of trees, gorging themselves until their biological clocks ring and they descend on fine threads of silken material to pupate on the ground. They usually can be found dropping to the ground throughout the summer months. Not knowing any better, many of these inchworms rappel directly into the water, becoming tasty trout sausages. When it is windy, inchworms can be carried for a distance when their long thread gets caught in the wind. This is perhaps the time they are most important for trout. Small streams with thick overhead canopies are the most likely places to imitate inchworms. Inchworms will float if the water's surface is relatively flat and calm, but a riffle will quickly drown them. Some studies have revealed that trout do not prefer to feed on some species of caterpillars, because their body chemicals create a foul flavor. So if trout are refusing your inchworm imitations when you see plenty of naturals about, don't stick with them too long.

For a long time, I thought these insects were far overrated. Every pattern book had a pattern for one, but I didn't know anyone that hooked fish with them. I always carried two deer-hair imitations in my box, but on every large stream that I tried them on they were ignored by the trout. So, eventually, they were demoted to my small-stream fly boxes, along with other unproven and prototype patterns. One day, I observed trout rising pretty consistently in a flat run on an alder-lined coastal stream. I threw an ant pattern expecting immediate acceptance, and was sorely disappointed when my fly trickled back through the run unscathed. I noticed a trout rising to a small spruce needle, and figured that this fish might just be game for an inchworm imitation. I tied on the chartreuse stick and lobbed it into the run, shocked that two fish both moved up from the bottom to take a shot at it. After that experience, I tried it on several other small streams and saw similar reactions from trout. I have since always carried both dry and wet inchworm patterns on every small stream I fish.

Deer Hair Inchworm

> *Hook:* Dai Riki 270, #12-16
> *Body:* Chartreuse or bright-green dyed deer hair
> *Ribbing:* Chartreuse thread

Inchworms compose a small fraction, 3-6% in most studies, of terrestrial food sources for trout. However, an easy-to-tie pattern like this one belongs in every small-stream angler's fly box. I like to fish inchworm imitations under low-hanging conifers, which seem to contribute the majority of these little critters.

Bead-Thorax Inchworm

Hook: Dai Riki 135, #12-14
Body: Green or yellow-olive ultra chenille or micro chenille
Thorax: Tungsten or brass bead

Not all inchworms float when they hit the surface of the water. In swift currents, they drown and drift freely until devoured by trout. The bead in the thorax allows the fly to get deep, and the bright color seems to get the attention of trout.

Fish Eggs

Fish eggs are an important food source for trout at certain times of the year. Though they often compose only 2-4% of the annual consumption by trout on small streams, they can make up as much as 30% of the food consumption during cold winter months. This is because most small streams serve as spawning sites for fish in large streams, so the eggs are an "input" into the food supply of resident fish. Eggs are most available during active spawning periods, and this time can vary depending on species (see figure). Eggs can be dislodged, either by nature or by wading anglers, and will continue to provide occasional treats for trout until they hatch. Fish, like whitefish, that spawn by just releasing eggs over gravel rather than building a redd, are particularly important, because their eggs are more readily available.

Drifting eggs and egg-feeding trout are most prevalent at the lower ends of riffles. Riffle water is the universal spawning habitat for salmonids, so it is only logical to look for egg-feeding trout here. You can fool some fish on egg patterns in other parts of a stream, but if egg patterns are not working in the riffles, they will generally be totally worthless anywhere else.

Most fish eggs are smaller than the big Glo Bug style patterns we see in the shops. Salmon eggs are the largest, at about 5-7 mm in diameter, then come trout eggs at 4-5 mm in diameter, and finally whitefish eggs are 2-4 mm in diameter. Keeping your patterns small will really increase your catch, especially in small streams where fish and their eggs are smaller. Also, the colors are more muted than the flashy fluorescent oranges, chartreuses, and reds we see on most fly patterns and artificial eggs. If fish eggs really looked like they originated near Three Mile Island, trout would see them glowing through the gravel and just dig out their dinner, rather than wait for them to drift down. By imitating the natural peaches, pale pinks, and pale yellows of most eggs, you will see much more success with egg-feeding trout.

Scrambled Egg

Hook: Dai Riki 135, #12-14
Tail: 2-4 strands white marabou
Body: Peach chenille

This is an egg pattern that imitates a drifting clump of milt attached to an egg. It seems to work well when I can't catch anything on the standard egg. The Scrambled Egg only works well when there are actively spawning fish, so you only have a 2-3-week window each year to throw it. This fly works especially well for spawning whitefish that cast their eggs and milt over a riffle without building a true redd.

Egg A' La Muck

> *Hook:* Dai Riki 135, #12-16
>
> *Egg:* peach, pink, red, orange, tan, or white medium chenille

Another very simple pattern to tie, given to me by guide Gary Muck. It is very effective when fishing below spawning whitefish, trout, salmon, or steelhead. It can be good tumbled into lake inlets in the early spring and late fall when rainbows or brookies are spawning. It should be fished unweighted below a heavy bead head and allowed to tumble freely near the bottom.

Comb Over

> *Hook:* Dai Riki 135, #12-16
>
> *Body:* McFly Foam pulled over a bead

This is another quick pattern to tie that offers a little sparkle and flash to the standard egg pattern. It can be spruced up even more by adding some Krystal Flash in with the Fly Foam. This pattern came from Deschutes River guide Jim Koudelka.

Alevin

> *Hook:* Dai Riki 075, #10-12
>
> *Tail:* Pearl sparkle material
>
> *Body:* White Antron, colored with waterproof marker on back
>
> *Ribbing:* Pearl or root beer Krystal Flash
>
> *Egg Sac:* Orange Glo-Bug yarn
>
> *Eyes:* Silver bead chain

Freshly hatched fish are an easy-to-capture delicacy for larger trout, for they cannot escape quickly (until the egg sac is absorbed) and are larger than eggs. This fly should be used about three weeks after spawning, then for about a month. While this pattern has a short-lived use season, when the freshly hatched fingerlings are abundant, it can be deadly.

Other Small-Stream Trout Foods

Trichoptera: Caddis

Hydropsychidae (Spotted Sedge)

Netspinning caddis like those in the Hydropsychidae family are common where there is an abundance of tiny things to filter from the drift. This makes them much more common in spring creeks and tailwaters, or in larger streams where other insects and bacteria have had plenty of time (or more importantly, distance) to break down organic matter into tiny pieces that drift with the current. Netspinners are only common on a few small streams, but where they are present, they are usually abundant, so it is good to carry a couple imitations so as to be prepared.

Ephemeroptera: Mayflies

Pale Morning Duns (*Ephemerella spp.*)

The most popular mayfly in the West is not nearly as important on small streams as large streams. Their bodies aren't as flattened nor do they cling to the rocks as well as the Heptegeniidae family of mayflies. However, PMDs can be important in gentle meadow streams and low-gradient valley creeks. While the adults and spinner fishing is well known, I prefer to imitate their nymphs in May, June, and July. These critters have no respect for the angling writers who claim they are olive-brown in color, and continue to exude a reddish-brown hue during their nymph stage. This nymph is easily distinguished from other mayfly nymphs because of its color alone. I use a reddish-brown or rusty-colored Hare's Ear in a size 14 or 16 and have had excellent fishing where I can find pale morning duns on small streams.

Green Drakes

The large green drakes are the most common of the large mayflies on small streams, but are so well known that I figured I could skimp on this section and go watch wrestling.

Gray Drakes (*Siphlonurus spp.*)

The gray drake is a swimming nymph that can appear in slower waters throughout the West. The nymphs seem to prefer slower and weedier water than its cousin *Ameletus*, making them less important on small streams. The fact that they crawl out of the water to emerge does nothing to enhance their importance to the trout palate.

However, wherever gray drakes do occur, the spinner falls can be extremely important to the trout. Because of its large size, 10-15 mm, an imitation or two should always be in your box. Gray drakes also have a peculiar habit of emerging only during a short period (2 weeks), but that span could be anytime between April and October. Even streams in the same region can have radically different emergence periods.

Brown Drakes (*Ephemera spp.*)

The *Ephemera* genus of burrowing mayflies is rarely found on small streams, because they require a silty substrate to hide in. However, slow, deep, and meandering meadow streams can hold a large number of these insects. Many anglers miss them in bottom samples because they don't kick up the bottom enough. The lower Gibbon River in Yellowstone has the perfect habitat for these insects. The brown drake nymph is a pale or tan nymph with plenty of gills that create a seductive motion when the nymph swims. Because it spends most of its life buried in the sand, it is rarely important to the angler. The adult emerges and lays eggs in the evening, though when ovipositing many females drop their eggs from well above the water's surface, never coming into contact and getting stuck. But, the large size of this insect, 14-20 mm, makes it a major hatch wherever it occurs. If you are fishing a slow small stream, you should be always prepared with at least a couple imitations.

Plecoptera: Stoneflies

Salmonflies (*Pteronarcys californica, P. princeps*)

This western behemoth (30-50 mm in length) is the most common insect associated with the word stonefly, but unfortunately for small-stream lovers, it is quite rare on creeks. The salmonfly is abundant only on large, fast rivers like the Deschutes and Madison. There are occasionally some found in smaller streams, but they are nearly always a 5-1 minority compared to golden stones. An overly cautious angler, like myself, might carry one just-in-case pattern, but don't hold your breath for a hatch.

Annelidae: Leeches

Most small streams have very modest populations of leeches, and they are often only found in numbers in slower, weedy water that is much more hospitable to bass and panfish than to trout. Leeches can, on rare occasions, be found in older beaver ponds on slow, slough-like streams, but most streams are bereft of this Annelid. Despite their rare appearances, some anglers catch no shortage of trout on black Woolly Buggers, which leaves us to ask what the hell all this entomology crap is worth anyway.

Zygoptera: Damselfly

These slow-water insects are extremely rare on small streams that are inhabited by trout. They can be found in weedy spring creeks, occasionally in dense numbers, and imitations of their nymphs are essential. I have actually had excellent success at times in parts of the Firehole River, both dead drifting and stripping beadhead nymph imitations. Damsel nymphs are world-class swimmers, and rarely get caught up in the drift. It is best to imitate them with a stripping retrieve through eddies, frog water (slack water), and slow, but shallow, pools. Small streams that contain large numbers of damsel nymphs are often good streams for sight fishing, so do that whenever possible. Damsels can also be important in beaver ponds, where there can be surprisingly large populations of the nymphs. For this reason alone, you should carry at least a half dozen imitations in your just-in-case box. The adult damselflies are of negligible importance to small-stream trout.

Odonata: Dragonflies

Putting dragonflies as a marginal food source was a tough call for me. There are some genera of dragonflies that will live in calm pools, camouflaged amongst the leaf litter on the bottom, waiting to go medieval on any insect that gets too close. Where these guys are common, a size 8 olive or black Deschutes Special (a variation on the Woolly Worm) can be a deadly pattern. Beaver ponds can also gain a quick population of dragonfly nymphs, as the adults are renowned for their ability to cover great distances. Here you absolutely need a couple dragonfly nymph imitations. After a couple of strikes, you won't ever forget them. For the most part, however, dragonfly nymphs are much more important to fish in stillwaters and bass rivers.

Nondescript Fly Patterns

Tan CDC Czech Nymph

> *Hook:* Dai Riki 135, #10-14
> *Abdomen:* Tan Hareline caddis and emerger Dubbin'
> *Shellback:* Tan Wapsi Thinskin
> *Ribbing:* 4X monofilament
> *Legs:* Dun CDC feathers
> *Thorax:* Natural fox squirrel dubbing
> *Head:* Copper, black, or gold bead head

Europe is filled with killer patterns that American anglers, taught by their corporate structure of the sport to fish only their basics, have never even heard of. This may be the best of them all. The CDC captures a nice bubble of air under the

fly, and the body looks incredibly buggy. This fly is a perfect imitation of *Hydropsyche* caddis larvae.

Olive Czech Nymph

Hook: Dai Riki 135, #10-14
Underbody: 15-20 wraps .010 lead wire
Abdomen: Insect-green Hareline caddis and emerger Dubbin'
Shellback: Olive Wapsi Thinskin
Ribbing: 4X monofilament
Thorax: Natural fox squirrel dubbing

The Czech nymph series has an infinite number of variations, and this is one of the more effective styles. I like to add Krystal Flash down the edges of the shellback to give it a little more of a flashy look. Legs can be added, but it is just an extra step that really won't produce that many more fish.

Pink Czech Nymph

Hook: Dai Riki 135, #10-14
Underbody: 15-20 wraps .010 lead wire
Abdomen: Pink Scintilla Hare's Club Dubbing
Thorax: Dark hare's ear dubbing with plenty of additional guard hairs
Shellback: Brown Twinklebraid or Antron
Ribbing: Pearl Krystal Flash

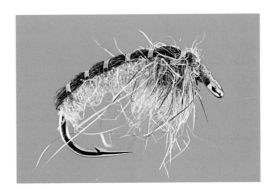

The Czech nymph series is a popular European style used for grayling and trout in rivers. The silhouette looks like that of either a scud or a caddis larvae, but it works even when either of these foods are absent. I am not a big fan of attractor patterns, but this is a dense pattern with plenty of flash, so it can even attract curious fish that aren't interested in feeding.

Partridge Soft Hackle

Hook: Dai Riki 305, #12-20
Body: Orange, yellow, or green floss
Thorax: Hare's ear dubbing
Hackle: Partridge, grouse, or quail

The floss body on this can be substituted with either fur dubbing or Krystal Flash, offering an enormous variety of color and silhouette combinations with one simple fly pattern. Beads can also be added for the thorax or for the head. A wide variety of soft hackles in various sizes and colors is essential on streams of all sizes.

Double Bead Grub

Hook: Dai Riki 135, #12
Body: Tan, olive, or brown sparkle dubbing
Ribbing: Fine gold wire
Head: 2 brass beads, gold or painted

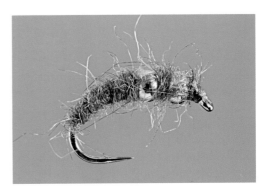

Sometimes depth and density is more important than exact replication. This pattern only emerges from the corner of my box when I need something that can punch through a deep, short run or a small plunge pool. Trout that live in these places don't see any frauds, and all you have to do is put something in front of them to get some action. If you really need to get deep, change the brass beads to tungsten.

Irresistible Wulff

Hook: Dai Riki 305, #12-16
Tail: Dark moose
Body: Antelope hair, spun and clipped
Wings: White calf tail or Antron
Hackle: Mixed brown and grizzly

I would rather box Mike Tyson than tie a dozen Irresistibles. Despite the frustration and headaches that arise during the construction of this pattern, it is truly a phenomenal small-stream pattern. It is an unparalleled floater and has good visibility.

Shadow Mayfly

Hook: Dai Riki 300, #12-16
Body: Grizzly hackle, palmered (can substitute brown or olive-dyed grizzly)
Wings: Brown hackle tips, clipped to shape

While this fly is named "mayfly," I think it is a better imitation of a fluttering caddis. It meets all the criteria of a good small-stream fly: easy to tie, good floater, and excellent visibility on the water. After giving this unorthodox pattern a shot, I have fallen in love with it and use it extensively whenever I am searching water on a new small stream.

Bright Bastard

Hook: Dai Riki 305, #12-16
Body: Peacock herl or Natural Arizona Peacock Dubbing
Shellback: Yellow craft foam
Wings: Black Antron and peacock Krystal Splash
Head: Black sparkle dubbing

Another adult blackfly imitation that is simple to tie and deadly when fish are welcome to all sorts of unorthodox terrestrials. You would be surprised to see how well heavily-pressured fish will respond to this and other low-floating, unusual terrestrial patterns.

Überbug

Hook: Dai Riki 305, #12-16
Body: Brown, yellow, rust dubbing or peacock herl
Wings: Blue dun, grizzly, brown hackle tips
Thorax: Dubbed CDC (use a dubbing loop and trim to shape)
Wingcase: CDC feather or hackle fibers to match thorax

This fly is an excellent imitation of nothing in particular. It looks exactly like a bug trapped in the surface film, with the CDC offering the low floatation and surface imprint to match struggling legs. Surprise! This fly comes from overseas, where the exact visual mimicking of coloration and static body shape comes second to imitating the motion and "life" of aquatic foods.

The Small-Stream Fly Box

As explained earlier in Chapter 2, the myth holds that you can fish any small stream with only a Humpy (in the West) or an Adams (in the East). That is it, right? These fish are dumb, inexperienced, easy, stupid, and willing to strike at any random piece of flotsam that is brought down to them by the chance of fate.

Any veteran of small-stream fishing is probably enjoying a hearty belly laugh at the insane notion that small-stream flies are totally insignificant. Rather, fly design for small streams is of the utmost consideration for the serious fly tier. Most large rivers have a uniform flow: flats, runs, riffles, and pools that all flow at a consistent rate. Your fly doesn't have to be the best floater, or the most visible, or the quickest sinking, because a long enough drift through consistent water allows you to pick up on where your fly is, or allows it to sink to the appropriate level. This is luxury that the small-stream angler lacks.

Small-stream anglers are forced to develop flies that can float through white water, or instantly sink to the bottom of a three-foot-long plunge pool. They must also be prepared with flat-water flies, because many small streams have selective trout sipping insects in the tailouts of long, flat pools. Many small-stream anglers who venture far from the road have also experienced the frustration of not packing stillwater patterns when happening upon a large beaver pond filled with cruising, active trout. Small streams also have a much greater diversity of insects than large streams do, thus an angler may need a wide selection of flies in order to find an appropriate imitation. These are all considerations that the big-stream angler is not concerned with. They pretty much know what is emerging where and when, and what they need to imitate it. Thus, it is their fly selection that is rather basic.

To most anglers, it is a surprise that most commercially tied patterns are quite inefficient for most small-stream applications. Small-stream fish are nothing special, right? Small-stream die-hards insist on tying their own patterns, sculpting them to match the very specific and often demanding conditions of their favorite little creeks. Commercially tied patterns are commercialized because they are effective over a very large area (which justifies the mass production), not because they are the best fly where you fish.

Many fly shops, guides, or other experts often recommend the old- guard flies (Adams, Royal Wulff, Elk Hair Caddis, Hare's Ear Nymph, and Woolly Bugger) for any nondescript small stream due to ignorance of the particular water. I am not condemning this, I do it often myself. These suggestions are bastioned by success over dozens of years and millions of fish. But I can promise you, after I fish a water, my top-five flies rarely correspond with my pre-trip predictions. If you do not tie your own fly patterns, and have specific waters, it is a very good idea to seek the services of a skilled local tier. Here you can place a specific order for flies with characteristics that conform to the small streams near you.

Here are aspects of fly tying that must be considered by the tier of small-stream fly patterns:

Floatability: Most small streams are fast, that is something the small-stream angler must come to terms with. Oftentimes, you have to fish pocket water and plunge pools, which will sink your standard commercial patterns. Unless you want to waste fishing time drying soaked patterns and reapplying floatant after every fish, you must find ways to design flies that float well. There are a number of material options a tier has to increase the floatability of his patterns, such as foam, CDC (Cul de Canard), and elk/moose hair among others. In addition to materials, the tier can alter many structural features to increase floatability. Tying a splayed tail, using palmered hackle, and making underwings or overwings of buoyant materials can all be effective structural changes when trying to maximize a fly's floatability.

Density: Nymphs and streamers fished on small streams do not have the luxury of a twenty-foot drift to descend to the trout's nose.

They need to get deep, STAT. Friends of mine are notorious for developing flies that can drop to the bottom of plunge pools formed by the pounding of 150-foot waterfalls. These double (and triple) tungsten beaded flies, with thick underbodies composed of double-wraps of lead, can sink literally like a rock to the bottom of any pool, regardless of the turbulence, while standard bead heads drift well above the snouts of bottom-hugging trout. Different fly densities are necessary for different situations and water conditions. Sometimes lighter weighting is necessary on nymphs you intend to sight-nymph with, while heavy weighting is necessary for high sticking a nymph. In addition to simply adding artificial weight to the fly, density and weight can also be altered by tying techniques. A tightly dubbed body will sink much faster than a loose, picked-out one. A palmer-hackled fly will descend slower than one with a collar hackle. These facets of tying can easily be tweaked to produce the exact density and sink rate you need on your favorite small stream.

Durability: A small-stream fly must hold up to a number of strikes and fish. Anglers in small streams often hook and land a much greater quantity of fish than their large-stream brethren, and the small-stream fly must be able to survive being chewed by dozens of mouths during the course of a day. In addition to just the sheer number of fish caught in small streams, the terrain of small streams must be considered. Flies fished on small streams are constantly bounced off rocks, stuck on limbs, ripped through riparian grasses and brush, and, unfortunately, imbedded in skin and clothing. Flies on large streams, with clear backcasts and deeper water face few of these perils. This considered, a Swisher-Richards No-Hackle is a bad choice for small streams not because it is a flat-water pattern, but rather that it would be rendered unfishable in minutes by a combination of fish, streamside willows, then a couple bounces off rocks at the end of a tailout.

Flash: Never underestimate the value of a little flash, just ask the stripper at the corner bar. Stream trout are no different than adolescent boys, and are often eager to go after an otherwise-standard pattern if it has a little pizzazz. The additional flash can come from metal bead heads, glass beads in the body, Krystal Flash or Flashabou, a Flashback, or even just sparkle-blend dubbing. Many old-school anglers think the flash is unnatural, and nothing could be farther from the truth. Flash is everywhere in the aquatic world, from the glimmer of light off the wet wing of a freshly emerged dun, to the reflection of the sun off the gas trapped under the skin of a rising Chironomid pupa, to the flash of an ant's bulging abdomen. Adding flash means adding realism, which means adding more fish to your daily totals.

Visibility: A small-stream dry fly must be visible in all light and water conditions, or else you will miss strikes. Visibility is something that is rather taken for granted on larger rivers, where uniform lighting and a general lack of white water allows the angler to use patterns that lack really good visibility. Small streams are often shaded much of the day, and fast water often won't allow you to see your fly, and sometimes can conceal a rise. A size 18 Black CDC Caddis is not a bad choice for a small stream because it won't catch fish (it actually imitates one of the most common small-stream insects, the *Glossosoma* caddis), but you could almost never see it on the water!

Visibility can be enhanced on your patterns by using contrasting colors (like the 3-color approach of the Cascade Flying Ant), tying parachute style, and making sure the fly is a good floater. Your fly is invariably easier to see if it is on top of the water, rather than in the surface film. Visibility does not always mean a light fly either. Sometimes glare or white water makes a dark fly much more visible than a parachute pattern. Visibility is also important when you are fishing nymphs you want to sight-nymph with.

Thoughts on Pattern Styles for Small Streams

Dry Flies: On big rivers, I fish dry flies only about ten percent of the time. On small streams, the inverse is true. Dry flies are made for small streams: the fish are aggressive, the drifts are short, currents are swift, the pockets are small, and the strikes are quick. The vast majority of angling days spent on a small stream are during the summer months, when hatches and terrestrials are abundant. Dry flies are easy to handle with the typically light lines and rods used on small streams.

When selecting a dry fly to fish in absence of a hatch, most people choose a basic attractor like a Humpy, Royal Wulff, or H&L Variant. All these flies will do is catch just enough fish to lull you into complacency. A better choice could be something like an Elk Hair Caddis, since it imitates an insect that is common along the shoreline brush throughout the season and is just as visible and floatable as the generic attractors. Other flies like a Parachute Adams or a Goddard Caddis will do the same thing. Between midsummer and early fall, my first choice is either of them and ant or beetle patterns. Again, more searching patterns, but visible and realistic. Hopper patterns should be used with restraint on heavily-fished waters, and I will keep them in reserve everywhere but the most lightly-pressured meadow streams.

When fish are picky, a parachute pattern that approximates the size and color of the natural is usually all you need. Parachutes are good choices because they still float well and can be seen easily, and they give the fish a better silhouette. Thorax-style patterns can also work well, as long as the hackle and tails are of good quality materials to keep them floating. I love to fish CDC or Comparadun patterns in slower currents, but neither are very durable or float well after a couple fish. Unless you are working a few particular fish, you can go through them at a wallet-burning pace.

If you plan on fishing dry flies on small streams, pre-treat them all with a permanent fly floatant (like Gorilla Proof) before hitting the water. Then, surgically implant a tube of paste or gel fly floatant into your arm because trying to fish dry flies on a rushing small stream without floatant will leave you frustrated when fishing is normal and suicidal when fish are rising. Without floatant, you will spend more time changing flies than actually fishing.

Nymphs: Nymphs are difficult to fish on small streams because the depth is constantly changing. Small nymphs will also increase the number of small fish you catch. The complexity of an indicator nymphing setup is a magnet for every snag within your casting radius. Yet, if you want to catch bigger fish on small streams, nymphing is the way to go.

Your nymphing selection for small streams should be, if anything, eclectic. If you think you are always missing the right fly on a big river, then just wait until you hit a small stream with a huge abundance of some random insects. Besides bugs, diverse water types require a variety of fly weights and sizes so you can fish deep pools, pocket water, and most importantly, slow flats.

I generally tie 70% of my small-stream flies as bead heads. The flash of the bead doesn't hurt, but this kind of fly gets the bug to the bottom fast and that is what really counts. With some patterns—stonefly nymphs, some Hare's Ears, and grubby-looking caddis larvae—I use two beads to aid the descent. Tungsten beads are ideal, but most pocketbooks can only afford so many of those beads. I keep the rest of my flies non-weighted or with a few wraps of lead under the body, so that I can use them at a variety of depths.

Always pack a few light-colored nymphs (Hare's Ears, tan scuds, etc.) that you can use to sight nymph. Many times you can sight nymph without spotting fish, by just watching the fly as it drifts downstream. This technique is deadly on many small streams.

Unweighted nymphs also have a place in the small-stream repertoire. Dave Hughes often talks about fishing unweighted nymphs like wet flies just under the surface. When I have tried it in hatch situations, I have been shocked at how lethal this simple adjustment can be. Unweighted Hare's Ears, Zug Bugs, and Pheasant Tail Nymphs have all fished well for me just below the surface. When I tie unweighted nymphs, I make sure to tie a red butt on them or use a different color of thread head so I can distinguish them in my fly box.

Wet Flies: Wet flies can be fun to fish through fairly uniform currents. Wet flies are often a happy medium, offering the simplicity of the dry fly without the worries of drag or snagging the bottom. It is a traditional way of fishing small streams, and there has been some resurgence of interest in it.

The original wet fly I fished on small streams was the Elk Hair Caddis pulled under at the end of the drift. I kind of held it in the current, giving it a couple jigs and letting it swing near boulders and under overhanging brush. The strikes were far too ambitious for six-inch trout, and I didn't even need to set the hook.

The great thing about wet flies for many people is that they wad up all the scientific mumbo-jumbo and

Latin terminology, and throw it all away. A friend of mine, Jack Lynch, catches fish on soft hackles and wet flies with infuriating frequency. Regardless of the conditions, whether fish are rising freely or anchored to the bottom, he ties on a size 16 soft hackle and just catches fish. That is the joy of these flies, you can know nothing about anything going on around you, and you will still likely catch a couple fish.

For wet flies, I recommend many sizes and colors of soft hackles tied with partridge, grouse, starling, and quail. These are essential anywhere, and really can be money-makers on some small streams. A few traditional winged wets can also be thrown in as well, but remember, those beautiful duck-quill wings will be reduced to shambles after fifteen minutes.

Anyone planning on fishing wet flies on streams of any size, absolutely must read Dave Hughes' book *Wet Flies*. In what is perhaps his finest book, he describes extensively how to fish wet flies and soft hackles under all sorts of conditions and situations. He even devotes a chapter to wet-fly fishing on small streams, where he discusses much more than the basic downstream way of fishing a team of wets.

Streamers: Streamers, while used on small streams on rare occasion, should never be omitted from the small-stream angler's fly box. When conditions are tough, they are often the only thing that can produce fish.

During spate flooding periods, few things will outfish a simple black Woolly Bugger. Its bulk and dark color is easy to pick up in muddy water, and its suggestive appearance could make it appear like one of many tasty things washed into the stream during the flood. Muddler Minnows are also a good choice during floods because their bulky head displaces a lot of water and it allows fish to feel it even when they cannot see it.

Speaking of the Muddler, it is an essential small-stream pattern. It can imitate a sculpin when fished wet or a hopper when fished dry. In smaller sizes, it can be an excellent caddis imitation in fast water. I always tie my Muddlers on a light-wire hook so I can fish it as a dry fly if the conditions warrant.

Pre-spawn fish can often be coerced to strike with a streamer while all other patterns drift by without pause. You don't always need to carry the eight-inch-long streamers used for spawning bull trout, but a couple small Zonkers, Sculpins, or Double Bunnies should always be kept in the dark recesses of your small-stream vest.

Resident fish, particularly the hefty ones, often can be coerced into striking small streamers. Small-stream fish are particularly territorial, and another fish encroaching on its hood is likely to be quickly dispatched. I always carry a few size 12 and 10 streamers, throwing them into prime lies and waiting for the inevitable assault. Between mid-fall and mid-spring, a streamer often offers enough bulk for fish to move a little way for a strike. Dries and nymphs have to be fished with nauseating thoroughness, while streamers allow you to cover a large section of prime water with minimal casting.

Now that we have discussed various parts of a small-stream ecosystem, let's look at the larger picture. The following is a discussion on how all those parts come together to influence a trout stream, and what to expect and understand on small streams near you. Because of logistical problems and the overlap involved with discussing small-stream regions across the country, this format should provide a good overview for your favorite small streams. Later on in the book, we'll look at case studies of several small-stream ecotypes and how each should be properly fished.

High-Gradient Mountain Streams

High-gradient mountain streams really fall into two categories: the kinds you love to fish or the kinds that are barren.

If you are from anywhere but the Midwest, you can remember at least one great little creek that tumbles down a series of little pockets down a mountain ravine. This is the dream situation for a small-stream angler: with abundant pools deep enough to hold several trout of respectable size, while requiring little expertise or effort in reading water or approaching fish. This is my perfect model of a small steam.

High-gradient mountain streams experience perpetual evolution. Hydraulic forces in swift streams are constantly moving rocks, shifting gravel beds, eroding banks, and dredging pools at a much faster rate than in lower-gradient waters. Combine this with the abundant and transitory large woody debris that litters these streams, and change is accelerated even more. Swift, high-gradient streams can be radically transformed from one season to the next.

This perpetual evolution makes finding fish a task to be re-learnt each time you fish it, something most anglers find

High-gradient mountain streams are dominated by swift water and it is important to concentrate on the few slow pockets.

less than desirable about these creeks. Some anglers are fond of this kind of habitat, however, because it has a limited number of lies, reducing numbers and leaving more of the limited food supply for a few fish. Usually swift streams will hold fewer trout, but they are larger than fish that could be found on a similar-sized lower-gradient stream.

Extremely swift mountain water can be tricky for the beginner to fish, because visually deciphering which currents are too fast and which ones are just slow enough to hold a trout is tough to master. To make it even more difficult, trout habitat in these environments is relative. What would be considered much too fast on a medium-gradient stream may be the best a trout can find here. Patience and a little guesswork will slowly reveal the right combination of current and depth that will hold fish on a particular creek.

Many high-gradient streams are mostly rushing white water, with few places for a trout to rest comfortably. However, the best high gradient streams are composed of stair-stepping plunge pools. Here, trout can rest comfortably in the slow/slack currents of the pools and wait for food to just drop in. These pools are not excessively deep, so there is usually plenty of insect activity in the shallows, and the plunging water keeps oxygen levels for both fish and insects quite high. Fish are almost always opportunistic feeders in these kinds of pools since fewer insects are found in the drift.

One of the most common things in high-gradient mountain streams is an abundance of large woody debris. This woody debris has a number of influences on the small stream. It controls the flow of water, albeit temporarily, and creates and destroys habitat every season. The wood also causes an input of trout food into the stream, mostly for boring insects like beetle larvae and wood-eating terrestrials like carpenter ants. The abundance of wood in a small stream jumps greatly following a fire, a clear-cut, or heavy storms (which cause landslides). For several years afterwards, large woody debris can litter a stream and radically change the fishing in it. Knowing about wood is critically important, for it creates the vast majority of current relief in many small streams.

Insect populations in these waters occasionally surprise the beginning entomologist, especially in plunge pool habitats. I was shocked to find typical slow water/spring-creek type insects grazing on the leafy detritus of plunge pools. These pools are rich in accumulated organic matter, so look for shredder and collector species—*Alloperla* stoneflies, *Paraleptophlebia* mayflies, and *Amiocentrus* caddis—in these habitats. These smaller streams often have more woody debris in them, and this means more *Cinygmula* mayflies, which are the only mayfly genus that feeds on wood during their nymph stage. There is rarely enough current here for filter feeders to do well, and few shallow riffles where grazers can thrive. If a plunge-pool fishery has a thick canopy, look for 60% of the insects to be collectors. Keep an eye out for terrestrial insects, because in this slow water trout will pounce on even the smallest ant that slips in.

Plunge-pool waters are exceedingly simple for the angler to fish. Simply sneak upstream, working from pool to pool. The structure of plunge pools usually allows you to make casts overland to the pools, so you don't have to worry about drag and mending your line. Plunge pools also increase competition for foods, so trout will aggressively strike at flies, if not put down by poor approaches or sloppy casting. Concentrate on hitting the most aggressive fish and moving on.

Medium-Gradient Mountain Streams

Medium-gradient mountain streams are probably the most common small-stream flyfishing situation faced by anglers. We have all seen them, with their eclectic mix of pocket water, riffles, pools, and runs, nurturing a bewildering variety of microhabitats, insects, and fish. This type of stream is abundant throughout the country, wherever there are hills and water flowing from them. This is the textbook small-stream model and the one most often on the mind when small-stream assumptions are made.

The medium-gradient stream can be the easiest to fish. A high canopy combined with bouldery pocket water allows for easy spotting of lies, simple approaches, and few casting obstructions. Of course, these waters can also be some of the toughest to fish; especially when thick canopies hang ominously a few feet above the water's surface or when the reduced flows of summer wean the stream down to a series of shallow, flat pools.

This kind of water often flows linearly without the braiding of meadow streams or the pool-chute structure of a high-gradient stream. The water in these streams usually gurgles around the rocks with a pleasant harmony, rarely exhibiting the urgency of steeper waterways. Fish habitat is more diverse, with pocket water and deeper traditional pools holding the best fish. Because of the overhead cover, there can be decent fish holding in shallow riffle water, though often only during low light or hatch periods. A trained angler can usually spot the good lies in this kind of water, making it easy to catch a large number of fish. However, the hydrology is suited to sustaining a modest number of average fish, not a plethora of fingerlings and few large fish (like a bend-pool in a rich meadow stream). Catching lunker resident trout out of a medium-gradient stream is something to be very proud of.

While they may not often grow huge resident fish, these medium-gradient streams are often ideal for spawning. They have an abundance of clean gravel because of the fast flows, but are not too swift that young fish are overwhelmed. Large fish may enter into the stream system and remain there for several weeks or more during their spawning season.

Medium-gradient streams have the greatest variety of insect species, with the limiting factor being the density of the canopy. Streams with a thick canopy of leafy plants have a lot of shredder insects like *Paraleptophlebia* and *Amiocentrus* that dine on all the leaves that descend during fall. These streams also have more collectors and filter feeders (like *Brachycentrus* and *Hydropsyche* caddis) have fewer algae grazers (like *Baetis* and *Glossosoma* caddis). Streams with a more open canopy have just the opposite populations: less shredders and collectors, and more grazers. Streams with thick canopies also introduce more terrestrial insects (particularly ants, beetles, alder flies and inchworms) to the stream, and provide a more enticing habitat for adult crane flies, which love shade and cool, moist air. Besides the canopy, the velocity of the stream and the kind of substrate can be major factors in the insect make-up. With all these variables, the insect make-up on medium-gradient streams is often the most diverse of all kinds of trout streams.

Medium-gradient streams are also where the "you can fish any old fly on a small stream" myth is nurtured. Because of the diversity in aquatic and terrestrial insect populations, the trout have seen almost everything and your fly is bound to resemble something they have seen before. Of all stream types, fly choice on medium-gradient mountain creeks is at its lowest level of importance.

The greatest challenge for anglers on medium-gradient streams is not fly choice or hatch matching, but rather avoiding getting too close to the fish. On pocket water with big rocks and logs, your wading can be more lax, but when fishing exposed water, beware. The flats of a meadow creek or the opal pools of a stair-stepping mountain creek scream stealth, but the open riffles and broken runs of a medium-gradient stream lull the angler into a false sense of security. Because you cannot see fish fleeing, many people assume that they aren't spooking fish. The largest, oldest, and wisest trout are the first ones to move out of harm's way, leaving you to catch all those small ones that so many people get frustrated with on small streams. Use patience, stealth, and long, accurate presentations on these medium-gradient streams, and you will soon see the average size of your catch rise. However, as we mentioned earlier, don't hope for lunkers because this biome is just not suited for it.

Slow Meadow Streams/Sloughs

Slough conditions and slow meadow streams are perhaps the rarest of the small-stream trout habitats that we will discuss here. Slow water rarely remains cool enough to sustain a good population of trout. When it does, it is often due to coldwater springs, and we will discuss spring creeks later on in this chapter. This type of water also is a little lacking in other things important to trout, namely spawning gravel, dissolved oxygen, and an abundance of trout food. Though not a trout Shangri-La, slow meadow streams offer some different challenges to the angler, so we will discuss this water type briefly.

One of the most frustrating things about slow creeks is reading the water. The location of a big fish and the location

*Low-gradient streams provide one of the more challenging fly-fishing habitats,
pitting the angler against clear water, slow currents, and exposed trout.*

of dead water seems almost arbitrary. The water looks flat with the occasional small boil of a deep rock or the more pronounced "v" of a rock closer to the surface, and most importantly, you cannot perceive the depth of the water. I am often frustrated myself after I stalk a spot, present the fly repeatedly without success, then walk up to find the water only ankle deep. Yet, the angler cannot walk right up to see the depth, lest they spook the trout. Long casting is required, because there are few weeds or rocks to make fish secure. This leaves the angler to maintain a high degree of concentration and exert a lot of effort (approaching, crouching, and making long casts) for an arbitrary reward. However, no rise is more welcomed by the angler than the nose of a trout slowly penetrating the thick meniscus of a slow creek.

Slough water that contains trout is most common in high alpine meadows or the semi-permafrost streams of Northern Canada and Alaska. This kind of water has a short growing season, and rarely grows impressive trout. Of course there are the exceptions, most notably the aptly-named-for-this-section-I'm-writing Slough Creek in Yellowstone Park. Slough conditions are also common where big streams braid around islands. During the low water, a side channel often becomes a slow trickle that is effectively a small stream of its own. One of my favorite "small streams" is a side channel on the Clark's Fork in Montana near the "footbridge" in Missoula. I spent my freshman year of college working that water when I grew tired of the swift currents of the main river. Big brown trout and rainbow trout finned the slow channel, educating me in the importance of casting and approach.

Insects in slow meadow streams and sloughs are also different from what we are used to encountering on small streams. Midges abound and become the staple of the trout diet. Many midges grow to impressive size in the silty bottom, requiring the angler to pack imitations upwards of size 10 just to be safe. Burrowing mayflies are also important, so don't be surprised by Brown Drakes or *Hexagenia* emergences, which can turn dead water into a churning feeding frenzy. Swimming mayfly nymphs like *Isonychia*, *Siphlonurus*, and *Ameletus* are also more common in these slower waters. Caddis and stoneflies are of much less importance in these areas, except in the short riffle sections. The caddis that are present are almost always filter feeders or collectors. Insects usually considered stillwater insects—like leeches, damselflies, and dragonflies—can pop up in the stomach samples of slough-like small streams.

The unique insect fauna of the slow slough creeks require the angler to come prepared with a different selection of flies than he or she would normally pack to a small stream. Because of the slow water, the style of fly also becomes more important. Full-hackled attractors that worked great on a pocket-water stream are not worth a wooden nickel on these waters. Flat-water patterns (parachutes, thorax patterns, spinners, emergers, and CDC flies) can prove invaluable in slough conditions. I usually carry a special box for these slough-type waters with me whenever I explore new waters, because they pay off both on slough water and picky fish in faster streams.

During hatch periods, the current in sloughs or slow streams is rarely fast enough to bring the bugs to the trout, so the trout start to cruise. Many fish cruise all the time regardless of emergences. When trout cruise in slow water, they form a tight ellipse, feeding on the way upstream, then turning around and swimming quickly downstream, rarely pausing to take an insect. Cruising trout tend to keep the same cruising pattern, especially on small streams where their home ranges are restricted. This means the angler is usually not erring by taking a few moments to observe the rise patterns and cruising rhythm. Patience on these waters is warranted, since the fish are usually larger than average.

I have noticed that fish cruising in open water tend to be more selective to particular food sources, while those that leisurely patrol the steeper bank water are much more opportunistic. These fish likely encounter a large number of terrestrials and are curious to expand their palates. The bank fish are also more likely to break from their path and rhythm to take a fly than their more-focused companions in midstream. This makes the bank-dwelling trout my desired targets for slow-water fishing. Cruising fish tend to be quite obvious and consistent in their feeding habits: fish breaking the surface are taking adults, fish boiling below the surface are taking emergers, fish darting side to side are taking rising nymphs or pupae, and fish rooting along the bottom are taking nymphs. A trout that is cruising is doing so for a reason: it is finding more food in that manner than with any other behavior. Don't mistake their consistency for gullibility. A trout has no reason to change its energy efficient behavior, regardless of how often you plop a grasshopper next to it.

This kind of water is suited to a two-person, or tag-team approach. This way, one person can observe the trout from a hidden, elevated position while the other angler can remain at a safe distance, undetected by the trout. Though only one person is actually fishing at a time, you will find that your individual success will be greater by taking turns and working together.

Riffle Meadow Streams

Few things scream "Trout Here, Must Fish" like a tiny mountain meadow stream weaving its way through a field of Indian paint brush and brown-eyed Susans. Yet small rushing meadow streams are rarely as good as they appear, until you take the time to really understand them.

For many anglers, riffle meadow streams seem to be factories of fish-stick-sized trout, and using standard approaches, casting, and flies, they will always be. The best fish are often only spotted as they dart from a shoreline lie or a shallow tailout. Even expert anglers spook well over 75% of the quality fish they run into on a small riffle stream. Patience is essential when dealing with these streams.

Hydrologically, riffle meadow streams tend to take on a similar structure. Most seem to wind through a meadow with riffles in the straight-aways and deep pools at each bend.

This is excellent trout habitat for large fish, for the ample riffle water cultivates an aquatic buffet and the pools offer security and sanctuary for large fish. Riffle water is also the motherland for the legendary (to angling) undercut bank. The meandering nature of these streams, combined with the lack of weed growth, makes these habitat structures quite important to trout. If the riffle meadow stream you are planning on fishing is just one straight riffle with a couple deeper pockets, don't waste your time. These streams produce mostly small fish that are easy to spook and not worth the frustration they can cause.

Large fish in riffle meadow streams will often take up different positions during the course of a day. In the mornings, they will be near the head of the pool, eating up the last of the insects undergoing their nightly diurnal drift. During the sunlight, they will tend to hold in the deep water, with the security of a log snag or undercut bank to conceal their presence. In the low light of the evening, they will rise freely near the undercut or at the tailout of the pool.

Since these bend-pool habitats are so much better than the surroundings, they will nearly always sustain the largest fish in the stream. These large fish, especially brown and brook trout, can be fiercely territorial and will defend their homes against smaller fish that encroach. This means the angler can quickly ascertain whether a particular pool has a big fish by just cruising through with a dry fly during the daylight. If you catch or get rises from a couple smaller fish, the odds are that there isn't anything special down there. If your fly drifts unscathed through a good-looking pool, and you are sure you didn't spook everything in the pool before your cast, take a mental note and return later in the evening. The odds are, there is a hefty trout in there, chilling in the depths, waiting for low light to resume active feeding. Some days I will cover four miles of stream during an afternoon, doing recon with a dry fly, only to spend the last couple hours of light concentrating on a half-dozen pools.

A winding meadow stream offers changing habitats with every bend.

Riffle meadow streams have one thing in abundance for aquatic insects to eat: algae. Without the canopy to block the sun, the cobbles in the riffles become coated with a generous layer of algae for insects to dine on. While many streams have a lot of shredders and some collectors, riffle meadow stream insects are often 70+% grazers. The Heptegeniidae mayfly family is common, as are many species of *Baetis* mayflies. Caddis in these streams are mostly *Glossosoma*, but there are usually some grazing species of the Limnephilidae family. There are also many midges, and all life stages are important depending on where trout hold. Because of the homogeneous nature of the habitat, these riffle streams can often have thick hatches of a single insect, making fly choice a little more important. Outside the water, there is usually no shortage of terrestrial insects, especially hoppers, crickets, and crane flies. This kind of water is the only place where I fish hoppers extensively, since fast water seems to enhance the urgency which the reactive strikes come. High water will also input a disproportionate amount of terrestrial worms and crane fly larvae, which love rich, moist meadow soils. If there are areas of stagnant water, adult mosquitoes and black flies/horse flies can contribute significantly (3-4%) to the trout diet.

Because meadow streams, regardless of speed, lack a canopy, they are quite difficult to fish during the oppressive sunlight of midday. Wild small-stream fish are smart enough to remain modestly in the depths during the direct sunlight hours (9 AM to 4 PM), and this means the angler who wishes to not chase runts will avoid these streams during these hours. Unfortunately, indirect sunlight hours often mean intense surface glare on the water and inability to spot fish. However, these problems are happily endured because the rising trout are less spooked.

Small riffle meadow streams are some of the most difficult streams to fish. Why? Since you cannot spot fish as readily as a smooth-surfaced spring creek, many more fish are spooked without the angler noticing. The open canopy makes a standing angler (and their rod and line) into a glaring inconsistency with the natural scenery, and trout perceive this with ease. Riffle meadow streams also tend to be shallower than smooth spring creeks and they lack weed growth, eliminating escape possibilities for trout and making them even more paranoid.

Approaches must be made with infuriating patience. I say infuriating, because you often must fish totally blind if you hope to catch the better fish in a riffle meadow stream. Those bend pools are best fished with an overland presentation with only your tippet and fly plopping on the water.

Riffle meadow streams are the epitome of what I discussed in the first chapter. You can either fish a Humpy, stand up, and happily catch smaller trout; or you can crawl, crouch in to position to throw a #18 CDC Ant on a 15-foot 7X tippet for fourteen-inch trout. Either way, you can enjoy an unprecedented experience in beautiful surroundings.

Spring Creeks

Spring creeks are the hallowed grounds of fly-fishing. Like Yankee Stadium, Madison Square Garden, and Soldier Field are for their respective sports, spring creeks across the world have nurtured many of the legends of our sport. Our old friend Izaak Walton composed his magnum opus within earshot of a gently gurgling spring creek. The great dry-fly/wet-fly debate launched its first literary mortar shots with the works of Frederick Halford and G.E.M. Skues, both spring creek aficionados. The post war American transition to scientific fly-fishing was kick-started by Pennsylvanian spring creek masters Ray Bergman and Vincent Marinaro. The angling genius of Ernest Schwiebert may never have been realized without spring creeks as constant inspiration. Though we as anglers have expanded our scope to freestone rivers, big reservoirs, and even the open ocean, we must remember the central role spring creeks have played to the heritage and development of our sport. No matter what new fish we pursue with flies and where we chase them throughout the twenty-first century, we will continue to come home to the spring creeks.

Spring creeks are not simply the flyfishing equivalent of a country club, with the wealthy and legendary anglers sipping Scotch and frowning at nymph anglers. They are a place where any Joe Blow can find extraordinary fishing on small streams. Spring creeks are neither as rare nor as exclusive to fish as first thought. There are spring creeks supporting trout in almost every region of North America, and many receive little pressure because of inaccessibility or simply because anglers don't know about them. Many small spring creeks (in the 4- to 10-foot-wide range) are totally ignored because passing anglers are put off by their size without even giving them a chance.

What many anglers forget about spring creeks is that they are generally small streams. There are a few large spring creeks around, the Henry's Fork in Idaho and the Metolius in Oregon come to mind immediately, but for the most part, spring creeks are less than twenty-five feet wide, and thus fall under our broad definitions of a small stream. A majority of spring creeks are very small trickles (under five feet wide) that often support fine trout but are ignored by anglers.

The formula put forth by small spring creeks—clear water + slow currents + ample weed growth—makes sight fishing the only viable solution most of the time. Weed growth consigns blind nymphing to an endeavor reserved for people seeking perpetual frustration. Clear water breeds wary trout that will sulk towards cover if they have a dry fly dropped right on their heads, a common by-product of blind casting of dry flies.

When you are looking for a fish in a spring creek, don't look for fish to match the image of a James Prosek painting. There are several keys you want to look for when spotting fish in spring creeks. First, look for movement. If trout didn't move the way they do, you couldn't distinguish them from rocks or pieces of wood. A trout moving side-to-side are easy to see, and generally much easier to coerce into a strike than a sedentary fish hugging the bottom. Secondly, look for silhouette. (A long, tapering oval is the shape you are looking for.) Next, look for the shadow. If you think you

are looking at a trout, spotting the shadow underneath the fish is a sure fire way to be positive the movement is not a thick clump of weeds or the silhouette is not that of a gray rock. Needless to say, if you are trying to spot trout without a good pair of polarized glasses, you need to go out and make your wallet about $100 lighter.

Once you spot a fish, make sure it is feeding. This simple step will save more migraines than a case of Valium. Many anglers (including myself for much too long of a time) will spot a trout, and devote the better part of an hour trying to fool it. If it's a larger than average trout, anglers will spend even more time working it. If this trout is not moving around when you first spot it, keep on moving. Often you will see trout holding in a prime lie, but not actively feeding. Trout will usually not vacate their prime lie when they are not feeding, they will simply sit there lethargically until insect activity sparks their interest once more.

Often it is easier to approach a fish holding nearer to the surface than one holding in 2-3 feet of water. This is because their window to the outside world is smaller as they move closer to the surface. Also, trout holding near the surface are often focusing on food in their binocular area of vision (right in front of them), thus you remain out of focus. This doesn't mean you can cartwheel into position, but it does give you a little room for error. Also, staying directly behind the fish can keep you in the fish's blind spot. Don't let a light ripple on the surface make you too bold in your wading or approach. Human eyes are not nearly as adept as fish eyes when it comes to coping with the dancing, flickering effect of sunlight on rippled water. I made this mistake for years and wondered why when I waded closer to the stream to spot fish under "ripple" conditions, the only fish I saw were the ones swimming off in fear.

Any nymphing done on a spring creek must be accompanied with overflowing patience. It will be a humbling experience. Sight nymphing is the obvious choice, for you can target your prey and avoid the weeds, rocks, and logs that will be detrimental to your presentation.

Blind nymphing, though tempting, especially when there is no surface activity or when it is too windy to spot fish, is often a quick ticket to Parkview Mental Hospital. Make sure weed growth is minimal, or at least confined to large patches you can avoid, before digging out the indicators and weights. I used to try to wage war with the trout like this on a small spring creek near Woodstock, NY, usually with little success, until I met an old man just sitting watching the river flow. That man, Quinn was his name, told me that he spends those times looking for bugs in the stream, inspecting the terrestrials on the shore, and looking for rises (to reveal potential fish to target when good conditions return). These things, he said, were more beneficial to his long-term success on the stream than trying to squeeze one or two trout out of the stream while getting all tangled up blue with an unproductive nymphing rig. While I thought he was just a little strange, his advice was great.

Spring creek trout live in lavish abundance, yet avarice is not above these creatures. These trout don't always wait for the natural drift to bring insects down to them. It is widely reported that spring creek trout will root through beds of watercress and other aquatic plants, then circle around downstream to pick off the scuds, sowbugs, and other insects expelled by their dredging. This feeding behavior can be frustrating at first glance, but with some creativity, it is simple to deal with.

If you are an American and under the age of 100, you probably have seen at least some part of the Star Wars series. Remember when Han Solo and the Millennium Falcon escaped the detection of a Star Destroyer in The Empire Strikes Back by hiding in the discarded space junk released by the same Star Destroyer? This is what you want to do with your fly. Toss your fly into the hodgepodge of drifting debris emitted by the rooting trout. This way your fly lands behind the trout, far from the trout's momentary attention. Then when the trout circles back your fly will be inconspicuously drifting, waiting to be consumed.

Because of the vast differences in current speeds and available foods, the insect base of spring creeks is often quite different from other streams of similar sizes and environments. Spring creeks often have a greater abundance of weed and algae growth, slower water, and a finer substrate. As far as mayflies go, you may find that the usual small-stream suspects—*Epeorus*, *Cinygmula*, and *Rhithrogena*—are noticeably absent. In their place, you will likely find many more *E. infrequens* (pale morning duns), *D. grandis* (green drakes), *Siphlonurus* (gray drakes), *Tricorythodes*, *E. simulans* (brown drakes), and the stillwater mayfly, the *Callibaetis*. Our little turtle-cased friends, the *Glossosoma* caddis, make room for the net-building *Hydropsyche* and *Cheumatopsyche* who filter out their food from the rich broth of the spring creeks. In addition to these critters, spring creeks also usually abundant with scuds, sowbugs, damselflies, and chironomids. To complicate this even more, the lush shorelines of most spring creeks also contribute a much more diverse and plentiful supply of terrestrial insects for trouts' palates. Take the density and diversity of insects that inhabit the small-stream ecosystem, and add the slower, clear water, and you have the makings of a frustrated angler.

With slow, clear, and weedy water, spring creeks challenge the skills of even the most accomplished anglers.

Here is where flies can make a big difference. Many times, we discount the importance of the fly, but when you are targeting pressured fish under tough conditions, fly selection can make a huge difference. Perfect presentations with the wrong pattern will simply drift by trout with little fanfare. When I am heading to a spring creek, even one that doesn't fit the classic ideal of a spring creek, I often take out several of my boxes of standard small-stream flies and add boxes full of Comparaduns, thorax-style patterns, CDC patterns, emergers, spinners, and midges.

You don't need to be on Silver Creek, the Letort, or Big Spring Creek to make these patterns part of your small-stream arsenal. One time I was fishing a long, nearly stagnant pool on an otherwise rowdy small creek in central Montana. All day long, I had no trouble coercing fish with the least subtle of flies, big black Foam Beetles (size 10) and the Improved Madame X. However, as I approached this pool I noticed several brown trout feeding just under the surface film near a large boulder. I generously offered them the beetle, with full confidence that they would accept it like all the other trout did. After nary a look, I knew I was in for a battle. I wove through the pines with unusual grace and settled into a recon position, where the trout and their prey could be observed. I came to the conclusion that the fish were feeding on tiny emerging cream midges, ignoring the occasional *Heptegenia* mayfly and *Glossosoma* caddis drifting by. This came as a shock, because we all assume mountain trout will feed on anything emerging, never exhibiting selectivity. However, here I was sitting on a rock, 6500 feet up in the Rocky Mountains, watching fifteen-inch trout do precisely that. Fortunately, I spent the day before fishing Buffalo Ford on the upper Yellowstone River, the closest thing to a limestone stream that isn't, and being lazy, failed to remove several of my boxes of slow-water flies. Tearing into them like a kid on Christmas morning, I found some size 20 CDC midge emergers in the appropriate hue. A couple bad casts and one good cast later, and I tied into a fifteen-inch brown, a fish I should have had no business hooking in a small stream. That incident proved to me the value of packing a small selection of spring creek flies everywhere I fished.

Geothermally-Influenced Streams

Of course, all spring-fed creeks are geothermally influenced—either hot or cold. When I say geothermally influenced, I am referring to those streams receiving warmwater inputs. These streams offer unique fishing opportunities, and because hot springs tend to affect smaller streams more dramatically, I figured that I should include a brief section on these special kinds of streams.

The first thing that comes to mind when we talk about geothermally-influenced streams is Yellowstone. The Firehole River is the archetype for any discussion of geothermally-influenced streams, though there are dozens of streams in that region that receive a significant portion (between 1 to 5% of their flow) in the form of warm spring water. All these streams share similar characteristics in terms of productivity, trout behavior, and biodiversity. These Yellowstone streams are not the only ones that exhibit unique characteristics because of hot spring inputs. There are thousands of hot springs across our country, many of which occur in mountainous areas and drain into trout streams. The results are a great boon for anglers.

One of the obvious benefits of the warmer water is that it allows trout growth to extend through the winter months, a time when most mountain trout are struggling to survive. The spring waters also bring an abundance of nutrients and minerals, which helps the growth of algae on the rocks. More algae means more bugs and more bugs means more trout. It is that simple.

The glowing words often tossed about when discussing geothermal streams often resemble the psychedelic world imagined by the Beatles. The realities of geothermal activity are often more muted. One of my favorite small streams is subtly named the "Hot Springs Fork of the Collowash"—leaving no secret about the hot water that contributes to its flow. This stream is not like the Firehole, with trout growing fat over the winter and fleeing for cooler waters during the summer. Rather, it has stream temperatures about 4-5°F warmer than its neighbors and a nice coating of algae on its rocks. This merely means that it fishes well later in the season and there are modestly better hatches than in the Hot Springs Fork's neighbors. On this stream, the hot springs are not miracle makers. All the hot springs do is turn just another mountain creek into something a little different amongst a sea of otherwise indistinguishable mountain creeks.

It is possible for streams to be thermally influenced by manmade factors. For instance, many mills and factories use stream water to cool off equipment. In this process, cold water is run through pipes around the machinery, then returned to the stream 5-20°F warmer. Most of these factories are situated on larger rivers and in areas of heavy pollution, whereas fly fishing is an activity practiced only in the more wild hinterlands. However, there are a few of these factories on smaller streams, and when they are not accompanied with unmitigated pollution, anglers should take notice. The water return areas can be rich in weed growth and are magnets for trout in the winter months, when the rest of the stream feels like a cold Slurpee.

Tailwater Streams

When anglers think of tailwaters, their minds immediately revert to big streams like the San Juan, the Bighorn, the Green, the White, or the Colorado. As far as I am concerned, we small-stream lovers should do all we can to perpetuate this myth, in the hope that most anglers will overlook the fine tailwater fisheries created by dams on smaller streams.

Considering the number of high dams, those higher than 30 feet (the height necessary to create the conditions we all think of when we say "tailwater"), across the country, relatively few are on small streams. This is because the four most common purposes of these dams—power, navigation, flood control, and irrigation/water retention—are rarely achieved by constructing them on smaller streams. However, there are enough of these

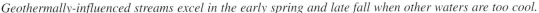

Geothermally-influenced streams excel in the early spring and late fall when other waters are too cool.

smaller tailwater fisheries in the West to provide a number of fine hidden fisheries to haunt the dreams of small-stream aficionados.

If you have missed out on the last 20 years of American fly-fishing, there are some serious benefits that tailwaters offer trout. First of all, they offer a consistent source of cool water. The water in most big tailwaters range from about 42°F in the summer to 54°F in the late fall when the reservoir turns over and the warmer surface water is mixed throughout the depths. This temperature range ensures that the water is almost always in the prime growing range for trout. Tailwaters also provide a generally constant flow of water, which prevents the spate flooding which scours out plant growth and aquatic insects. Big reservoirs also act as a silt trap, allowing clear, nutrient-rich water to flow out of the base of the dam. Even the famously roily Colorado River looks like a pure alpine stream after being tamed by Hoover Dam. The productivity of tailwaters is renowned, though often misunderstood. Tailwater streams have simple, but very prolific, aquatic communities, with filter feeding chrionomids, caddis, simuliids, oligochates, scuds, and sowbugs.

However, there are also many problems that accompany dams. Since productive trout fishing is rarely the motivation to construct a $400 million piece of engineering, water flows from peak-power dams can vary greatly daily, weekly, and monthly depending on power demand. This water fluctuation prevents natural reproduction, and as a result, many tailwaters must be supplanted with hatchery fish every year to compensate for natural reproduction. Tailwaters can also have very low oxygen levels when oxygen is depleted in the upstream reservoir.

If you are from the Northwest, you are very aware of all the threats to steelhead and salmon caused by dams. Between chopping up smolts, disorientating smolts so that they are easily preyed upon by birds and other fish, and inhibiting the upstream migration of adults, dams are a nightmare for migratory salmonids. Just like the people who deny global warming, there is a strong contingent of people who will argue that the effect of dams is minor or has shown no influence on salmon survival. Those who argue that "techno-fixes" like barging smolts, smolt passage improvements, and new hatchery rearing practices will improve everything are no better. Since dams and hatcheries were initiated, we have always said the "new thing" would be the answer, and in ten years, the salmon situation will be all good. It has never worked, and the wise money will say that it never will.

Let's get off of that sore subject and return to the topic of dams on small streams. What is essential with dams is that they are sufficiently deep (greater than 30-40 feet) and that they have a bottom-release method of releasing water. If these two criteria are met, the stream below has a good chance at benefiting from the changes caused by the dams. The flows below the dams are often clearer, richer, and cooler than without the dams.

With the increased nutrients in the water below the dam, an increased amount of algae, moss, watercress, and other aquatic plants welcome the angler. These plants, in turn, provide habitat for scuds, sowbugs, and crane fly larvae. The presence of these three insects is always an indicator of a quality fishery.

Water fluctuations below dams are slower and generally less severe than those on free-flowing rivers (see figure). After a quick rise in water level, the stream will usually offer poor fishing for a day or two while the trout seek shelter from the storm and move into their new shoreline habitats. During a flood, most fish move to slow water areas, especially the flooded shoreline vegetation. Due to the off-colored water and the shelter afforded by the plants, they can comfortably hold here feeding on dislodged terrestrial foods like crane fly larvae, worms, and terrestrial sowbugs, beetles, and ants. One of the most productive areas for fish to hold during flooding are in "angler's trails" along the shoreline, where they can hold near the plants on either side of this artificial channel, and pick off the food drifting by in the swifter, uninterrupted water of the trail. Once the fish has located a quality lie, they will usually return to a normal feeding regime until the water level changes again.

In extremely low flows, which can occur both during the winter when water is being stored in the reservoir or during the summer when water is diverted for irrigation, fish will change their holding habits. Many trout will seek the riffles and runs at the heads of pools during this low water. Here there is plenty of food and enough oxygen so that they don't get asphyxiated while seeking it out. Anglers often target pools during low water, but sometimes exploring the riffles can be more productive.

Swift tailwater fisheries are welcomed by the angler, because they offer the abundant insect life of a spring creek without the headaches of meticulous approaches and ultra-stealthy casting. Though the weed growth is less than in slower waters, and the insect populations are not as abundant, swift tailwater creeks are usually far superior than their freestone competitors.

Spawning Streams

Of course, all of the above streams could also qualify as a

Water pressure from the nearby high dam makes this small stream originate in a spectacular rooster tail emanating from the pump house.

migratory spawning fish will have a much different cycle of nutrients. As a standard rule, any stream that is heavily used as a spawning refuge has smaller-than-average resident fish.

In a regular stream, young trout grow up eating the food in the stream, and continue to consume food as they grow bigger. In contrast, spawning streams see the young trout from another lake or stream consume food that otherwise would be consumed by resident fish. Thus, when those migratory fish leave, it is a "leakage" in the net stream biomass. The resident fish also have to deal with fiercely territorial migratory trout that move into the stream for a couple months out of the year to spawn. When these large fish move in, they force the resident fish out of their preferred holding and feeding areas, thus limiting the growth of resident fish even more.

Of course, there is one major benefit offered by these spawning streams . . . they offer unusually large fish at certain times of the year. For trout, this means either the spring or the fall.

Spawning fish behave differently than the resident runts we are used to. First of all, these fish do not feed regularly. Many trout and steelhead will eventually feed once they reach their spawning grounds, but rarely stop to snack en route. Also, these fish are extremely territorial. They have one thing on their mind—chasing tail—and if some little fish is darting around its nose, the big spawner will give it a bitch slap. Fortunately, the only kind of bitch slap fish can offer up is with their mouths, so it gives us a chance to catch them.

Many spawners move into their spawning tributaries well before they actually intend to spawn. Summer steelhead will come into a stream during August or September and not spawn until the following spring. Brown trout will start their spawning run in October on many streams, and not actually get around to their business until mid-December. This offers anglers plenty of time to pursue these fish.

For most fish species, the ideal spawning habitat is not the tiniest headwater streams. This is good for us anglers, since hooking and landing big fish under these conditions is very tricky. Most species of trout and salmon prefer to spawn in streams between third and fifth order—about the size of most of our larger small streams. All these fish will spawn in shallow, fast riffle waters with gravel bottoms. Many fish will stack up in pools below these prime spawning beds while recovering from their migration and waiting for the actual spawning to begin.

When targeting these pre-spawn fish, I generally leave my dry flies at home. Many anglers report success with repeated drifts of large, buoyant dry flies over spawning-run fish. While the prospect of a four-pound brown trout devouring a four-inch-long mouse pattern gets the blood pumping, the rarity in which it actually happens will cause you to fall asleep. I have had a lot of success with standard indicator nymphing rigs for these fish. Repeated drifts, up to fifteen or twenty, with larger nymphs like October Caddis Pupae, Pupatators, and Bead Head Bitch Creek Nymphs can often induce a strike from these territorial fish. By adding a smaller dropper, you can also target the smaller resident fish.

The real weapons wielded in the war against the spawning run fish come in the form of streamer patterns. Streamer patterns will consistently aggravate strikes out of territorial spawning-run fish, and in their smaller sizes will also entice the resident fish to strike. Streamers allow you to put a realistic fly down deep next to a fish and dance it there until the fish moves or strikes. The aggressive spawner is most likely to opt for the latter alternative.

During spawning, and for several weeks after the actual spawning has finished, there will be no shortage of fish holding at the tail of a riffle or the head of a pool gobbling up all the eggs that didn't quite end up where they should. This source of food should not be ignored, and on infertile streams, it can account for as much as 15% of the food consumed by trout. This is a great time to be on the water; with a box full of an assortment of egg patterns, you can catch as many fish as you please. A mistake many anglers make when going after egg-feeding fish is to use large, steelhead-sized Glo Bugs and cluster egg patterns. Most of the available eggs are single eggs, which are only a fraction of the size of the morbidly obese Glo Bugs we find in most fly shops. Tie your single-egg imitations on size 12-16 hooks, and keep them no larger than a pencil eraser. Also, use muted colors. Pale yellows, oranges, and peaches dupe more trout than the loud fluorescent reds and chartreuses we see on many egg patterns.

Like I mentioned earlier, many spawning streams are inlets to lakes and reservoirs. In the West, most reservoirs are intended to benefit many things, but rarely the fishing. One problem with reservoirs intended for flood control is that they spend much of the year at a low level, only to fill up for a couple months, then let out most of that water to sustain summer irrigation. This process has a dramatic effect on the trout that live in the inlet stream below the high-water mark. The fluctuation of water creates conditions that few aquatic insects can proliferate in. A stream that is a rushing, boulder-strewn chute most of the year is suddenly inundated under fifteen feet of water. Few insects can tolerate this drastic change in their habitat, and you end up with a river full of midges and not much else. Of course, some insects will drift down into this temporary stream under low water, but rarely enough to make it great fishing. The moral of all this is try to avoid inlet streams to reservoirs below the high water mark.

Once fish move onto their redds and begin to actively spawn, it is best to let the fish do their thing, rest, and recover while returning to their home waters. Some fish will stay and feed for awhile, while most will get the heck out of these little waters as quickly as possible. Many of these fish are emaciated, fight poorly, and taste worse. It is best to leave them be so you can have a shot at them on their next run, when they are more energetic.

Of course, there is the eternal ethical debate whether it is right to pursue pre-spawn or actively spawning fish. There is no "right" answer to this one, and every angler must reflect on just how important catching a fish is to her (or him). I am in the camp (probably the majority) that believes going after pre-spawn fish is okay as long as all fish are played as quickly as possible and immediately released with no handling. If targeting pre-spawn was unethical, then what about salmon, steelhead, and shad fishing which is exclusively the pursuit of pre-spawn fish. Notwithstanding the philosophy of others, I strictly adhere to the rule that actively spawning fish are totally off limits. Once a fish arrives on its redd, it has earned the right to pull tail in peace. Regardless of what you choose to do, for the sake of the future fishery, all pre-spawn or spawning fish should be released unharmed.

Sculpted/Civilized Streams

Not all small streams flow through unmolested forest and meadowlands. Many streams are part of the urban and suburban landscape. Rather than flow along willows and under maples, these streams flow along backyards and under decks. As suburban areas continue to encroach on rural lands, these types of waters are growing more and more common. A good small-stream angler won't immediately think that all the development has totally killed the trout fishing. Some very good small streams lie hidden in the suburban jungles of America.

How can a stream flowing past houses remain a good stream? For one, angling pressure surprisingly is diminished to only a few neighborhood kids dunking worms after school. "Real anglers" would never waste their time on such a close-by trickle. Many of these streams get extra nutrients from garden fertilizers, and this artificial eutrophication can spark weed growth and larger insect populations than nearby waters. There is also an infusion of garden insects (and others which are more numerous around homes), that can amble into the water like ladybugs, other beetles, ants, honeybees, and wasps. All these things can help out a little stream that is flowing through a suburban area.

Now I don't want to make this sound like development along streams is necessarily a good thing. Most construction along streams is motivated by efficiency, short-term profits, and speed. Poor or non-enforced land-use laws allow contractors to take short cuts that can destroy stream habitat. Many times, these creeks are permanently destroyed by siltation when vast areas of land are cleared in order to build subdivisions.

However, in places like England, where they have been building and farming alongside streams for two millennia, there are dozens of handbooks on how to build along streams and how bad historical practices can be remedied. Planting certain plants for shade and riparian stability, building tiny log-dams and adding boulders to break up the current, and adding lime to counter acid precipitation are all techniques used to improve stream habitats. Flyfishing clubs here in America can improve local streams by using these techniques and in less than five years experience a noticeable improvement in the fishery.

Some of the following techniques can be used to improve riparian habitat on a small stream near you:

Creating "Margins": Margins are the damp areas between the normal water level and the dry land. These areas are exceptionally important for wildlife, and they also support riparian plants that shade the water offering shelter and terrestrial foods for trout. Margins can be created either

Creeks flowing through small parks and rest areas often harbor nice trout just a short cast from picnic tables.

through engineering procedures, like narrowing the stream with piles and adding riparian plants, or simply just fencing off livestock that graze on the riparian plants.

Deflectors: Deflectors are nifty little pieces of engineering that both create and control scouring. They can accelerate the current to create more spawning habitat and to offer more current velocity during low flows. They also offer shelter for young fish during flooding conditions. Deflectors can be made out of logs or boulders; whatever suits your finances or equipment. Often alder or willow should be planted near the point of emergence from the riverbank to add additional support and reinforcement. I know a family that turned a two-mile section of a poor low-gradient trickle into a fine reach of trout habitat with nothing more than various kinds of deflectors placed every twenty feet in their stream.

Wiers: Wiers can be ugly and harmful if used in the wrong manner, but they also can create riffle-pool habitats where none existed before. Wiers (and their relatives, the log-step dams) create a slow, uniform flow above the wier and a turbulent and varied current below it. This structure can help settle sediments in the pools, allowing more habitat for burrowing insects like brown drakes or chironomids, while the fast-water below can harbor good populations of stoneflies and caddis.

Tree planting: Planting trees along streams serves several purposes. First, they stabilize the banks, reducing erosion and siltation. Secondly, they shade and insulate the stream, keeping temperatures cooler in the summer and warmer in the winter. When trees wash out during flooding, they can offer excellent in-stream habitat for the trout. Trees also offer cover to trout, as well as support plenty of insect life that can fall into the water as terrestrial food.

If you would like to read more about this for your fishing club to improve the water quality on a stream near you, two excellent resources are *The River Scene* by S.M. Haslam and *The New Rivers and Wildlife Handbook*, put out by the National Rivers Authority. They offer realistic and practical ways to repair streams. The National Rivers Authority book is written from the point of view of a landowner, so their suggestions look at both the social and private costs and benefits of the various projects. Both these books are from England, so they may be difficult to locate in bookstores but are available on the Internet.

Beaver Ponds

Few things fire up the wintertime imagination more than the thought of beaver ponds. It might be because they are so secretive and ephemeral; the pond you discovered last fall could be blown out by the next spring. It might also be the magical appearance of large trout and flat water, where once only fingerlings swam through rushing riffle water. Either way, beaver ponds hold a special place in the memories of small-stream devotees.

If you think finding out about good local small streams is difficult, just try to get information on local beaver ponds. Rumors from anglers are often misleading, because a pond might be silted in or blown out in less than a year after it is constructed. Maps generally are worthless when seeking ponds because most beaver ponds are gone by the time the map even goes to print. A combination of their short-lived nature and tight-lipped anglers means the only way to really find beaver ponds is to actually get out and hike up and down streams.

In my mind, there are natural beaver ponds that I like to call "artificial beaver ponds." These artificial ponds are often constructed on private lands for aesthetic purposes or for irrigation or livestock feeding. The underwater hydrology of these ponds is similar to that of a beaver pond, but there are some distinct differences. First of all, these ponds are often more permanent than beaver ponds, often taking fifteen to fifty years to silt in. The concrete or earthen dams also prevent blowouts during spring runoff and summer thunderstorms. This permanence allows stillwater insects (like *Callibaetis*, leeches, damselfly and dragonfly nymphs) enough time to reproduce and grow in number to the point where they can be a significant source of food for the trout. These ponds are also quite easy to fish, as part of the shoreline is often left open for aesthetic purposes.

Beavers tend to select segments of a stream characterized by wide valleys with low gradients and a sufficient supply of forage to establish successful colonies. Of course, there must be wood in the vicinity, especially aspen or alder, though other trees will suffice. Western fur trappers automatically associated aspen stands in flat country as beaver territory and often would set traps regardless if they could find a pond or not.

Once established, beaver ponds influence many short-term factors on the stream: they alter riparian vegetation, slow the water flow, buffer flood events, impound transported sediments, and create new side-channel habitats. All these things have a significant influence on the trout in the pond and downstream of the pond.

The life of the pond depends on the available food sources for the beaver. If the beaver runs out of food or if the dam is severely damaged by floods, the beavers will move on to a better site. Oftentimes, beavers will take up a

Sculpted streams often have small dams and small ponds, which can produce surprisingly large trout that will cruise through shallows.

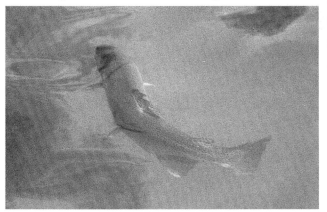

cyclical process of abandonment and reoccupation of several sites on a stream. The limiting factor in this process is the available food supply and the length of time it takes everything to grow back. Sometimes beavers will abandon a damaged dam, then come back in a couple years, improve it, and once again call it home.

Beaver ponds affect the fishing in many ways. For one, you have a stillwater situation, so longer, finer tippets replace the shoelace-diameter leaders common on the creek below. Wind also becomes a concern for the casting angler, and longer rods become more useful.

Reading the water is also different on beaver ponds. The currents are much more subtle, and it can be quite difficult to discern depth on these stillwaters. If the surface is calm, I immediately try to locate the main channel(s) by looking for color changes in the bottom and watching floating debris (objects will sometimes float faster through the channel water). Once this is done, I look for surface and subsurface structure that trout may relate to. I have always been kind of perplexed when fishing beaver ponds, because these trout seem to hold tight to structure like largemouth bass. Maybe they are just cruising near this structure, and pounce as soon as a fly is cast their direction. Regardless, make sure that you fish the major visible structure of any small pond—beaver created or otherwise.

Consistent success on beaver ponds, especially when fishing dry flies, really depends on how well you can fish cruising trout. Many times this is easy, as trout are cruising in relation to some sort of structure (like a brush line), other times it can be more difficult. Patient observation before casting will almost always pay off, since trout tend to cruise

the same pattern repeatedly. If you watch a couple cycles you can often predict the speed and direction of the trout, making accurate presentations a snap. This kind of watching for 5 minutes and catching a fish on each cast is far more productive than casting 5 times a minute and spooking far more fish than you catch.

The small stillwaters formed by beaver activity offer a different palate of foods for the trout to feed upon. Many anglers immediately think they should turn to their traditional stillwater patterns—scuds, leeches, Woolly Buggers, damselfly nymphs—when they happen upon a beaver pond. This is a big mistake.

You must remember that every bug in a beaver pond had to come from the creek from which it was created. Most small streams lack enough slow water and weeds to produce enough freshwater shrimp and leeches to populate a beaver pond. Even if a couple *Callibaetis*, damselflies, or dragonflies fly over from a nearby stillwater, it would take more than two or three years (the average life span of a pond) for them to take hold and become a reliable food source for the trout. Look for good populations of marginal water insects who normally inhabit the leaf-strewn eddies and pool. *Paraleptophlebia*, *Ameletus* or *Siphlonurus* mayflies, *Amiocentrus* and *Limnephilid* caddis, and midges should provide the backbone of the aquatic diet for the trout. Ponds with more current may have greater populations of fast-water insects than we are used to encountering on small streams. Also, like on reservoirs, it is not uncommon to see trout feeding on stoneflies or caddis that emerged in the fast water, yet were knocked into the pond by either wind or their poor flying skills.

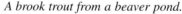

A brook trout from a beaver pond.

Chapter 6
Small-Stream
Fly-Fishing Technology

Finding Streams

Before you can string up your fly rod, spot trout, or tie on your fly, you have to find a place to fish. This pursuit can range from something mind-numbingly simple, like fishing that creek you drive over on the way to work each day, to the detailed, like thumbing through Ph.D. dissertations looking for streams with the best populations of Trichoptera. While a guess-and-check system is serviceable, developing a system of finding productive streams will save you many wasted trips and allow you to focus attention on small streams capable of producing large trout.

Many anglers think that all the good streams have been been explored and discovered. You certainly won't be the first person to ever wet a line on a particular creek, but there are thousands of productive secret streams that flow right under the noses of shops, guides, journalists, and the hordes of big river anglers. For example, a group of researchers in Yellowstone Park recently wrote a book on the waterfalls of Yellowstone. One would think that in a place like Yellowstone, where both professionals and amateurs have thoroughly explored for over a century, all the waterfalls would be documented. In fact, they discovered over a hundred previously undiscovered waterfalls in ten years of research, and claim there are hundreds more still to be discovered. Since where you fish is likely not as crowded as Yellowstone, you can be sure there are a few hidden gems not exploited by the local angling community.

When looking for a likely creek, look first at small streams that are on the routes to some of your favorite waters. This way you can take an hour or two to fish the stream on the way home, content after hitting a comfortable stream and you don't waste a tank of gas and a day of valuable fishing time exploring some remote stream with no success. The next step is looking for groups of new streams. These areas allow you to fish two to four new streams in an afternoon, spending more time on those that fit your taste. Finally, after you have exhausted these possibilities, and are comfortable on small streams, look for remote streams that are tributaries of productive big streams. Big streams don't magically become good (unless they are a tailwater), they are good because of what flows into them.

Many times, anglers who are disappointed with small fish on small streams are spending too much time on unproductive creeks. Putting a little research time in before hitting the water, just like we do before we travel to large waters for the first time, can really separate the proverbial wheat from the chaff. Here are some tips that may aid in your locating of more productive small streams.

Maps

When looking for potential small-stream destinations, your first move should be to get a map. Maps are great, and I can think of few things better than kicking back, watching a Knicks game, and browsing through maps during commercials. Thoughts about what some unexplored stream looks like, the canyons and meadows and other scenic wonders are enough to wash away February cabin fever.

I usually pack two kinds of maps: DeLorme's State Atlas and USGS Green Trails maps. The DeLorme Atlas is a good road atlas that gives you what you need to get to your stream. The only problem with this series is that sometimes the road names are antiquated, so you must rely on distances and road intersections to catch the right turns. Once I'm on a stream I use a Green Trails map to navigate it or nearby trails. These maps show springs, waterfalls, canyons, and other features that will dictate how, when and where you fill fish.

When I search for streams, I use both of these map series. I'll use the smaller scale map (the DeLorme) to locate good potential, and then use the Green Trails map to scrutinize it. Are there springs contributing to the stream? Big springs are often named and can be a good boon to the fishery. Are the topo lines close together? This could mean a canyon, good pocket water, and tough hiking. Are the topo lines far apart? Might mean a meadow and stellar hopper fishing. Is there a lake or reservoir downstream or upstream? Spawning-run fish and constant releases are often the benefits of a nearby reservoir. Is there a trail or road next to the stream? Easy access often means increased pressure and the likelihood that other anglers could provide information on the creek. All these things can be discovered with nothing more than a quick look over a map.

Reading a map is simple and there are easy things to look for that can help you locate good small-stream fisheries. Often, the best small streams are tributaries to blue-ribbon trout rivers. This is because the underlying geologic, climatic, and ecological features that make the larger river system productive, render the small streams good as well. Using a map to scan major tributary systems of popular streams can reveal many productive small streams. Another benefit to locating productive tributary streams is that they are often overshadowed by the glamour water, and you can have a great stream all to yourself.

If you have a general idea of the climate and vegetation, maps also can give you an idea of how large the stream is: simply look at the length of stream above where you are looking to fish and the size of the watershed. A 25-mile-long stream in a coastal forest may be 100 feet wide, while the same length of stream in northern Arizona might be only 100 inches wide. Maps also show you the size of the watershed and the size of the tributaries. A short stream can carry a lot of water if it is fed by several large tributaries during its brief existence. Knowing the size of the stream is important because stream size affects the amount of sunlight that reaches the stream bottom, thus influencing algae growth and insect populations. Stream size also dictates many equipment choices, including your rod, line, and fly choices.

Also, maps allow you to locate and identify difficult-to-reach areas of popular small streams. Good streams don't just become bad at some point, so when you can get to unfished water on a good creek you could be at the doorstep of some phenomenal fishing. Look for areas where you can stop along a road and (easily) hike into an unseen stream, rather than parking at the fishing access sites, and sharing the water with everyone else. This brings me to another good use of maps: they let you see what land is public and private. This can come in handy, especially if you don't enjoy running from Jethro and his shotgun, when you innocently cross his unposted private property.

If you want to take your map browsing to another level, try geologic and vegetation maps. These maps can give you additional clues to the quality of the fishery in the section you are targeting. They can also tell you how streams react to hot droughts and heavy thunderstorms. During hot droughts, streams lined with large, deciduous trees can stay cooler because they receive much more shading than those with an open canopy. A map of general vegetation patterns can easily give you this information, so you don't have to waste a day of driving just to find out. During a heavy rain shower, sedimentary rocks like shale or sandstone can quickly erode and render a stream off color. A geologic map groups different rock types into different colors, so a quick glance at the geology upstream of your target fishing area can tell you if it is worth fishing after a spate. Geologic and vegetation maps can be located at local universities or be purchased at your local USGS office.

Many people who fish casually say they don't want to try these hard-to-find places and spend days searching maps. They want to fish, not plan. That is fine, but they should not be surprised that disappointing trips are the result of guess-and-check fishing. By taking an extra three minutes to look at some geologic or vegetation maps, you can save days of trying to blindly explore new streams under adverse conditions.

Since we are now in the twenty-first century, using a compass is a lost art. Now, many people use a GPS (Global Positioning System) to help them explore new waters. A GPS uses satellites to give you an exact latitude, longitude, and elevation. This information can be important if you find yourself disorientated when bushwhacking to a small stream or hidden lake. A GPS is also nice for marking the exact area you caught fish on a lake or stream, so you can return at your leisure, or direct friends to the exact site of good fishing.

Books and Magazine Articles

Granted, small streams are rarely the subject of books or articles, but often you can use these resources to piece together some basic information on the stream or streams that you are looking at.

When looking in a book, don't waste your time reading it. Wait, that sounds bad. Reading is good, but not when you are looking for a couple shreds of information. Simply pick the book up, go to the index, and look for the stream names you are researching. If you do this, you can literally go through fifty books in a couple hours. In addition, you don't run off on tangent subjects, which distract you from your research time.

If you are planning on fishing a region, go to the local university or large public library and pull every likely book that may contain information on the streams you are looking for. (Fly Shops are good destinations too, but they often lack out-of-print books, and understandably don't take kindly to people flipping through their books and taking notes without at least buying a couple of them.) The first books to use are the big, encyclopedic state fishing guides, though this may often give you nothing more than a location, size, and types of fish that inhabit the stream. Next, look for detailed regional books, that may have a bit more information on prominent small streams. Then look for books on particular lakes and rivers, which your target streams are tributaries to. Rather than notes, simply photocopy the pages with pertinent information, highlight them, and put them in a file folder for that stream/region.

Regional guidebooks are the most controversial of fishing books because they overstate and understate at the author's discretion. Some anglers are fighting mad when they find their favorite little stream lauded in print, while others get mad when their favorite creek is badmouthed as a poor producer of quality fish. The authors have to walk the fine line between getting their readers onto good water and letting the cat out of the bag about their own favorite waters. These angling checks and balances make guidebooks a modestly reliable representation of the stream. Most authors are writing them out of a service to other anglers, sharing the knowledge they have gleaned over years of searching, and hoping to prevent you from making the same mistakes they made. One thing is for sure, they aren't writing these books to get on the NY Times Bestseller List, make their millions, and retire to a prime stretch of the Madison. Trust me, I wrote one, and I'm still eating Top Ramen and saltines.

Magazine articles are useful for many things, but not for locating small streams. Since magazines are generally nationally distributed, it is tough to get a Washingtonian all riled up about Footwide Creek in upstate Vermont. Remember that you just may find something, so don't ignore them entirely. Magazine articles can often be found via search engines on various magazine websites, conveniently available for purchase. If you don't have a bottomless bank account, then find a library that carries back issues of that magazine and pull them up there.

Academic Journal Articles

Most anglers draw the line when it comes to looking for information in journals, which have the aesthetic quality of a calculus equation . . . by the way, they also usually have a calculus equation in them. Despite their imposing appearance, journal articles are packed with detailed, well-researched information that has been refereed by other professional researchers. Sometimes you have to wonder about the "facts" espoused in some fishing books and magazines, and this is rarely a problem in academic journals.

Though on my "hit list" for several years, I had never fished Cache Creek, a small stream in Yellowstone Park. When researching the 1988 fires in the park, I came across several articles on this small stream. Upon more research, I found over twenty articles about the creek since 1989! I knew the relative abundance of insects, the type of water fish held in, the type of substrate, as well as the kinds and size of fish, before I even set eyes on the water. Not surprisingly, my first trip there was quite successful.

Journal searches are best done at a library that has a subscription to journal databases like Article First, World Cat, or Agricola. These databases allow you to locate a few article citations by just entering a key word or subject. Once you get these citations, locate the articles and then immediately look in the bibliography. The bibliography is your treasure map for research, often more useful than the database. By going article to article, you can often find the information you are looking for.

Good journals to research:
The Canadian Journal of Fisheries and Aquatic Science
Transactions of the American Fisheries Society
Aquatic Insects
The American Midland Naturalist
Ecology
Oecologia
Journal of the North American Benthological Society
Journal of Freshwater Ecology
Freshwater Biology
Hydrobiologia

Government/University Reports

There is plenty of information that is made available to the public for free, or at a small fee, by the Fish and Wildlife services, EPA, National Forests, BLM, or university extension offices. These are the best print resources that you will find, much better than books and magazine articles. Many of these records can be found on the departments' websites as well.

One of the best reports to look for are the USGS streamflow records for various streams. In western North America, where water is as scarce as literacy at a NASCAR event, close tabs are kept on even the smallest streams for irrigation

purposes. These records give you an excellent idea of how much water you can expect on a new stream. More importantly, it can give you a great idea of how a stream you have fished before looks at different times of the year.

Internet Research

Looking for information on small streams on the Internet is often difficult, because few websites are devoted to them. Regional fly shops may post some information, and some locals do put up information on small streams, but finding these sites often requires using a number of different search terms.

If you want to access insect information, the EPA and county water districts often keep records on insect populations on small streams. This information is used, along with many other factors, to assess the overall stream health. By e-mailing the website, you can often get instructions on where and how to formally request the information. Oftentimes, you can get reams of information on dozens of streams with a single e-mail.

Internet bulletin boards, the ones where you post a message and wait for someone to post a response, can be a good way to hook up with other anglers and their knowledge of small streams. Most small-stream anglers keep their secrets well hidden, but all it takes is one loose-lipped person to let you in the door with plenty of information. Be critical of some information you find on here, however, and don't get your hopes too high when people promise twenty-inch trout rising everywhere.

Interviewing

Calling up a guide, fly shop, or an aquatic biologist can be a good way to get answers to your small-stream questions. Guides can be a little tricky, for some spend most of their time mastering the streams they guide, and don't want to waste time on the piddley tributaries. Other guides guard their small streams ferociously, for the creek is a refuge from the crowds they deal with every day on the big rivers. But, keep trying and you may get lucky. Also, use e-mail rather than calling them: if they know something, they'll write, if they don't, at least you're not clogging his line while a potential customer is trying to get through.

Fly shops can be wonderful if you talk to the right people. Every shop has a couple employees who explore all over and a couple employees who specialize on the glamour water. The right guy or gal may be able to steer you in the right direction, or give you some contacts where you can find out more information.

Biologists are a great resource, and biologists who fish are even better. Every land grant university has experts on small-stream ecology, entomology, and fish (or similarly related fields). Dropping an e-mail or a phone call to these guys and gals can give you reams of information, for most are more than happy to share their research with anyone who will listen. If you are really nice, many will give you copies of their articles or bulletins for no charge. They can also direct you to the ideal books, articles, and reports that may aid your searching. If they also fish, their information can be more valuable than any other you receive.

Analyzing Prime Lies and Hunting Big Fish

You could have a combination of the casting skills of Lefty Kreh, Patrick McCafferty's entomological knowledge, and the fly tying ability of Oliver Edwards and it wouldn't be worth a rat's ass if you didn't know where the fish were. For all the talk of the importance of different flies, equipment, casts, and retrieves, it is all worthless if you are fishing water that is barren of trout!

Fortunately for us anglers, finding fish in a small stream is not too much different than finding fish in a big stream. Many of us think that it is even easier on a small stream! Big streams have only a couple habitat types—broad riffles, long shorelines, and big eddies all contain fish—but is very difficult to distinguish microhabitats that could help focus your attention. There are riffles on the Yellowstone and the Clark's Fork of the Columbia that are the size of a football field . . . there you are just covering water, hoping to put your fly in front of a fish. On a small stream, you can have a riffle the size of a pool table, but a couple exposed rocks will help you refine your casts to the most likely holding areas for trout.

Finding big-fish areas on large streams has always been difficult for me. I am never the guy with the monster fish you see on the covers of all the fishing magazines. All the water seems to look the same and catching a big fish seems to be the result of pure luck, like hitting pocket aces in Texas Hold'em. On small streams, it seems like big-fish areas are trimmed with Christmas lights and flashing arrows. You have the option, if you wish, to totally ignore small fish, and concentrate all your efforts on the larger-than-average fish.

Fishing for big fish on small streams is a patient, quiet endeavor. Sometimes if you are gunning for big fish, you may make only two-dozen casts and cover five miles of stream in an afternoon. I find this kind of fishing exciting and a nice change of pace from the machine gun casting and deliriously fast action that characterizes most small-stream fishing. Catching ten twelve-inch fish on a relatively infertile stream is a much greater accomplishment for me than picking up a bucketful of fifteen-inch rainbows while roll casting on the Madison.

When looking for big fish on small streams, concentrate on prime lies. (Prime lies are places that afford trout current relief, overhead protection, access to deep water, and food.) However, some streams, because of their structure, will have prime lies that don't really fulfill all four of these criteria. If you do catch a big fish in a particular kind of structure, look for more of that structure to produce similar fish.

You rarely see big fish rising freely on small streams, and you rarely see them holding in exposed areas (pool tailouts being a notable exception). So much of your big fish hunting comes from fishing the water and not necessarily the fish. So, usually, I will seek out some good-looking water,

take care approaching it, and then settle down and observe for awhile. Are there any rises? Are there too many rises (a sign that there are many little fish with no big fish to chase them off)? Are there insects emerging? Can you make a presentation that won't spook the fish if the fly is refused? Are you in the best possible presentation position? There are many more questions that should drift through your mind before you commit to making a presentation.

Big fish in small streams are easily spooked, for they only grew to ripe old age through years of avoiding the predators that captured their slower brethren. I once crossed a large, rather deep pool on a medium-sized mountain creek by walking across a fallen log that spanned the length of the pool. As I was crossing the pool, I had an open window to all the trout. The young of the year and fingerling trout held at all depths of the pool and swam around without much care to my presence. The juvenile and smaller adult fish hung around for awhile, then darted off when I got too close. The largest fish in the pool wasted no time getting to cover. I only saw them when they were dashing around looking for a chance to escape, for they had spotted me before I saw them. This incident reinforced the importance of stealth when approaching big fish.

Approach Techniques

Ask most flyfishing professionals for the most important part of fly-fishing and they will tell you: "Presentation, presentation, presentation." Presentation is a good answer because it encompasses everything: from flies to leaders to casting to retrieve. But before the presentation comes the approach, so this has to be more important. For you could have a perfect presentation, but if you already spooked the fish you are going after, you are wasting your time.

The first key in any approach is to do so slowly. I am just as susceptible as everyone else to taking shortcuts as my fishing time is coming to an end: ignoring non-prime lies,

This is how NOT to fish a flat, exposed creek. Wading puts down trout that otherwise would confidently cruise this slow pool. Stay out of the water unless necessary!

not observing trout during a heavy hatch, and most importantly, accelerating my approach. Doing these things will allow you to maybe cover more water in your waning moments of fishing, but it surely won't help you catch any more big fish. Remember, nature has all day to do what it's doing, and you will have more success if you take it at its pace.

Another important factor in the approach is the decision to wade or not. This is a hotly debated topic between experienced anglers. There are advantages to both sides of the argument: a stealthy out of water approach allows you to target larger, more difficult fish and have a much higher cast-to-catch ratio, while wading in the water allows you to make more casts and hook more, albeit generally smaller, fish.

Wet Wading

The most basic method of approaching fish on small streams with densely vegetated shorelines is to simply wade right up the middle. As simple as this seems, there is some methodology to this technique. When wading I am always trying to be sure of how my approach is affecting trout. If I see trout shooting upstream 30 feet of where I'm wading, it is a sign that my wading technique has leaks in it.

To minimize alerting trout of your presence, wade where you are least likely to cause waves or vibrations that will sound like a fire alarm to the trout. This usually means wading in the very shallow marginal waters along banks or bars, or wading in the thickest, whitest white water you can find. Wading through swift turbulent water causes almost no upstream vibrations, thus allowing you to approach lies with incredible stealth. As unorthodox as it sounds, I have found that wading through white water is actually easier than wading through a fast slick, since the force of the current is dissipated in all directions. Wet wading (without waders) is also the safest method to wade through white water, because your bare legs have less resistance and less buoyancy than, legs in waders.

When wading it is important to fish upstream, because the silt you kick up wading will alert trout to your presence for quite a distance downstream. This is something to remember when fishing slower, silty streams or spring creeks. While fish may continue to feed after the cloud of mud dissipates, they likely will be more wary than usual for several minutes (up to a half hour). This consideration should be taken into account as a courtesy to other anglers, so that you don't put down fish that they are working.

Water conditions often dictate the optimal wading technique. Faster water allows you to approach fish closer than will slower water. Look at the ripples that come off when you wade: fast water creates a narrow "v," slower waters create a wide "v." (The ripples in the "v" are simply the trout-alerting vibrations that emanate from your wading.) In addition, wading in faster water you don't alert trout off to your side that you are approaching.

The only time wading is an obvious choice is in rocky pocket water. Here the water is so broken that you can get very close to fish without spooking them. I have even stepped on modest-sized trout residing in pocket water, who were oblivious to my approach. Even stumbling around won't alert fish to your presence. Since this kind of water allows a close approach, you don't have to worry about mending or long casts.

Wading should be a technique of last resort when fishing in slow runs and shallow pools. Mentally exhaust all other possibilities before hopping in this kind of water. Unless you plan on making 90-foot casts within a second or two of entering the water, your vibrations will reach the fish long before your fly does.

Pool Jumping

Pool Jumping is often a technique reserved for the highest headwaters, though I have used it on rivers as large as the canyon section of the Lamar River in Yellowstone. I'm not really sure where I first heard of this technique, but I think it was in some ancient (early 1980s) issue of Fly Fisherman magazine concerning terrestrial fishing in the Adirondacks. Pool jumping is a technique used on plunge-pool fisheries, where the creek simply descends a hillside in a series of pools, and the only real holding water is in these pools.

The basic premise of pool jumping is to throw your fly into a pool that is significantly elevated from your casting position. This is no more than a straight upstream presentation with a couple of twists and advantages. First of all, a plunge pool has two key holding spots, the head and the tail. By casting from below, you can remain out of view of the trout, increasing the likelihood of success. Secondly, often you can position yourself to present to the tailout almost without drag. These two benefits of remaining downstream and out of view make this technique much more desirable than fishing a pool below you.

Often, the gradient will be less severe, and pool jumping will require making longer casts and casting to the second pool upstream of the one you are in. This is the most common type of pool jumping situation, and a place where pool jumping will greatly increase your catch rate. When you fish a small pool while standing over it, fish have nowhere to go and panic trying to escape your presence. The last thing they want to do is feed with a clear and present danger a few feet away. By putting a pool in-between you and the fish, you won't alert fish and they will move further for your flies. Also, if you cast overland, you don't have to worry about drag or mending the long cast.

Belly Crawling

This technique is reserved for those areas with open canopies and little riparian brush, most importantly meadow streams and beaver ponds. It is also extremely effective on the open spate type of stream, but the wear and tear on the body caused by crawling over these rocks is rarely worth the trouble. In those cases, I would recommend simply relying on crouching and long casts to mask your approach.

Belly crawling is a technique that is geared towards individual fish holding in particularly vulnerable or exposed

Crawling into position allows the angler to closely approach trout in vulnerable shoreline lies, creating shorter and more effective first-presentations.

lies. I usually restrict my use of this approach for when I have spotted a fish or when I am absolutely certain there is one holding in a particular lie. If I approached every fishy-looking spot, I would probably have a high cast-to-catch ratio, but I sure wouldn't catch a large number of fish in the course of the day. If the conditions require the use of this technique, I will walk downstream right along the river looking for fish fleeing out of lies, make a mental note of them, then come back upstream using belly crawling to approach the best lies.

Once in position, I usually like to make my cast lying on my side. It looks as weird as hell, but it works. On the Little Firehole in Yellowstone, big fish from the Firehole stack up in a large pod near the confluence of Iron Spring Creek during July and August. These fish are quite visible and get hit hard with every imaginable fly pattern all day long. The only way to get them is with tiny nymphs and an invisible approach. After two middle-aged men fished the run for an hour with no success, I moved in. I started crawling about 100 feet from the shore, the last 50 feet on my elbows. It took me five minutes just to get into a position where I could cast. As I nestled up behind some long tufts of shoreline grass, I heard one of the guys yell, "Incoming!" followed by a laugh and a scornful wave of the hand. It was tough to ignore the comment, but if I'd got up to rock bottom his ass in the water I would have spooked the fish.

Turning to my side I stripped out enough line and parted the grass so I could see the drift of my tiny, sky-blue painted indicator. After one false cast, I dropped my indicator ten feet above the pod, and it immediately shot under. I set the hook, played the fish, landed and released the perfectly spotted fifteen-inch brown while still lying down. Because I didn't stand up to play the fish, I landed two more rainbows, both over thirteen inches. After a couple unsuccessful drifts and deciding the pod was sufficiently spooked, I got up and walked past the old guys (who by now were only forty feet away, trying to see what the hell I was doing) and mentioned, "Stick with the hoppers, they're easy to see." It was money.

Belly crawling takes practice. Not the actual crawling, any infant or drunk can do that, but the casting, retrieving, playing fish, landing and releasing fish can be tricky unless you have done it before. A little practice on a meadow stream with soft grass can be an excellent way to work this technique into your angling repertoire. Many people find it much easier to do everything when propped up on an elbow, and if this is more comfortable for you, then certainly do it.

Belly crawling is a slow way of fishing, requiring patience that few of us can summon. It isn't perfect for all situations. The angler who insists crawling into position for every fish is going to end up as sore as a NFL running back on Monday morning with relatively few fish to show for his efforts. Despite this, when a belly-crawling approach is made to a spotted fish and done correctly—complete with a good cast and drag-free drift—it will nearly always result in a hooked fish. Knowing when and where to use this technique will consistently put you into larger fish than any other approach style.

Tag-Team

This is a simple technique that requires only two anglers and a pair of polarized glasses. One angler is the "spotter," whose goal is to spot feeding trout, and if possible, discern that they are feeding on. The other angler is the "angler," whose goal—surprise—is to catch the fish. Though this

Tag-teaming a trout requires one angler to get into a high position to spot a nice trout like this, while another angler carefully gets into casting position.

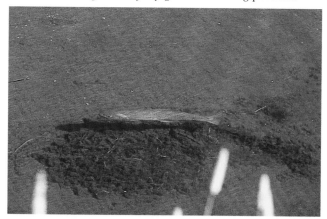

technique is often used on large, clear streams, stillwaters, and salt water, it is possibly most effective in small streams where there is not enough water for two anglers to fish in close company. It also is one of the best ways to catch unusually large fish in small streams.

This technique is most effective on clear, slow streams on sunny days: when the potential for spotting fish is at a maximum and so is the potential for spooking fish. The slow, flat water will reduce your chances for an undetected approach, so the angler is much better off having someone spot fish for them, rather than trounce through the water in an attempt to see the fish themselves. An individual angler in this situation is at a significant disadvantage, and may spook 75% of the trout without even being aware of their presence. This technique is least effective on fast streams, where spotting is difficult and turbulence facilitates a close approach.

My favorite way of using this technique is sending the spotter (with polarized glasses) upstream to the next pool, trying to gain an elevated position where visibility is maximized. Coincidentally, this technique is only effective when an elevated viewing position can be obtained: it is virtually worthless on a meadow stream with low banks. (It is possible on meadow streams, if there is tall grass along the banks and the spotter belly crawls into position. Because this is infuriatingly slow for the angler, who must sit and wait for the spotter to get into position, I wouldn't recommend it.) The spotter should move into position with great stealth, using bushes, rocks, and trees to conceal the approach. It is surprising how close one can get to fish, when you are not immediately concerned with casting and the complications casting causes! Once in a comfortable position the spotter has several tasks: look at all the current lines, look for obstructions that could cause snags or otherwise screw up a presentation, locate all the fish in the pool, prioritize them by size, and deduce which are actively feeding (and subsequently worth the effort of casting too). A small pair of binoculars can be surprisingly helpful on small streams when it comes to looking for fish and what they are feeding on.

The spotter then instructs the angler to the optimal casting position and tells the fisher where to cast. The job for the angler is simple: do what the spotter says. Obviously, the burden of skill is on the spotter, and a good spotter will surely increase the quantity and quality of your catch. I personally enjoy being the spotter more than being the angler; it is very rewarding to help people catch fish that they would never have a chance when fishing alone. For most anglers, catching fish is important, so it is a good idea to set up a rotation system so each person shares spotting and fishing duties.

This approach style allows for techniques that are much more difficult for individual anglers, such as fishing Woolly Buggers on an upstream dead-drift. As effective as this technique is (try it sometime, you'll like it!), it is very difficult to detect strikes without visual contact with your fly. Having someone to watch your fly and tell you when to set the hook can greatly improve the effectiveness of the technique.

Sniper Approach

This method allows you to move into position by any means necessary. This differs from belly crawling, because you can be standing, crouching, sitting, or even straddled on a large tree branch (it has happened). The sniper philosophy is to use boulders, tree trunks, brush, or whatever else is handy to mask your approach and casting position. Many big-stream anglers laugh at this, but it is probably the greatest reason that they do not catch many fish on creeks.

The structure that you are using to conceal yourself can, and should, also conceal your casting. A big boulder that hides your body can be worthless, if the trout, five feet away, can see your nine-foot shiny wand flailing in the sunlight. Before you cast, look and try to see what the trout sees. If it is an open sky, consider taking another angle or using a different cast to avoid spooking the fish. One of the best camouflages for your casting is a background of small trees or large willows swaying in the wind. All this may seem rather picky, but we lose most of our fish not on the cast, not with the fly, but on the approach.

Of course, when using obstructions to conceal your approach, you have to learn more than the overhead cast. Often sidearm casting is the only way you can pull off a cast with a large obstruction in front of you. Learning these approaches and casts will greatly improve your large river fishing. On the Clark's Fork River in downtown Missoula, Montana, there are numerous places where willows and ash trees allow you to closely approach rainbow and cutthroat trout feeding on tiny Trico spinners in the surface film. Without utilizing trees to mask your approach, you can easily spook the large trout, which hold only a few inches below the surface while feeding on the tiny spinners. After years of small-stream fishing, I was able to pull off some radical wrap-around casts (thus landing some beautiful trout) while my college buddies had trouble just getting close enough to cast with the standard approaches.

Resting a Pool

When I first read Gierach's writings on the virtues of pool-resting, my first thought was, "He is old and needs an excuse to rest." I was thirteen at the time and couldn't comprehend to wasting any precious moments on the water by sitting around making coffee while waiting for a pool to recover. How crazy is that? Later I read Dave Hughes' book on Yellowstone, and he mentioned that he took a nap at Buffalo Ford and when he awoke, there were fish rising everywhere. Maybe this insanity is infectious.

After I tried it, I found that it was.

How many times have you taken great care to approach a fish, but something in your presentation or approach put the fish down? I know I have done it more often than I care to remember, and so has anyone else who has spent a lot of time on small streams. The proximity in which you ply your trade magnifies your errors. On most small streams, if you put down a fourteen-inch fish, you just wasted your biggest fish of the day.

Resting a pool is difficult, but essential if you want to consistently catch large trout in small streams.

Pool resting is one way to give you a shot at fish that otherwise would have eluded you. Pool resting comes in two forms, the pre-cast rest and the post-cast rest. Look at a pre-cast rest as preventative medicine, and the post-cast rest is an elixir for errors.

The pre-cast rest is shorter in duration and used to let everything get back to normal after stumbling into casting position. Often, the pre-cast rest can be used for "productive" purposes like observing the trout, checking current lanes, observing insects, and choosing and tying on flies. I use the term "productive" in contrast to "unproductive" ways of resting the pool: eating, watching birds or flowers, or humming the annoying song you heard on the radio on the ride up. The pre-cast rest can be anywhere from one minute to ten minutes in duration, unless you fell in the water or kicked a bunch of rocks in, the fish will be comfortable again after only a couple minutes.

The post-cast rest is reserved for when you spook a big fish during a presentation. The post-cast rest should be used to figure out what you did wrong and how to avoid repeating the error. This is also the time to do all the sweet nothings that we all enjoy about the outdoors. Kick back and look at the birds or scan the tree line at the edge of the meadow for moose. Give the pool or fish—anywhere from fifteen minutes to an hour to allow the fish to resume feeding constantly. If the fish comes back out making splashy rises—when before you arrived it was casually sipping insects—do not immediately start casting to it. The odds are that it is still nervous from whatever happened earlier, and the increased urgency in rising is a sign of this. Given enough time, the fish will return to its casual feeding regime and you will get another shot to fool it.

Regardless of which type of rest you are trying to do make sure you use at least a portion of it observing the nat-

ural processes around you. Look at the trees, soil, plants, terrestrial insects, and rocks. These things are quite significant to mastering a small stream, but are overlooked in the rush of casting and catching. Who knows, it may just reveal something that will prove valuable on your next cast.

The-Let's-Not-Break-Another -Freaking-Rod-Tip Approach

This is my favorite, because I have learned through years of guess and check that rod tips lose when they do battle with the earth. Small stream maneuvering all too often requires crawling, climbing, and scrambling, which is hard enough without adding a $500 piece of graphite to compound the situation.

Let common sense dictate your practices. ALWAYS carry the rod butt-first when not fishing, because if you slip forward and your rod is pointed in the same direction as you are you will most likely break your rod tip and do a face plant while fruitlessly trying to save your rod. Some people carry the rod with the tip forward, claiming that they throw it to safety before they land. Great theory, but not nearly as neat in practice. Another thing to remember is to set your rod up or over an obstacle when trying to climb over it. Finally, use a rod sling rather than trying to hold your rod in your teeth or in some other awkward place when you must use both hands to climb. The rod sling will fit in the back of your vest taking up minimal space, and it makes it much easier to make treacherous moves while on the water.

Casting Techniques

First of all, let me clear up something right now. I suck at distance casting. Like the divot flying past a golf ball, I can lob my fly rod about as far as I can throw a fly line. Needless to say, you will never see me leading a distance casting competition. Fortunately, the key to small stream casting is accuracy on the very first cast. Being able to hit your target with a minimum of false casts will allow you to catch more and larger trout on small streams.

On small streams, precision on the very first cast is essential if you hope to catch large trout.

I have always loved the fact that small streams force you to throw out the playbook of traditional fly casts and come up with a few creative spontaneous casts of your own. Big rivers let you fall back on standard overhead, flip casts, and roll casting 95% of the time, yet brushy small streams don't afford the angler this luxury. I will assume that you already know the basic overhead and roll casts. If not, there are many good books that discuss those topics with much better detail and photography than I can. These are the casting techniques that I use most extensively in my small-stream fishing, though you should also be prepared to come up with all sorts of variations when the water dictates.

Reach Cast

The reach cast, also known as the reach mend, is an essential part of the small-stream casting repertoire. The reach cast can be used to put your fly on the other side of an obstacle, while your line all lands in the water. The reach cast also can be used to keep all your line in a similar current line, thus reducing drag on your fly.

The reach cast is achieved by simply making an in-air mend of your fly line. As you make your final forward stroke on the basic overhead cast and your fly reaches its maximum distance, just tip or reach with your rod to the side you want the mend to go. This is not a hard motion! You should only make a gentle reach so you don't pull your fly too far back from your intended target.

Sidearm Cast

This is nothing more than an overhead cast that is made parallel to the water's surface, but few things should be practiced more than sidearm casting. Why? The sidearm cast is most often used to put your fly under overhanging brush, grass, logs, or rock. If done properly, the sidearm cast is a lethal weapon to put your fly where most anglers cannot or will not, and oftentimes the trout takes your fly with little hesitation. If done improperly, you will splash your fly down short of the target (occasionally forgivable by the trout) or you'll put your fly in the overhanging tangle and almost certainly spook the fish getting the fly out of there. After you shake your fly free, or wade up to unhook it from the branch, your fly will certainly get the silent treatment by the trout for quite awhile.

A sidearm cast can place your hopper imitation where nobody else can put it.

The angle cast is very similar to the sidearm cast, and while the sidearm cast is usually used to put your fly under a forward obstruction, the angle cast is used to avoid casting obstacles behind you. This cast is another invaluable tool on small streams where casting obstructions are the norm rather than the exception. It's true, it's true.

Puddle Cast

The puddle cast is a great way to achieve slack on those long downstream presentations—not to mention upstream presentations and all the other uses. It is better than the wiggle cast because you can achieve more accuracy, which is important when you are making casts to current lanes and pockets the size of a punchbowl.

To achieve the puddle cast, make a normal cast (angled at 45 degrees) and when your forward stroke is at the end, drop your rod tip to the surface. The line will drop to the surface and this will stop the fly line, creating "s" curves. (You will get more "s" curves the higher above the target you make your final cast before dropping your rod tip.) The puddle cast is one of those used extensively on weedy waters where you need plenty of slack line to get a good drift.

Galway

I first read of this Irish cast when flipping through the pages of Gary Borger's excellent book, *Presentation*. It is a great way to avoid snagging brush when making your back cast.

The basic premise of this cast is that you are making two forward casts, rather than one forward cast and one back cast. The caster achieves this by turning his or her body about 45 degrees to follow the line during the entire cast. This allows the caster to observe the line and its path, manipulating it where necessary. Of course, with ample experience, the angler will learn how the line will fly on a normal cast. By observing the territory the backcast must traverse, the angler can fish comfortably and confidently without watching the line do its thing.

Half-and-Half

Like New York Knicks basketball, the Half-and-Half is ugly but effective. It allows you to make a long cast, without worrying about drag.

The goal of the Half-and-Half cast is to throw your line so that only your tippet and fly land on the water, while your line lands on the grass, rocks, or logs. The advantages of this technique are many. First of all, without your line on the water, you are almost guaranteed a five- to ten-foot, perfectly drag-free float. Secondly, you do not spook the fish by letting your line drift over it or by slapping the water particularly hard with your line. Third, it allows you to make the cast far from the stream, so that you do not have to crawl, squat, or make another kind of uncomfortable approach.

The benefits of the Half-and-Half lend themselves to stealth situations, as opposed to long drifts, or drifts through multiple currents. It is particularly useful when you are working a single fish. I use it when I am fishing upstream and see a prime lie or a good rising fish. I then move over to twenty feet or so below the fish and between five and twenty feet from the bank. Here is where I like to execute the cast, though it can be made from almost any position, though downstream presentations with this cast do not get very long drifts. I like to also use this cast when I am even with the fish, standing twenty to forty feet back on the bank. This position usually requires fishing blind, which I will discuss later in this chapter.

This cast is usually used on particular fish or lies, but you can effectively search the water with it. I like to use it blind on open-meadow streams during midday, where approaching right up to the water is the recipe for a fishless day. By working up the bank, make your false casts over the grass, and with your final stroke make a change of direction cast so that just your fly and leader land in the water. After the drift, walk up about ten feet, do an off-land mend (see below) so that your line is on the water and you can pick it up to cast again without pulling your fly through the grass. Take a few more steps and repeat the process. This is often the best way to fish a meadow stream when the fish aren't rising for a hatch.

The biggest problem with this technique is that if you screw up, more often than not you will snag up in the grass or rocks right next to the water. Besides looking less than smooth when walking up to undo your snag, you will likely spook the fish that you were working so hard to fool. If you crawl up to remove your fly, sometimes you can salvage both your fly and fish. If not, at least you can give the trout a heart attack when you pop up right next to it. I actually had a fish splash me with water on the upper Firehole when I appeared only a foot above the surface to work my fly out of a piece of stubborn grass.

Off-land Mending

Off-land mending is related to the Half-and-Half, in the sense that part of your cast is made over some sort of terrestrial structure.

The term off-land mending may be a misnomer, since I most often use it with large rocks in pocket water. In swift pocket water, drifts can be complicated because of the maelstrom of currents and obstacles. When you have an obstacle, or dangerously deep and swift water between you and good casting position, a normal drag-free drift is nearly impossible with standard casting techniques. This is where I rely on the off-land mend to keep my line off the water and out of the conflicting currents. I use a rock like a grannie is used in pool, in order to keep my line off the water. As the fly reaches the end of its drag-free float, I can extend that drift by mending the line off of the rock into the current. This technique can often extend your drift two or three times beyond that which you would receive from a normal presentation.

This technique can also be easily done off the shoreline too. I will often use it to extend the drift of a fly I made a Half-and-Half cast with. My only recommendation is that you do not try to use this technique over a log with any branches or snags on it because your line will find them with the precision of a smart bomb.

A Bow-and-Arrow cast is perfect for prime lies like this slow, deep overpass.

Bow-and-Arrow Casting

I like the bow-and-arrow cast when I am trying to make a cast under a low bridge or under branches that hang only a couple feet above the surface. This cast is the only way to go when brush or other obstructions prevent a sidearm cast. On small streams, this is the rule rather than the exception.

Simply grasp the fly in your hand, pulling it back so as to flex the rod tip. Then point to where you want to cast and let go. Usually your fly goes where your rod tip was pointed before you pulled the fly back.

Obviously, the downside of this technique is that you are restricted to rather short casts, usually only the length of your fly rod. If you pull the fly back by your ear, and hold your rod arm out extended, you can often add another four feet to the cast, for a total of about 22 feet with a nine-foot rod. Also, try to do this cast only with dry flies; nymphs and indicators can be contorted into Gordian Knots if you screw up with this cast.

Slap-Drop

This presentation is important when an angler wishes to make a downstream presentation to fish holding under a bridge or other low-hanging structure. Since most fishermen start their small-stream fishing endeavors at a point of crossing (i.e. bridge), and a low bridge is one of the best holding lies for trout, an angler would greatly increase his/her catch rate by mastering the bridges. This presentation is one of the tools to achieve that goal.

The greatest challenge to making a downstream presentation is to a fish under a bridge, especially a wide one. To present to fish holding in the rear 1/3 of the sheltered water, a slack-line presentation is necessary to get your fly downstream. However, the bridge occasionally prevents a good parachute or S-cast, which would give you the desired drag-free float. Some anglers would recommend a sidearm cast, which would place your fly deep under the bridge, then follow with a number of roll-mends which would throw slack line into the current seam, which are intended to give the fly a drag-free drift. However, every time I have tried this, I seem to give the fly a minute jerk with each mend, and I always seem to make the fly drift a tad slower than the current. For fish that are regularly pressured, as fish holding under bridges always seem to be, a tad slower will seem like a bimbo at an astrophysics symposium. Maybe a better caster could execute this perfectly, but for myself and others of less-than-Krehian casting ability, there must be another option to fool these picky fish.

My solution to this problem is a cast called the slap-drop, which is a basically a poorly executed sidearm cast that is allowed to hit the bridge and drop straight into the water. This gives you a nice pile of leader that will let the fly drift naturally until it straightens out. For dry-fly fishing, you can simply hold your line in place so that it doesn't drift down to the fish before the fly. The current and your fly will do all the work. When nymphing, this allows the fly to plummet straight down on a slack line, whereas on most casts the sinking fly is slowed by the tension on the leader. You can often eliminate the need to mend your line by making this kind of cast.

Blind Casting

One of the most advanced skills that any fly angler can acquire is the ability to fish totally in the blind. This requires the angler to be able to assess a potential lie, cast to it, and detect a strike, all without actually seeing the fish, the lie, or the fly. Impossible you say? "Contrare," reply many small-stream experts.

In many situations, it appears impossible to approach a fish without spooking it or at least alerting it to the degree that anything but the most flawless presentation would be rejected. In these situations, it can be surprisingly productive to make a presentation to a fish you cannot see. This involves first inferring where a good potential lie exists. One of my favorite examples is on a bend on a very narrow meadow stream lined with knee-high willows. You cannot see it clearly without sticking your head up and sending all the trout scurrying, but you assume it is deep and fish-worthy. Now, the problem is how to get a fly in that spot. If you wade downstream of it, you are in clear sight of the trout. If you back up too far, you must cast over too many willows to set the hook cleanly. If you approach from upstream, you will kick up too much silt to not spook the fish. If you approach from the inside bend, you are in total view of the trout. Damn! One solution to this problem is to back up 15 feet from the outside bend and prepare to make a cast to the unseen pool. Of course, from this position, you cannot see your dry fly on the water. This is enough of a conundrum to cause 99.9% of anglers to give up and move on to other fish.

The key now is to select a fly that will elicit a strike that could be detected without actually seeing the strike. This "indirect" strike detection can come in the form of seeing rings on the surface of the pool, seeing spray from a splash, watching your line get pulled by the fish, hearing the sound

of the rise, or even watching the trout hit the fly by jumping out and landing on top of the fly. Obviously in this situation, you would not pick a fly like a floating nymph that would be taken with considerable nonchalance by the trout. My favorite choices are insects that are large enough to warrant a vigorous rise or insects that are likely quick to escape: grasshoppers, crane flies, and adult caddis.

Your cast must be clean on the first shot. A mistake after all this work can cost you the fish. If you are short, you can snag the willow branches, and if you cast long you may "line" the fish or get your line caught in multiple currents, causing the evil drag to appear. This situation is where the good casters bring home the bacon. The casting step of this technique is the difference-maker between those anglers who catch big fish on small streams and those anglers who only catch the five-inch runts.

Now, your presentation requires keen attention as your fly disappears from view behind the curtain of willow branches. Ears must follow your fly when your eyes are no longer sufficient. Listen for a rise, and look on the other side of the pool for the spray or rings that indicate a rise. If your approach, fly selection, and cast were sufficient, you should have no problem hooking into one of the best trout of the day. Of course, there are times when all of this effort results in only a six-inch fish. At first, it is a good idea to laugh at yourself over all the hoopla you went through, but in retrospect, a good angler will think about how and why they caught a small fish. Good questions include: Am I spooking the larger fish, Am I not reading the water properly and falsely classifying lies as prime? Am I just wasting time? Don't let the last thought enter your head. Fishing, like poker, should be judged in the long run, not on a case-by-case basis. In the long run, this technique will land you more and larger fish than just passing up difficult lies.

False Casting

Avoid at all costs. Anyone who has spent an appreciable amount of time on a small, brushy creek knows all too well the perils of false casting. Big streams allow us the luxury to false cast until our arms fall off, but there are few occasions where a false cast should be executed on a small creek. False casting is used to both dry your dry fly out and to help pay out line for longer casts. Since roll casts are often used on small streams where regular casting is prohibited by vegetation, the only practical purpose for false casting on creeks is to dry your fly.

Why not false cast? Most obvious is the fact that many small creeks are extremely brushy and excess casts, given the law of averages, will leave you spending more time untangling snags than actually fishing. Many beginning anglers who are learning how to cast are quickly frustrated by the constant snags, and swear off all small streams altogether. Even good casters should avoid false casting on small streams, even where possible. Small-stream fish are jittery crack addicts compared to their large-stream cousins, and a misplaced false cast will send these spooky trout immediately to the nearest pool or log tangle. The flash of the rod, wave of the line, or tap of the fly on the surface will also put down fish that won't vacate their lies, leaving you wasting time working trout that are alerted to your presence and unwilling to rise.

How can you get around false casting? There are several techniques. First, is choosing a fly that requires no or little casting to dry adequately, like the Deer-Hair Daddy or the Shadow Mayfly. Another technique is to carry a little suede patch to dry your fly and powder desiccant. The combination of these two things can often dry your fly just as well as several false casts. If you must false cast, you can move away from the stream to make a couple false casts over dry ground, then return to the stream and continue fishing. This technique is only viable when the stream has a broad riparian zone, such as meadows or gravel bars. Finally, if you must false cast over the water, do so where you have already fished or cast to before. Never cast over where you intend to make your final cast or over fresh water that you have yet to cast to.

Nymphing Techniques

Indicator Nymphing

Indicator nymphing should be the backbone of any stream angler's repertoire, for most trout consume over 85% of their calories within eight inches of the bottom. However, most anglers treat indicator nymphing on a small stream as something akin to baking chocolate chip cookies rather then buying them at the store. Why go through the trouble, when you can get a similar result with less effort? Once the skeptics try it under the correct conditions, the improved size and quantity of their catch is enough to convince them that the slight amount of added effort is more than worth it.

When to use nymphs on a small stream? This questions is crucial because nymphing small streams can be maddening if you involuntarily throw nymphs every chance you get. Nymphing is almost always the most effective technique when streams are swollen with rain or snowmelt run-off. Under these conditions, few trout will

This rainbow fell to one of the more underutilized techniques in small-stream fly-fishing, indicator nymphing.

be rising and the only way to catch anything is with nymphs. Nymphing is also good on streams that are a series of modest-sized pools or deep runs. In these places, trout may be unwilling to swim four to eight feet to the surface for a tiny morsel, but will freely accept any fraud that is drifting by at their level. My other favorite place to fish nymphs is along deep bend-pools that are undercut. A dry fly may not even enter the field of view for a fat trout holding deep under the bank, while a properly drifted nymph can be lethal on these fish that have seen it all.

In contrast, where should you not fish an indicator nymph rig on small streams? Places where you must make short, accurate casts in brushy conditions can cause enough complications to make you swear off indicator nymphing altogether. Streams with rapid depth changes can also be real headaches to nymph with an indicator and weights, because you always seem to be drifting too shallow or snagging the bottom. Also, I rarely use indicator nymphing on tiny streams—less than five feet wide—opting instead for a dropper nymph off a dry fly when a nymphing situation comes up.

When planning to go indicator nymphing on any small stream, it is important to bring the whole supply of gear: indicators, weights, extra tippet, etc. As I mentioned earlier, I prefer corkies with a toothpick because they are easy to use and I won't have to turn tricks on the corner to afford more than one. All the gear is essential, because small-stream nymphing is as, if not more, demanding on your equipment as on larger streams.

If you plan on indicator nymphing, make sure you have plenty of backcasting room. With all the terminal gear on your line, snags and tangles are much easier to come by when your line hits an overhanging alder branch. Also, remember to keep your loops open and your casting simple so as to avoid casting problems with the indicator rig.

I always fish multiple nymphs when I use an indicator nymphing setup, but when you are catching small fish, they can really get wrapped up in the leader causing more problems than it is worth. If this keeps occurring, it is a wise choice to trim back to a single nymph, though multiple nymphs still have their benefits. Multiple nymphs can easily result in multiple fish per cast, because once a fish is hooked on one nymph the other fish think it is chasing the other one, and they'll try to strike at it first. This unique experience is a great novelty of anglers of all skill levels, and a sure way to give a kid a great story to tell his friends at school.

Visual Nymphing

Visual nymphing is an art that is disappearing quickly with the popularization of indicator nymphing. Many times, visual nymphing is far superior to indicator nymphing, especially on pressured fish in shallow waters. Visual nymphing generally requires that you present to a sighted fish, for many clues of a strike come from the fish. Of course, visual nymphing can only be used in clear waters where you can see the action take place.

The first part in visual nymphing is the choice of fly. The fly should be chosen so that it can be easily spotted under water. On some streams, this may require a light fly and others on a dark fly. The deciding factor is the color of the substrate: in a stream with a dark, leafy substrate, you want a light-colored fly, and on a sandy substrate, you want a dark pattern. The fly should also be weighted, so that it sinks without extra shot. The fly can be weighted to different degrees to achieve the proper sink rate, and I usually tie my favorite sight-nymphing patterns in three different weights. I distinguish between the weighting by using different colors of thread head. Generally, you want a medium-sized pattern (rarely smaller than size 14 or 16), so that you can see it at a distance. Smaller flies can be extremely effective, but you must be able to decipher a strike from the movement of the trout. Much easier said than done.

The second part of visual nymphing is getting into position so that you can see the trout and your fly. Often this means moving into a place where there is little shade or glare. Like I mentioned earlier, using logs, brush, and rocks, you can move very close to trout, which is essential with this method.

The third part of this technique is strike detection. There are two ways to do this: watching your fly and watching the trout. If you plan on watching your fly, you have to be able to keep it in view from when it hits the water until it reaches the trout. This is not easy. If you lose sight of the fly, you can give your fly a little tug and often this can recalibrate your eyes to it. If you lose sight of the fly, then turn to watching the fish. When watching the fish, you must have a vague idea where your fly is, so that you can tell if the fish is reacting to your fly or to something else. Watch the fish and see if it makes any side-to-side darts, and/or opens its mouth when your fly is in the general vicinity. The opening of the mouth is the key thing to focus on because the inside of the mouth is white and easy to spot.

Visual nymphing is an advanced technique that will allow you to fool very difficult fish in any size stream. I have used it successfully on everything from big rivers like the Yellowstone or the Green down to tiny alpine trickles that can be leapt across. Small streams are the best places to hone the technique, because there are more fish to practice on and you have to use a lot of stealth to approach them.

High-stick Nymphing and Czech Nymphing

This technique is a favorite all over the world—from the grayling streams of Norway to the brown trout rivers of Czechoslovakia. The latter is where it originated and the country that consistently wins international flyfishing competitions with it. Yet, many American anglers have forgotten it with the advent of indicator nymphing. It is best suited to large streams, where you can approach fish quite closely. However, in swift, deep runs and pools, it can be a killer small-stream technique.

Fly choice is key to the technique. There is no lead attached to the line, so the fly must be able to descend on its own. A dense, heavy pattern is essential so that your fly

sinks quickly and so you can feel where it is at all times. The Czech nymph style is popular for this technique, though woven-body patterns and other flies with little water resistance work quite well too. I will also use a dense stonefly nymph pattern for this kind of nymphing, as it is easy to feel the aggressive strikes that those big flies bring on. Finally, using a double-bead pattern can be effective, especially a double tungsten bead pattern.

This nymphing style is traditionally done with a team of three flies: the heaviest pattern in the middle, with the lighter patterns ahead and behind. This way the heavy fly keeps the others down deep near the bottom.

This technique rests on making a short cast with only a little amount of line extending from the tip. The rod should be held high, with the fly drifting directly below the rod tip. The rod should follow the nymph downstream, and another cast made when the fly reaches the end of the drift. Your drift is quite short (only ten to twelve feet), so it requires you to get quite close to the fish. Because there is little to no slack in the line, the strike can almost always be felt once you know what a strike feels like. If you cannot feel or see the strike, you can also always throw on an indicator.

While there isn't a lot of slack line, the fly is still dead-drifting! Don't pull the fly through too fast or too slow—just go with the flow of the current. If done properly, you can actually achieve a better dead drift than you can with an indicator. The water on the bottom of a stream is always slower than the water on the surface, yet with an indicator and line on the surface (as is done with indicator nymphing), your fly will rarely be travelling at the exact speed of the bottom current. This is because, even with perfect line control, your indicator will always be trying to pull your nymphs faster than you want to go. With Czech nymphing, you can compensate with your rod tip, and keep your team of flies traveling at the correct speed.

Dropper Nymphing

Dropper nymphing is a productive technique when there are no insects emerging, but there are sparse numbers of large food sources—stoneflies, large mayflies, October caddis, grasshoppers, crane flies—bumbling about. By using a big

This nice brown succumbed to two nymphs "Czech nymphed" through a plunge pool.

dry fly and a smaller nymph, you can target both aggressive fish that are looking up to feed, as well as passive fish that would ignore anything that doesn't hit them on the nose.

Dropper nymphing is not as simple as attaching a nymph to a dry fly; there are some considerations you should take into account. First of all, when looking for a dry fly, concentrate on a large, buoyant pattern that will be able to float well, even with a heavy nymph pulling down on it. Foam is the optimal material for the dry fly, but flies incorporating spun deer hair or palmered hackle do well if adequately dowsed in floatant. What you do not want to use are CDC flies or other low-riding or delicate flies. Low-riding or flat-water flies won't be able to support the weight of the dropper, and are easily pulled under. CDC flies are even worse once they meet a fish's mouth, and most have to be changed only after a couple fish.

The leader connecting your dry fly and nymph is a critical connection. It should be of lighter leader strength than the main tippet, because if you snag your dropper fly on something, you only want to lose that fly, not the whole rig. Also, using fluorocarbon for your dropper leader in this situation can be very advantageous. Many fish rising to your fly will pass very close to your dropper leader, and anything that makes it less visible will increase your catch rate. The dropper leader should be attached to the bend of the dry fly and the eye of the nymph. I prefer an 18-24-inch length of tippet for my dropper; too much more and you'd be better off throwing an indicator rig, much less and you are making your dropper ride pretty high in the water column.

The nymph choice for dropper nymphing is also a critical choice. The nymph cannot be so heavy as to sink the dry fly on every cast, nor can it be totally unweighted so that it sits on the surface film. The solution to this is a small, dense pattern that will get down quick but not so heavy that it will pull the dry fly under. You should never add weight to the dropper leader to help get the nymph deep, rather use bead heads and internal weights to bring the pattern deep. The other important factor in choosing a nymph for this technique is picking an insect to imitate. Since your imitation is probably not drifting on the bottom with the rest of the insects, it had better imitate a type of insect that is preparing to emerge if you want any shot at fooling a fish with it. Thus, I usually use a midge pupa (which are perpetually emerging) for my dropper, though I would turn to using a caddis pupa or mayfly nymph if either of these insects could be expected to emerge in the next couple of hours. Flies that you do not want to use for droppers include most of the trout foods that never drift more than an inch or two above the bottom: stonefly nymphs, caddis larvae, midge larvae, sowbugs, fish eggs, aquatic worms, crane fly larvae, and most scuds.

Oftentimes, my decisions to use dropper nymphs are spur-of-the-moment decisions. If I see a nice pool on a tiny stream and get nothing on the dry fly, I will just grab a nymph off my vest, use it on a dropper for that particular situation, then cut it off when I move on. If I am planning on doing this several times on a stream, I will prepare two or three dropper leaders (and flies) in advance and simply tie them on for the one or two casts where I might need to use them. When I am done, I cut off the rig at the bend of the dry fly, and stick the nymph and leader on my vest until the next nymph situation comes up.

Dropper nymphing is most productive in pocket water or riffles where fish do not have much time to inspect your dry fly. On flat stretches, approaching cautious trout can often spot the dropper leader coming off the dry fly, and some trout even get spooked by bumping into the dropper leader when preparing to rise to the dry fly. When fish rise to the dry fly in a dropper rig, unless they jump out of the water and land on top of the fly, they must come into contact with the dropper leader. If fish are rising slowly, they often can abort their decision to eat your fraud before getting the imitation in their mouth.

Dry-Fly Techniques

Skating

This technique on small streams is mostly used as a way to aggravate a strike from a naïve fish, rather than imitate a natural insect. I like to use classic skating both on open meadow streams, where the wind can give your fly a wild erratic action, and on small brushy pools, where you are dappling your fly in a restricted area. I also like skating flies when the wind is so strong that accurate casting is impossible, and the surface is so ruffled that trout would have difficulty seeing a small fly on the surface.

Skating on small streams is a secret weapon on small streams, and I treat it like my little atomic bomb: hold it in reserve unless the conventional forces don't work. I rarely use it the first drift or two past a likely looking lie. If a section of water looks exceptionally good, and repeated dead drifts bring nothing up, try to skate a fly over the area. By skating the fly right off the bat, you run the risk of spooking wary fish and simply not interesting inactive trout.

*Skating is an effective technique for caddis,
crane fly, and flying ant imitations.*

If you are planning on skating your fly, bring a long rod. The long rod allows you to get your line off the water so you can manipulate the fly directly or allow the wind to push your line around causing the fly to dance. Make your fly look like it was smoking crack. When you skate you want to impart random motion on your fly without pulling around so fast and erratically that a pursuing trout cannot strike at it. If you are bringing up a lot of fish but not hooking many of them, slow down your action and give fish more time to hone in on the fly.

Classic skating theory has always advocated two types of flies: caddis and spider-style flies. While caddis patterns have surged in popularity, spider flies have really fallen out of popular favor over the past decade, as we have seen more realistic imitations emerge onto the scene. For a pure skating pattern, however, few things can match the motion of a fine-hackled spider pattern. A small-stream regular will be sure to pack both of these styles whenever they are headed to the creek.

However, the most realistic pattern to go skating with is an adult crane fly imitation. A skating technique will perfectly mimic the bumbling, awkward flight of crane flies as they amble across the water's surface. If the pattern is tied out of the right materials (deer hair or foam body, and a stiff hackle), and greased up, it should be able to shimmy and glide with a Ginger Rogersesque grace all day long.

Dappling

Dappling, or dapping, is the technique most often promoted as "the small-stream technique" in angling books. It is a simple technique that requires no casting, and it can be used by even a rookie angler. This method requires simply hanging a length of leader from the rod tip, and letting the fly drift a short distance. Following the fly with your rod tip can reduce drag and allow you to extend the drift of your fly.

This technique is often reserved for conditions that prohibit standard casting: holes in brush, cutbanks, and pockets in logjams. However, it is also useful in pocket water and plunge pools, where swift and divergent currents cause immediate drag. Dappling can also be used on pools or beaver ponds where trout are cruising near the banks and you don't want to spook them with a cast.

One disadvantage with dappling is that it often requires a careful, concealed approach. Walking up to a location where dappling is necessary is like wearing bicycle shorts to the bar: you'll scare off your quarry. The exception to this is pocket water, where you can often wade very close to your target before casting.

Dapping almost always requires a large, buoyant dry fly that will bounce on the surface until the trout attacks it. Imitative patterns (except crane flies) are rarely used for this technique, for most trout that are in lies that require this technique are not in position to feed on a hatch.

Repeated drifts are not necessary with this technique. Make one drift, maybe two, and move on to the next probable lie. If a fish is there, it will strike, so making extra casts is usually a waste of time. After you catch one fish in an area, you may want to try it again... maybe lightning can strike twice.

The Twitch

This technique was advocated by Leonard Wright Jr. in his book *Fishing the Dry Fly as a Living Insect*, and it is an effective way to imitate adult caddis, stoneflies, and even grasshoppers. All of these insects naturally skitter or kick when on the surface. While caddis seem to dance in an erratic fashion, I have noticed that hoppers and stoneflies, when they land near the banks, nearly always re-orient themselves to the bank and kick in that direction. This is the direction you want to try to direct the motion of the fly.

After a dead drift doesn't produce for me, I'll use this little twitch just as the fly enters into the trout's cone of vision (of course I am just guestimating the moment the fly enters the cone of vision). By twitch, I don't mean pull the fly ten, five, or even three inches across the surface. About one inch, maybe two, is the size of twitch that you are looking to achieve. The movement should be almost undetectable at forty feet.

To perform the movement properly practice is essential. Moving a fly such a short distance from such a great distance is incredibly challenging and something that can only be actually practiced on water. But this is one of those techniques you'll be glad you practiced, because on both small and large streams it'll produce many fish you could not otherwise catch.

Under and Up

Many anglers are torn between fishing dry flies or wet flies on small streams. This technique is a marriage between the two. The under-and-up technique starts out as a classical up-and-across, dry-fly dead drift. However, when the fly reaches the end of its drift, you pull the fly under the surface, and strip it back upstream towards you. This is a good technique when you have to drift your fly downstream through thick brush and you cannot make a standard cast.

Some anglers and writers try to scientifically justify this method as an imitation of a diving female caddis, swimming towards the bottom to lay eggs. Though I always try to be a scientific apologist for my weird techniques, it just cannot be done in this instance. A diving caddis could never dart upstream against the current like a minnow, which is what this technique does. This technique puts the fly down next to or over a trout, and hangs around like a nagging in-law. I just think it simply pisses the trout off.

The best fly to use in this situation is a down-wing pattern like a caddis or midge imitation. My favorite pattern for this technique is an Elk Hair Caddis. It is bulky and causes a lot of displacement underwater, so fish can see it and feel it. The Elk Hair Caddis is also durable, which is important when you have 4-5 sharp hits for every solid hookup. You can technically use any dry-fly pattern with this method, but many up-wing styles will spin your leader tighter than Allen Iverson's cornrows.

Streamers in Small Streams

Like trolling flies in lakes, using streamers on streams is something that few anglers dare admit to. It causes ashamed looks like when you have to discuss your wild college days with your kids. The reason these people feel shame is because this technique can be so deadly. But also like trolling flies, few people even try it, for they buy into the "small stream=small fish" myth that burdens our sport. Thus, those of us in-the-closet small-stream streamer anglers can, fortunately, keep the monopoly on our deadly techniques.

There are some very biologically sound reasons for fishing streamers on small streams. First of all, small streams are often used as spawning grounds for fish from larger streams. This results in a number of small, fry-sized fish for the larger resident fish to prey upon. In any given region, there are usually more fry-fingerlings per square foot in small streams than larger rivers. In addition to this food source, there are also much larger migratory trout that temporarily inhabit the streams during spawning season and can easily be aggravated into striking a streamer. The opportunistic nature of the resident trout also makes streamers a good option. Few small-stream trout, even smaller 8-10-inch fish, can tolerate a smaller fish (a.k.a. lunch) holding nearby without at least taking a snap at it. Also, small-stream trout tend to guard their lies with much more aggression than larger stream trout. This makes them much more likely to strike at a fly that gets too close, even when hunger is not a factor. Combine these biological reasons with the brushy and jumbled nature of many small streams, where normal drifts are far less productive (and much more difficult) than just twitching a fly near some cover, and it becomes obvious that streamers can be deadly on some smaller streams.

Of course, those of you who target big brown trout in the Rockies with streamers the size of small automobiles may have to adjust your techniques and equipment slightly for small streams. First of all, the average size of the fly must be reduced, save when spawners are your goal. I try to keep my streamers in the size 8-10 range for most of the season, though some of the big size 2 Zonkers will come out to do

Streamers can be effective on creeks, especially creeks with migratory brown trout.

battle with spawning-run bull trout. Also, keep in mind the fish that inhabit small streams. Dace, darters, and small sculpin can be found, but the suckers, shad, shiners, and chub are less common. (This is in general. Depending on where you are, these other fish can be highly important to resident and migratory trout.) Your flies should parallel their shapes and sizes, which may require some creative tying for most streamers found in shops are tied to mimic the larger stream baitfish. Tippets, while still needing to be strong enough to withstand powerful strikes, need not be sufficient enough to anchor the *U.S.S. Enterprise*. A lighter 3X-5X tippet will add more movement to your fly, and if you add a piece of rubber shock tippet, like Lefty Kreh advises in his book *Presenting the Fly*, you should have no problem with overly enthusiastic takers. Finally, a full-sink or sink-tip line is not always needed on small streams, and can actually cause more problems than they solve. Unless the stream is over 20 feet wide or has pools/runs in deeper than four feet, keep these specialty lines in the car. Weighted patterns, especially bead heads and coneheads, should be enough to get your fly to the bottom on small streams.

My favorite technique for small-stream streamer fishing is sinfully easy. I simply crimp on a split shot right near the eye of my fly (which, by the way, is attached to a floating line and 8 feet of 4X tippet) and fish my fly straight downstream. The fly is brought to life with short strips and movements of the rod tip, stopping for several seconds along cover to bust a move, then moving to the next piece of cover. I usually start at one side of the stream, fish each piece of good cover in a thirty-foot section, then fish it back to the other side. Here is my secret—on the first pass I will drift the fly downstream to the cover before holding it in place, and on the second pass, I bring the fly up from behind the cover (when possible). My theory is that the fish who see the fly coming from upstream will take the fly out of hunger, while the fish who sees the fly as it approaches from behind will strike out of aggression or simply as a reaction to the surprise of a competitor blindsiding them. My reasoning for this untested (and probably untestable) theory is that many fish will ignore a pattern fished one way, but savagely attack it when it comes from a different direction.

Drifting flies broadside to trout in small streams can be effective, though it is rarely possible on small streams. Because of the short casting and complex current lanes found in small streams, the good drift needed to execute this maneuver is difficult to come by. I have found that simple downstream presentations are the most practical and productive way of fishing streamers on small streams.

Streamers are extremely effective during spate conditions following a heavy rain. Here visibility is reduced and trout move to the edges of the current to avoid the extra current velocity. A water-displacing fly (like a Muddler or small sculpin) will allow the fish to feel the fly even when it cannot see it. Sometimes streamers will be the only thing that can turn futile casting practice to actual fishing when tough water conditions prevail.

Fishing Behind Someone and Dealing With Crowds

Being stuck behind another angler on a small creek can effectively ruin your day. I have started many days on stream with high hopes, only to see them shattered by a surprising lack of trout. More often than not, simply walking upstream will reveal the source of your dismal success: a good angler who fished the water immediately before you.

Like I discussed earlier in this book, good anglers can fish small streams with devastating efficiency. Every good-looking lie will be full of reluctant trout with sore lips. A good angler can render a section of small stream worthless for fishing for several hours.

The quick detection of previous anglers can save your day on the water. Detection begins even before you get in the water. Are there other cars in the pullout or at the trailhead? Often, I will keep on driving if I see a car parked in a pullout near my target stream. That one is easy, but sometimes you can't tell which direction the anglers went, or if they were fishing another stream in the area. Fortunately, tougher reads can be done on-stream as well. Some of the most obvious things to look for are fresh footprints in sand or mud. Sometimes these can be tough to decipher, so if you are not sure, look for wet spots on shoreline rocks. These marks are almost surely the remnants of wading boots, and a sure sign that someone else is sharing your stream. Another, less objective method is to simply fish likely looking water and if it comes up fishless, wade through and look for fish scurrying away. If there are fish there and they didn't strike when you present to them, this could be a sign that someone has given them some sore lips. (This technique assumes you have fished the stream before and know how the fish "normally" behave.)

Often, once an angler is discovered above you, you have a couple choices. The first option is to jump well ahead of the other angler. This is often the easiest move, and I will discuss how to do that properly in the following paragraphs. The second choice is to change flies or techniques. Since most anglers fish dry flies on small streams, I try nymphs. If I want to keep fishing dry flies, I will switch to a medium-sized ant or beetle pattern. These subtle patterns work well on fish that have already been bombarded with hoppers and big attractors. Finally, if there are other good streams in the area, I generally find it easiest to move to a nearby, non-pressured stream.

On small streams—because of their compact nature and the devastating impact just one angler can have on another's angling—fishing courtesy is important. If you see someone sitting along the stream just observing the water, reel up your line and grant him or her a wide swath of the creek. They may be looking for fish, resting a pool, or simply observing and appreciating the beauty of their little spot: regardless, they beat you there; so let them have their moment.

When you must pass a slowly advancing angler, avoid walking right along the stream bank when passing them and give them plenty of backcast room. I have seen punches thrown on a small stream because an angler walked too close behind another one and got whipped on the neck. Curiously, this fight was started by the one casting, who was pissed that the other one messed up his cast! Make eye contact, wave, and say hello (at least) if you must pass within close proximity.

Also, don't start fishing right above the other angler. Nothing frustrates me more than someone who is concerned enough with their fishing to stop fishing 300 feet below me in order to pass, while they are so unconcerned with my experience so as to start fishing again only 40 feet upstream of me!

When you must cross the stream, choose the swiftest, most turbulent water downstream of the other angler before fording. This will keep vibrations to a minimum and reduce the sediment you kick up. It is amazing how seemingly gruff anglers will go out of their way to thank you and talk with you if you do this. They appreciate the respect it shows them and the knowledge and manners it shows you have.

Finally, there are never enough fish in a run or pool for you to hop in and double-team it. Don't walk up and pile on like Dave Megget. It doesn't matter if the pool has more fish in it than the Star-Kist Tuna Factory, nobody wants an unwelcome threesome. Let the angler who was there first spend all afternoon there if they want, and you can go ahead and explore without someone nipping at your heels.

Sometimes, when fishing crowded waters, you are forced to be Machiavellian in your attitude. If you must fish a stream with another car at the access point, walk or fish upstream and keep your eyes peeled for the angler. See him before he sees you. If you think that the angling has been adversely effected by being so recently fished, then simply reel up, and take a big detour around them and start fishing a quarter-mile above him. Stay far away from the stream so that you are totally undetected and he thinks he is fishing alone. The worst thing you can do is let him see you, which may lead to a game of angry angling leapfrog, with both of you spending more time trying to get ahead of the other one rather than enjoying the fishing. If he is oblivious to your presence, then he will be fishing merrily along unaware that he is hopelessly casting to water that you already fished through with General Sherman's devastating effectiveness.

Physical Training for Small Streams

Fly-fishing is not marathon running, it is more like bowling. You can be fat and drunk and have a mouth stuffed with M&Ms and a Swisher Sweet and still catch fish. If you want, you can find streams that you can fish all day and barely move an eighth of a mile. If you really feel vigorous, you might even hop into a boat with an electric motor and troll the afternoon away on a local lake.

On a small stream, you can do none of this. Feeble legs will slip on rocks or collapse under swift currents. Underdeveloped shoulders will not be able to hold the rod high to prevent drag. Weak arms won't let you climb over rocks and boulders, or scramble up a tree to elude a bear. A lagging cardiovascular system will make you hate the person who coerced you into the five-mile hike to this magic creek. Simply put, good fitness will make your small-stream experience much more enjoyable and productive.

I don't want to make you think you need to be Michael Johnson or The Rock to enjoy small streams. However, small-stream fly-fishing requires more walking, scrambling, wading, and yes, falling than the vast majority of our big-stream brethren deal with. Besides, being in good physical condition will let you live longer and fish many more days than you would if you led a sedentary lifestyle.

Fitness for small streams requires two parts: weight training and cardiovascular training. Diet is important for general health, but little can be recommended specifically for fishing. Besides, I am not the person to talk about good diets, considering I down 120+ ounces of Coke a day and usually chase it with red meat and Goldfish crackers.

Weight Training

Believe it or not, there are some weight-lifting techniques that you can use to help build muscles that are used in fly-fishing and wading. Weight training, for most people, should be done 2-4 times a week, allowing adequate time for muscles to recover. However, if you wait more than 5 days in-between workouts, your muscles will start to atrophy. Most of these exercises should be performed with low weights and high repetition, for you are pursuing muscle endurance, not necessarily power. Here are some good exercises and what they will do for your fishing:

Upper Body

Dumbbell Raises: These will improve shoulder strength and will allow you to hold your rod high throughout the day. Keeping your rod high will keep line off the water and reduce drag. Many people, including myself, get tired at the end of the fishing day and are less prone to use proper form when presenting to trout. This exercise will reduce this kind of fatigue.

Dips: Dips will allow you to push yourself up and over logs and rocks with ease.

Fingertip pushups: I hated my 8th grade basketball coach, Mr. Griffith, for making me do these, but I thank him today. Few things will strengthen your hands and fingers more than this exercise. This can help you when you must scramble over rocks and up cliffs. When climbing up some sheer rock faces, strong fingers will save your life.

Crunches: Crunches let you do everything better, as almost all strenuous motions in the course of fishing are somehow connected to the abdominal muscles. I find that crunches really help when making belly-crawling presentations.

Back Raises: The inverse of a crunch, this exercise strengthens your lower back. A strong back makes fishing, no matter where, a much more pleasant experience.

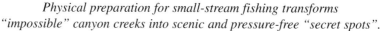

*Physical preparation for small-stream fishing transforms
"impossible" canyon creeks into scenic and pressure-free "secret spots".*

Leg Exercises

Calf Raises: Absolutely essential. If you do no other exercise, do this one. Even if you have to do this in the kitchen with jugs of milk in each hand, it is worth it. This exercise strengthens your calves and will allow greater stability when wading and walking on rocky shorelines. It also improves your jumping and dexterity, so you can hop from rock to rock easier. I have known people who have thrown their wading staffs away after doing this exercise for several months. It is most important to do this exercise both with the toes pointed in and pointed out, this way you work the lateral muscles that are central to your stability.

Squats: Strong hamstrings and glutes will help your wading greatly. If you plan on wading deep, swift water, this exercise will allow you to battle upstream and hold position in the water. Be sure to do this exercise with proper technique and low weight to prevent injury to your back.

Leg Raises: Often performed by women trying to tighten their hips, this exercise really improves the strength of your hip flexor muscle. When you lift your leg to take a step in fast, deep water, this muscle undergoes a lot of stress stabilizing your leg. A strong hip flexor will give you better control of how you wade, reducing falls and near-falls. This is another exercise you want to perform with high repetition and low weight to gain endurance.

Cardiovascular Training

Having a fit heart and lungs will eliminate the fear and pain that accompanies high-elevation and hike-in fishing, opening up thousands of miles of water that were formerly out of the question. You would not believe the numbers of anglers I encounter each year gasping their way up the Slough Creek Trail in Yellowstone Park. The miserable experience that many people go through to go up the trail unfortunately overrides the memories of good fishing at the end of it.

If finding more fishing holes is motivation to exercise, great, but general health should take precedence. Walking a mile every day, taking the stairs instead of the elevator at work, or jogging on a regular basis all will help make strenuous fishing trips less so. As always, check with your doc before exercising.

I jog on a regular basis, so I am usually good to go on low-elevation waters. When venturing into high-elevation waters, running stairs or adding an extra mile or two to the jog for a couple weeks before the trip helps make the thin air more bearable.

A good way to give your workouts some relevance is to make your hike-in a personal fitness yardstick. My dad and I always time our ascent to the First Meadow of Slough Creek, trying to top it each time we go to the park.

Playing Fish
Steering Out of a Pod

If you want to maximize the number of fish you catch out of a pool or run, it is essential that you get the fish out of the area as quickly as possible. When fish are under distress, like many other animals, they release certain chemicals and hormones that can alert other fish to the danger. The accumulation of these chemicals, after several fish being caught, can turn fish off from feeding, and it'll end your little joyride through the pool.

The first step in steering fish out of the pod begins even before you hook the fish. It is important to present first to fish holding at the edges. This allows you to get them out of the pod without dragging them through the other fish. My priority list is:

#1. Back of the pod
#2. Inside edge of the pod
#3. Outside edge of the pod
#4. Whatever is left over.

The tendency of most anglers is to pursue the most active fish first, regardless of position in the pod. This strategy will indelibly result in fewer total trout being caught.

Once you hook a fish in the pod, quickly steer it downstream. It is a good idea to move the fish into fast water that will accelerate this process. I usually turn my rod parallel to the water pointing downstream in order to increase the torque on the fish, turning its head and body broadside to the current, forcing it downstream.

The major exception to this rule is when you see an exceptionally large fish, which you would be willing to sacrifice the rest of the pod for. This has happened to me often, and I'll admit, after catching a bunch of 8-inch trout, there is nothing wrong with rolling the dice and shooting for a big one at the price of a bunch of smaller ones. Here you simply ignore the other fish and tailor your presentation for that one big fish, then play it to maximize your chances of landing it, regardless of how it disrupts the other trout.

Another exception to this rule, is to possibly allow the very first fish you catch to struggle in the pod before escorting it out. Though I haven't constructed a scientific experiment for this, it seems like the struggles of the first hooked fish gets the other fish excited. You will often see other fish chasing it around, with their little trout-brain synapses firing like crazy, trying to figure out what the hell Norm is chasing around the pool. Oftentimes after the first fish is struggling in a pod, I will hook another fish on the dropper fly. As effective as this can be on the first fish, it rarely works on subsequent fish, unless the pool is full of recently stocked hatchery trout.

Avoiding Obstacles

One of the greatest frustrations in small-stream fly-fishing is to go through all the effort to approach, present to, and hook a large fish, just to see it dive between logs, get tangled, and break the line. This frustration is not momentary, for you often must tie on a new fly and leader, detracting several minutes from your valuable fishing time. If this happens to you a lot, don't feel bad, because it happened to me for years until I learned some basic techniques to keep fish from enmeshing themselves in snags.

To keep a fish from diving down and burrowing in a snag, keep its head and pectoral fins above water. This way, the only direction the fish can go is up. Admittedly, this is easier said than done, especially with a freshly hooked trout, but this simple technique will prevent 90% of your problems with fish burying themselves in snags or rocks that are on the bottom of the stream.

If I am downstream of a fish, presenting upstream, and there is a large log or branch in the water between the fish and myself, I simply wait for the fish to jump. When the fish jumps, I just lob the fish over or around the branch, and let it fight it out below the obstruction. This is surprisingly simple, but unless you are keeping a constant tight line and paying attention for when the fish is preparing to jump, you can miss that quick chance to get out of your jam. This technique obviously works best for rainbows and cutthroat, known for their Jordanesque airtime, and decidedly less well for brook and brown trout, who prefer to slug it out underwater.

If you are upstream of the fish and it starts to turn to run into a snag or into rushing white water, hold your rod paral-

Rarely do small-stream anglers have the luxury of playing a big cutthroat over a clean gravel bottom. Be aware of how to land a fish before casting to it!

lel to the water's surface in the opposite direction than the fish wants to go. This increases the torque on the fish, and greatly increases the effort required for the fish to execute its desired maneuver. It will also tire out the fish quicker, thus allowing you to unhook and release it before it has a chance to cause more headaches.

One of most frustrating situations can be when you are pursuing a fish that is holding at the edge of a potential snag; for example, the edge of a fallen log that lies parallel to the current. Even if you can hook this fish, you won't have much luck landing it. What I do with this problem is try to get the fish to rise as far away from the potential snag as possible; this means making repeated drifts getting closer and closer to the fish until it takes. As the fish moves out to rise to the fly and is hooked, the fish will tend to shake its head and hold in place for a second or two before it bolts back to its shelter. Take advantage of the fish's pea-sized brain by turning your rod downstream immediately after hooking the fish. This uses the current and the rod torque to force the fish downstream and away from the obstruction you want to avoid. Once the fish is steered into open water, the fish is yours.

The best way to avoid obstacles is to play a fish as quickly as possible. This also allows you to release the fish with a minimum of stress, letting it return to its aquatic home. A win-win for both you and the trout.

Releasing Fish

In small streams, you generally catch many more fish than in large streams, so consequently, it is important to know how to get fish back in the water safely and quickly. The first step in the process is getting rid of that damn net. If you use a net on a small stream, you'll spend more time taking the net out and putting it back on your back than actually fishing. Most fish should be released by simply grabbing the fly and twisting it out of the fish's mouth. If the hook is barbless, it should be pretty easy to release fish this way. This is the optimal release technique, since the fish never leaves the water and is not touched.

If you can't release the fish this way, then pick the fish up and turn it upside down. This disorientates the fish and gives you a few seconds to pull out the fly without the fish hurting itself by squirming all over the place. Before you take the fish out of the water, be sure to take off any glove you may have on and wet your hand. This way you don't remove the fish's protective slime.

While the textbook fish-revival technique of holding fish in the water upstream to let them recover is a good idea, it is not always necessary on small steams. If you play a fish quickly in a small stream and get it to hand within a couple seconds of hooking it, you can usually just set the fish in the water and it'll just take off instantly. Sometimes it is impossible to release a fish in the textbook manner, and as long as you play a fish quickly, it will easily recover from a little lob into the water from a bridge or overhanging log.

OK we have hacked through the majora and minutia of small-stream fishing. The fish, the trees, the rocks, the bugs, the flies, the techniques, the approaches, the casting, and the kinds of water have been broken down and dissected. Looking at all these things independently is fine and dandy for a book, but in a stream, they are all blended and convoluted into deceptive complexion.

Now, it is time to look at all these things together in their interplay on the stream. We will include several case studies that will show a detailed way to approach and fish a stream, taking into consideration the ecological makeup of the fishery. Each stream will have a set of vital statistics that will reveal information ranging from substrate type, to riparian vegetation to average width and depth, to predominant insects.

These waters are actual creeks that I fish regularly. While all information is accurate and factual, like Desolation Row, "I rearranged their faces and gave them all another name." These are generally outstanding streams, and part of their greatness is that they don't have anglers lining their banks. Hopefully these depictions may spark memories of streams near you and add some insights that may put a couple more trout at the end of your line.

Stream Name: Five Rivers Creek
Type of Stream: tailwater meadow stream
Average Width: 6 feet
Average Depth: 22 inches
Predominant Riparian Vegetation: grasses, wildflowers, lodgepole pine, ponderosa pine
Geology: igneous, basalt
Substrate Type: large, gravel rocks
July Temperature: 51°F
Significant Insect Populations: *Baetis, Cinygma, Cinygmula, Glossosoma*, Limnephilds, *Alloperla*, terrestrials (carpenter ants)
Fish Species: brook and rainbow trout
Average and Maximum Fish Size: 8-inch average, up to 14 or 15 inches
Productive Fly Patterns: Cascade Flying Ant, Black Beetle, Olive Hare's Ear, Baetis Nymph, CDC Alloperla

This small stream is an alpine gem, starting out at about 7700' in elevation. Like many small streams, it is a combination of the ecotypes (tailwater and meadow stream) that we discussed earlier.

How does a tiny creek at such a high elevation produce fish in the size range that it does? What this stream has going for it is the relatively consistent water temperatures from the base of a 50-foot-tall dam. The water in the reservoir is fertile which makes it unsurprising that the water coming out the bottom is moderately rich. The water then flows for about a mile through an open meadow, where it can be warmed by the sun and receive the light needed to spark photosynthesis. Combine these ecological factors with the fact that most anglers ignore it because both the creek and the reservoir are at the end of a twenty-five-mile, one-way dirt road, and you have the mixings of a fine small stream.

When I fish this stream, it is usually during the mid-summer, simply because the high elevation and deep snowpacks keep the roads closed from late September through the 4th of July. Because it is summertime, I would go ahead with using terrestrial patterns unless a hatch made me think twice about it. Because I know the region well, I know that carpenter ants are abundant around the lodgepole and ponderosa pine trees that boarder the meadows. The fly, a #12 Cascade Flying Ant is chosen. While the stream is exceptionally clear and flat in places, the fish are so naïve (due to lack of pressure) that I can get away with a ten foot, 5X tippet. This type of stream screams for a long rod to battle the afternoon winds that kick up, so I would pull out my 9'9" 4-weight to punch the fly through the wind. Oh, I almost forgot, because it is a meadow,

Drifting small terrestrials near riparian grasses is a good technique for slow mountain tailwaters.

I would wear my olive-green shorts, blue shirt, and blue cap; this helps me blend into the background better.

As far as most open meadow streams go, a day on Five Rivers goes pretty much normally. The fish are opportunistic feeders during the daytime, though because of fear of predators, you need to use a careful approach to get the fly in front of them. In the evening, when adult insects are more abundant, they got pickier, even focusing their attention on a particular kind of caddis. This is where my boxes of not-quite attractors yet not-quite spring creek flies came in handy. I was able to fool fish that would have only given passing notice to something as usually effective as a Parachute Adams.

Stream Name: Golden Gate Creek
Type of Stream: geothermally-influenced stream
Average Width: 28 inches
Average Depth: 7 inches
Predominant Riparian Vegetations: sage brush, buffalo grass, willows
Geology: igneous
Substrate Type: medium cobbles and gravel
July Temperature: 63°F
Significant Insect Populations: *Glossosoma, Baetis, Cinygmula, Heptagenia, Brachycentrus*, brown and black ants
Fish Species: brook trout
Average and Maximum Fish Size: 7-inch average, up to 12 inches
Productive Fly Patterns: Cascade Flying Ant

Golden Gate Creek is the perfect example of how small streams are overlooked. This exceptional creek is a textbook anecdote of how stream size has much less to do with productivity than does insolation, water temperatures, water chemistry, and riparian makeup. Even though it is narrow, Golden Gate Creek appears even narrower because of scrubby willow bushes lining the banks and it can hardly be seen by drivers cruising by at fifty miles per hour. Yet, once an angler hops out and wets a line, it won't be driven past again.

The first time I fished this creek it was with skepticism befitting a Beat poet. I had caught nice fish on small streams before, but this was a Smurf compared to the others. As I walked up to the stream, I saw the shadows of dozens of brook trout shooting off under the willow-lined banks. Nothing new, right? I quickly became frustrated when I futilely attempted to cast through the narrow corridor of willows that lined the stream. If the smallest gust of wind blew up, it would blow my two-weight line off course into a tangle of willows. After a half dozen train wrecks, I finally dropped my beetle in the water and got instant gratification from the rise of a ten-inch brook trout. It seemed everywhere I dropped the fly in a fresh reach of water, I would hook a brookie between nine and twelve inches. After I hooked that alpha trout, I was able to still hook a couple smaller fish in each run. It was like this all the way through the creek.

Afterwards, I reflected on how this stream could possibly be so good, and how I could find more streams like it! First of all, the stream receives warm water from dozens of

The widest spots on many tiny creeks can be leapt over, this has little bearing on the size or number of trout it contains...only the number of anglers.

tiny springs, like many other streams in its region. These springs also add calcium and other minerals to the water that help the chain of life to grow. In addition to the springs, the stream has an open canopy, which allows plenty of sunlight to come down and spark photosynthesis. The result of all this is a thick carpet of algae, which harbors a large population of grazing insects like *Baetis* and *Glossosoma*. With all this food, it is no surprise that there are a ton of brook trout in here. I wish I could bring some electro-shock equipment in here and check the populations per mile, but I would guess it has between 300-500 trout over eight inches per mile. But, I kind of wish there were brown trout in there instead of brookies. With their lower fertility, there could easily be a hundred fish over 13 inches per mile.

Now, we have established that this stream has fish in it, but we haven't covered how difficult they can be to catch. Like most small streams, they aren't picky about things once the fly is in their window of view, but getting that fly there can be maddeningly tough. In a stream of this diminutive size, the fish have nowhere to flee to and will dart instantly to escape any sign of danger. Once one fish darts around to escape, the others panic too, setting off a chain of events that can leave you fishless.

Two things will help with catching fish in Golden Gate Creek: casting accuracy and casting accuracy. The opening between the willows above the water can only be a foot wide, and at forty feet with a crosswind, casting can become Mission Impossible. If casting this accurately does not sound difficult, it isn't on a big stream because if you miss you simply pick up your line and cast again until you get it right. On this stream, if your cast misses you will get tangled up in the willows will invariably put down the fish (and its thirty neighbors) when you go unsnag yourself.

Stream Name: Roy Creek
Type of Stream: medium-gradient mountain stream
Average Width: 10 Feet
Average Depth: 20 inches
Predominant Riparian Vegetations: Douglas fir,
   vine maple, red alder, mosses
Geology: igneous, basalt
Substrate Type: boulders and large cobbles
   (grapefruit to basketball sized)
July Temperature: 50°F
Significant Insect Populations: *Epeorus, Glossosoma,*
   Limnephilidae, chironomids
Fish Species: rainbow trout below waterfall;
   rainbow/cutthroat hybrid above the falls
Average and Maximum Fish Size: 5-inch average, up to
   10 inches
Fly Choices: BH CDC Czech Nymph, BH CDC Brassie,
   Combover Egg, Shadow Mayfly, Hot Butt Elk Hair Caddis

Roy Creek is a classic medium-gradient mountain stream, where the myths of small-stream fly-fishing are reinforced. In Roy Creek, the fish aren't large, there are few hatches, and it takes little sophistication to land many, albeit small, trout. A Humpy and a 4X might just be the best setup here. However, the knowledgeable angler can learn to avoid the smaller fish and concentrate his or her time on catching the larger fish that most anglers spook.

Roy Creek flows out of the Oregon Cascades to the Columbia River, and en route it carves a magnificent, deep canyon with hardy mosses and lichens clinging to exposed basalt faces. Because of geology and climate, most streams in the area have large basalt chunks and fallen trees lying in and around the stream, and Roy is no different. These large obstructions serve two purposes the angler should note: they create a varied trout habitat, and they allow the stealthy angler no shortage of places to sneak up on trout.

First of all, the large boulders and logs break up the current and allow large, deep (4-12-foot deep) pools to form amongst the abundant riffle water. In a fast, cold stream like Roy Creek, the slower currents are a welcome relief for larger fish. Besides breaking up the current, these obstructions provide security for the trout. Roy Creek is fairly exposed in the canyon section and since most trout don't aspire to be a fish stick for a hungry osprey, the large structures will make trout more secure. Thus, combine these two factors, and you know why the boulders and logs scream like an "x" on a map when looking for the larger fish in Roy Creek.

It doesn't hurt that these structures help conceal your approach to the fish either. I dream of streams like this one, where I don't have to get down on my knees to crawl within casting distance of a fish. Here I can crouch and scramble into position without much trouble, letting me focus my concentration on the trout.

Now that you know where the big fish are and how to approach them, catching them is the easy part! I usually fish this stream upstream with dry flies, then back down with nymphs. It can be difficult to pull fish up to a dry fly through 10 feet of water, so nymphs are usually the most productive technique for the largest fish. I would fish my nymphs about 8-12 feet below an indicator with plenty of shot to get the fly down to the bottom.

One other note on Roy Creek is that it has a large waterfall, about a 30-foot sheer drop into a pool the size of a softball infield. This draws relatively heavy pressure from anglers with spinning and bait gear. As we discussed earlier, this is a pretty poor place for the fly angler to ply his trade because of the great turbulence in the pool. So fight the urge to pursue the rumors of "the big fish under the falls" and spend more time on the gentle pools and runs further downstream.

Stream Name: Cool Creek
Type of Stream: high-gradient mountain streams
   (plunge pools)
Average Width: 8 feet
Average Depth: 18 inches
Predominant Riparian Vegetations: red alder,
   western red cedar, vine maple, crabapple
Geology: igneous
Substrate Type: small boulders to large cobbles

July Temperature: 57°F
Significant Insect Populations: *Alloperla* stoneflies;
   Amiocentrus caddis; *Paraleptophlebia* mayflies.
Fish Species: rainbow and cutthroat trout
Average and Maximum Fish Size: 8-inch average, up to
   10 inches
Fly Patterns: CDC Alloperla, Mahogany Dun Comparadun,
   Amiocentrus Larvae, Olive Czech Nymph

Like Golden Gate Creek, Cool Creek trickles under the road without much notice from the angling community. In fact, the little glen where it approaches the road looks similar to dozens of others in the area, none of which nurture permanent streams. Since it is quite short (only about three miles long) it only appears on the largest scale maps. With all the brush and trees, you actually have to look for the stream to even notice it. This kind of stream is extremely common throughout the United States, and for the angler willing to experiment, this kind of stream can also be extremely rewarding.

The first thing that may stand out about this creek is that there is little difference between the average and maximum size of the trout. This is not all that unusual for plunge pool fisheries, and one of their charms as well. Streams like Cool Creek are perfect for beginners; a place where they can catch decent trout even if they happen to spook a couple other fish first. You can also get away with sloppy casting, thick leaders, and attractor flies because of the competition for food within the pool.

Cool Creek requires neither great accuracy nor stealthy approaches and subsequently is a first choice for me when I take first-time fly fishers. This is a perfect stream for wet wading, because you can use the pool jumping technique we discussed earlier to keep vibrations to a minimum. By wet wading, you also give yourself a clear casting lane behind you. This is also a short-rod stream, because you generally only have to make short casts and you have a jungle of potential snags overhead.

To fish Cool Creek, simply make your casts from as far back as you can and try to keep your line out of the tailout, which will cause drag on your fly. It is really that simple. If you want, you can get close, crouch, and fish with your rod high, go for it. If you want to stand up and cast two pools ahead, give it a shot. It will all produce fish. The only time I would recommend "getting fancy" is during the early or late season, when the water is cold. During these periods, give a pair of weighted nymphs a shot and you would be shocked at how many more fish you will hook than with dry flies.

With the thick canopy, little sunlight reaches the surface of Cool Creek, so most of the food for insects is fallen leafy material. This means there are a ton of shredder insects and little of anything else. The preeminence of these bugs can cause selective feeding on them, something that may not be expected when fishing small creeks. When I am fishing Cool Creek and similar waters I pack along my spring creek boxes, loaded with flat water patterns. It is amazing how well these patterns will work when the fish target a specific hatch.

Plunge pool fisheries like this Cool Creek are tough to match anywhere in the flyfishing world for their combination of ease of approach, consistent size of fish, relative unimportance of casting accuracy, and easy fly choices. The easiest thing to compare it to is springtime panfish fly-fishing. But instead of beating the muddy water of a panfish hole with a bunch of other anglers, plunge-pool fisheries offer an Eden-like serenity and aesthetic that cannot be matched anywhere.

Stream Name: Pepper Creek
Type of Stream: high-gradient mountain stream
Average Width: 25 feet
Average Depth: 17 inches
Predominant Riparian Vegetations: rocks
Geology: igneous
Substrate Type: large cobbles
July Temperature: 56°F
Significant Insect Populations: *Brachycentrus*,
   Glossosoma caddis; *Isoperla*, *Hesperoperla*, and
   Nemouridae stoneflies; *Baetis* and *Epeorus* mayflies
Fish Species: rainbow trout
Average and Maximum Fish Size: 7-inch average, up to
   14 inches
Fly Patterns: People's Stonefly, CDC Isoperla,
   Golden Stone

Pepper Creek is one of those nightmare high-gradient mountain streams, with wide rocky riparian zones in many places. Yet, for some unbeknownst reason it still produces relatively good fish for its region.

Because it is so swift, most angling friends I know have had trouble fishing it. They expect fish to hold in "normal" water, yet there is so little of it on this Pepper Creek, that if they stick to the usual suspects they spend a lot of time walking and precious little time fishing. The key to Pepper Creek is to learn to analyze and read the water. If you can figure out the tiny slots and pockets that allow the trout a bit of rest, you can find decent, not great, fishing on Pepper Creek.

The wide riparian zones of Pepper Creek makes approaching fish, even with the fast water, something that should be undertaken with care. The swift water here has lulled me into complacency several times, but by now, I know that I can't just walk up and cast to the water ten feet away. If I fish in the daytime, I hang back and make overland casts over the rocks, allowing the tip of the fly line, leader, and tippet to fall in the creek. If I fish in the evening, this problem is lessened, and I will fish without this extra caution.

With the rushing water of Pepper Creek, matching the hatch is not critical, but that doesn't mean that fly choice is not important. If you fish flies that neither float high or sink quickly, you'll be disappointed. This is one of those waters where you get almost nothing out of prospecting the middle of the water column. Fish either hit dries when bugs are common or they stick tight to the bottom where they don't have to fight the current.

Because of the swift water, I like to concentrate my efforts on Pepper Creek during the warmwater seasons (late-May to September) and during emergence periods for large insects (*Hesperoperla* stoneflies, *Brachycentrus* caddis). This combination of factors means the trout have a higher metabolism (thus are prone to move around a little more) and they have large foods that will cause them to move around more to feed. If you fished the creek at these times you'd be pleased by the activity you see, but if you came in early October, you wouldn't think there was a fish within five miles. Sometimes, choosing when to fish contributes more to your success than how you fish.

Stream Name: Thunder River
Type of Stream: medium- to low-gradient stream
Average Width: 25 feet
Average Depth: 18 inches
Predominant Riparian Vegetations: willows,
    cottonwoods, sagebrush, grasses
Geology: igneous, basalt
Substrate Type: medium to large cobbles
July Temperature: 72°F
Significant Insect Populations: *Baetis*, PMD,
    PED mayflies; *Brachycentrus*,
    Glossosoma caddis, *Calineuria* stoneflies
Fish Species: rainbow trout
Average and Maximum Fish Size: 9-inch average, up to
    21 inches

The lake-fed, montaine Pepper Creek, while similar in flow to Thunder River, is about 15 miles long. Thunder River, flowing through sagebrush past grazing cattle and under the hot desert sun, is over 70 miles long. Throughout the Great Basin and American Southwest, there are other small trout streams, which over the course of a hundred miles may only grow to be ten feet wide.

Being a desert stream, Thunder River presents many problems not dealt with by anglers honed on more hospitable streams. First of all, it can be lethal for anglers and fish during July and August, where air temperatures routinely reach 100°F and stream temperatures push 75°F. Wintertime fishing, with driving winds and snowstorms, can also be ruled out of the potential angling schedule. This leaves spring and fall as the best times of the year to fish streams like Thunder River.

Water is also a precious commodity for Thunder River. The region receives about 12-14 inches of rain throughout the year, and much of this comes during summer thunderstorms. These gullywashers can turn the normally placid and gentle stream into a rushing torrent that could easily pick up a tent pitched too close to the stream and send it downstream. A constant eye must be kept on the sky to be aware of incoming thunderstorms or thunderstorms brooding upriver, lest you get stranded on high ground waiting out a flash flood.

Because of the lack of water, plant growth in the desert is confined to the riparian areas of streams like Thunder

River. The banks are choked with willows making shoreline approaches next to impossible. Where it is possible it isn't recommended, because the banks are often swarming with rattlesnakes, which are there feeding on all the rodents and amphibians drawn to the river banks. This means wading is essential, but as always, should be done so as to reduce the number of spooked fish.

When I fish Thunder River, I always pack the longest rod I have. The wind always blows, and a six-weight is almost always the way to go even when fishing small flies. There are no tall casting obstructions, and the longer rod keeps my line higher than many of the streamside willows.

Grasshopper and cricket patterns get pulled out of the dark recesses of my fly bins when I come to Thunder River. They are naturally abundant in the early fall and there are so few anglers that they still produce well. Of course, since most fishing is done early and late in the season, a huge selection of *Baetis* patterns is essential, as is a collection of nymph patterns.

Streams like Thunder Creek, which lie more than a four-hour drive from any town larger than 5,000 people, are the last "wild" streams left in the lower 48. With no other famous waters in the vicinity, very few anglers have the motivation to put up with the dust, winds, and heat to fish remote small streams like this one. Yet every person who fly-fishes really needs to spend time on waters like this one. In this open country, you can easily drive for a half-hour without even seeing another vehicle. Jack Kerouac would smile at Thunder River. Hitting the road for endless hours to fling a fly on a steam unburdened by fly shops, brand names, magazine editors, and hordes of anglers is something that can rarely be done these days.

Wintertime Case Study: Sherman Creek
Type of Stream: high/medium/low-gradient mountain
    stream, spring creek, spawning stream
Average Width: 8 feet wide
Average Depth: 22 inches
Predominant Riparian Vegetations: ponderosa pine,
    willows, grasses
Geology: igneous
Substrate Type: baseball-sized cobbles and large gravel,
    silt in pools
January Temperature: 48°F
Significant Insect Populations: *Baetis*, PMD (*E. inermis*),
    Isoperla, *Cinygmula*, *Glossosoma*, Grannom,
    Green Drakes (*D. grandis*), chironomids, Nemouridae,
    Capniidae
Fish Species: brook trout, brown trout, rainbow trout,
    bull trout, mountain whitefish
Average and Maximum Fish Size: 8-inch average, up to
    16 inches (brown trout), up to 26-30 inches (bull trout)
Fly Patterns: Pupatator, CDC Cap

Like many streams, Sherman Creek is a complex combination of several ecotypes. It emerges from stillwater origins as a rushing whitewater stream, with few lies for trout to fin in comfort. It rushes down about 1000 feet from the mountains over five miles, then it later flattens out and becomes as slower, winding stream with tall grasses and wide marshy banks. In this section, sporadic springs (a result of volcanic geology) feed the creek, enhancing weed growth and helping to buffer temperature swings throughout the season. It is the combination of mild winter temperatures and spawning brown and bull trout (from a famous nearby water) that makes creeks like this one a prime target for wintertime small-stream fishing.

First of all, I wouldn't be in any rush to get to the stream in the morning. Wintertime trout fishing is best between 10:00AM and 4:00PM, when the sun is high and warming up the water. (On small streams this window can be even smaller.) Usually I stay in a lodge near this creek, so I'll eat a big breakfast then head out after it settles. There is usually no competition from other anglers, for those who are willing to brave the harsh winter conditions will stick with the famous river which this stream flows into.

I would first target fish in the slower pools of the creek. This is where the larger spawners are usually holding since they moved into the stream during the previous fall. Drifting Pupatators, Rubber Leg Hare's Ears and other large nymphs is my tactic of choice, since they are large enough to elicit strikes from the invaders yet not put down the resident fish. Repeated drifts of these flies is absolutely essential, and the water should be fished more thoroughly than at any time of the year. The cold water limits the distance fish will cover to get your fly and you'll often need multiple drifts to elicit an "aggression" take from the fish.

Streamers are just as important as nymphs. Because this stream is relatively narrow, streamers fished downstream and twitched around cover in pools will be the most effective way to fish them. I have found that sight-fishing Bead Head Woolly Buggers in black or yellow can be deadly when water conditions are right.

Of course, the resident fish will be feeding on the eggs cast by spawning whitefish. Since the whitefish just shoot their eggs over the bottom without making a nest, many eggs

invariably get caught in the drift. These eggs provide a critical food source for the winter trout, and most trout feeding at the end of a riffle will not ignore an imitation. In fact, it is not surprising to catch all your resident fish with egg patterns. Because the stream is not particularly wide, but is deep, I would choose to Czech nymph with a heavy Czech nymph as my middle fly, with egg patterns as my droppers.

On the rare occasion (because of the high elevation and cold temperatures) you can catch a midge, *Baetis*, or Capniidae emergence on this stream. When bugs are coming off, use the marshy banks to closely approach fish, and make short casts to specific risers. Light tippets are essential to fish the imitations of these tiny insects specifically.

Flooded Stream Case Study: Black Creek
Type of Stream: medium-gradient mountain stream
Average Width: 20 feet (26' in flood stage)
Average Depth: 25 inches (29" in flood stage)
Geology: igneous, basalt
Substrate Type: grapefruit-sized cobbles
May Temperature: 54°F
Significant Insect Populations: Golden stoneflies, *Isoperla* stoneflies; Limnephilidae and *Brachycentrus* caddis; *Epeorus* and *Cinygmula* mayflies
Fish Species: rainbow trout
Average and Maximum Fish Size: 7-inch average, up to 13 inches
Fly Patterns: Black Woolly Buggers, The People's Stonefly, San Juan Worms, Cranefly Larvae, Pupator

Black Creek is normally a beautiful rushing mountain stream, with stoic pine trees and lush willows peppering its banks. It is an image straight out of a Tennysonian poem. Usually, that is. This May, my pilgrimage to Black Creek found me standing under a canopy of baby blue skyline, and as I hiked to the water, I dreamed of the small rainbows popping up to take small yellow stoneflies as they dipped to lay their eggs. Yet as I arrived streamside, I found myself gazing over a swarthy stream, swirling with murky water and the

Small streams can be surprisingly productive in the winter, when smaller resident fish feed on the spawn of migratory salmon and trout.

During high water, worm and crane fly larvae imitations can be deadly.

occasional piece of floating debris. Give up? Turn around? Not a chance.

Flood conditions can be daunting to even experienced small-stream veterans, because all the traditional rules of small streams are out the window: the fish aren't everywhere, the approach isn't as important, and wading is dangerous if not impossible. Yet once you adapt to how different flood-stage fly-fishing is, you will be surprised at how relatively easy the fishing can be.

When discussing a flooded stream it is essential to determine what causes the flooding. If it is snowmelt, the water is frigid and fishing is usually slow at best. If it is rain, the water is warmer and the fish are more likely to be responsive to patterns. Since it was a late-May flood after a mild winter, most of the water was from a recent heavy rainstorm.

Another question that is critical during flood conditions is the geology of the area? A sedimentary rock like shale will cause the water to be extremely off color and thick with sediment during flood conditions. Fortunately this creek flows through a basalt watershed, keeping it about as clear as one can hope (about 7 inches of visibility).

Where to find fish under flood conditions is critical skill that it takes most anglers several trips to figure out. Perhaps the most surprising thing for first-time flood anglers is that the deep pools rarely produce fish. This is contrary to what most people expect, since pools look like the slowest water in the stream. However, think, "What makes pools deep in the first place?" Scouring water! When is water volume high enough to do that scouring? That's right, during flood conditions! Though the water looks smooth on top, near the bottom the currents can be much faster and nearly impossible for trout to comfortably hold in position.

The best place to look for fish during flood stage is near the banks. The high water often floods the banks, which are lined with vegetation and debris, which in turn break up the current allowing fish places to rest. If you are fishing a stream that has a fishermen's trail shadowing its banks, this is the place you want to concentrate your efforts. Trout will hold in surprisingly shallow depths, because the murkiness of the water adds a degree of security for them. The flooded bank water also adds a banquet of terrestrial foods to the drift, and trout will feed on the increased numbers of worms, crane fly larvae, beetle larvae, and drowned terrestrials in the drift.

On Black Creek on that sunny May Day, I was lucky this flood came in the early season. It gave me the opportunity to fish large, dark flies like stonefly nymphs and cranefly larvae which are easy targets for these myopic trout. If I was fishing the same flooding creek in the fall, I would be hard pressed to find many insects larger than a size 14, and fishing would be tougher. With a big People's Stonefly and a San Juan Worm on 3X tippet, I proceeded to drop mortor shots along the banks of Black Creek. With the indicator hardly 10 inches above the first fly, I was able to drift my fly down the fisherman's trail as well as in short pockets in the riparian willows without hanging up. While the rainbows were neither as huge nor as plentiful as in more optimal conditions, it was better than quiting and going home.

Fishing flooded creeks is actually kind of relaxing for me. When clear water abounds, I become a neurotic with my approach, constantly fretting over achieving perfect non-detection. When the water is blown out and off color, I can do a little more standing and a little less observing the water. The fish are generally there or not.

One last note about fishing high water on small creeks: make sure that you don't fish on days of fluctuation. Fishing within about 36 hours of peak flow is rather poor, as fish are more worried about seeking new lies than eating. After this period of adjustment, fish will start feeding again fairly regularly on nymphs and other subsurface foods.

Low Water/Drought Case Study: South Fork Alsea River
Type of Stream: medium-gradient mountain stream
Average Width: 15 feet
Average Depth: 13 inches
Predominant Riparian Vegetations: red alder
Geology: sedimentary, sandstone
Substrate Type: grapefruit- to golf-ball-sized cobbles
September Temperature: 62°F
Significant Insect Populations: *Alloperla*, *Isoperla*, and Nemouridae stoneflies; Chironomids; *Paraleptophlebia* and *Cinygmula* mayflies; *Glossosoma* and Limnephilidae caddis
Fish Species: coastal cutthroat trout
Average and Maximum Fish Size: 7-inch average, up to 12 inches (resident), up to 18 inches (sea-run)
Fly Patterns: CDC Ant #16, Mahogany Dun Comparadun #16, Diving Glossosoma #16, CDC Alloperla #14, Ribbon-wing Caddis #14

The Western coast range mountains of the United States get drenched with rain from October through early July. In some places, like the Olympic Mountains of Washington, this rainfall can exceed 200 inches in a year, making this ecosystem, by definition, a true rainforest. Yet for all that rain, precious little snowpack lasts into the summer. So, when the rains stop in early July, many of these streams shrink to mere trickles. Creeks like the South Fork of the Alsea, between the months of July and September, will see only 4% of their annual streamflow during the entire three-month period.

When streams like this one undergo a radical shift in their flow levels, small-stream fishing becomes a daunting challenge. Where the stream once was an eclectic variety of riffles, runs, and pools, it is now is a pitiful series of long, shallow, and flat pools with a light riffle at the head of each. The water has receded from the banks, leaving a wide swath of no-man's land between the normal banks and the water. Because of the reduced flow, fish are nervous about overhead predators and the undisturbed surface gives them an unencumbered view of the terrestrial world.

Most anglers with any sense will pass up on fishing these waters because there is an immense amount of effort required for marginal rewards (seven- to nine-inch trout). Yet, what if you are on a vacation and this is the only option you have to get away from the noisy kids and irritating inlaws? Of course, you go fish it.

When I take people fishing on waters like this the first thing we do is figure out how far they can cast. If they can cast 50-60 feet with relative accuracy, the best way to get them into fish is to let them cast from the end of the pool to the riffle at the head of the pool. Most fish will hold in the disturbed water of the riffle throughout the day, because it offers more dissolved oxygen and a degree of overhead protection. All they have to do is stay far behind the riffle, plop an ant or *Alloperla* pattern in the riffle, and pull out each trout as quickly as possible before it can spook the other fish in the close confines of the riffles. Wet flies can also be fished with extraordinary success in this manner, for the fish are more likely to hit something safely below the surface.

If this long-distance casting cannot be achieved, the best thing to do is to fall back on the tag-team approach. With the reduced flows, there is not sufficient current to bring the trout enough food, so many trout will start cruising the pools to feed. When this happens, I usually go up to a high slope where I can spot cruising fish, and from there instruct my friend on where to approach and where to cast. Without

someone spotting fish, a lone angler will spend a lot of time fishing barren water or unknowingly spooking fish.

When fishing this flat water, there is no need for super-floating patterns like the Humpys, Elk Hair Caddis, or Royal Wulffs. I usually opt for low-floaters like the Mahogany Dun Comparadun or a Brown X-Caddis. These realistic patterns make a big difference when trout have an eternity to inspect your patterns.

I once sat with a friend working a pair of cutthroat on this stream. They were holding right at the end of the throat of the pool, with just enough current to supply food but not so much that they had to rush to eat it. They were actively taking foods both on the surface and below. With that kind of behavior, I had no doubt that we would get a rise out of one of them on the first cast. An hour and a half later, and after a dozen pattern changes, several adjustments to the leader, and many obscenities uttered, the trout continued to feed on naturals and refuse every artificial offered. We resolved ourselves to fool these fish, even if we never moved out of the pool until dark. Finally, a #22 CDC Baetis Emerger on 8X tippet fooled one of the fish. For years my friend bought into the small-stream/easy-fish myth, but this experience debunked that forever.

Late-season trout in low-water creeks often require long presentations with imitative dry flies.

LEARN MORE ABOUT FISHING WITH THESE BOOKS

TYING EMERGERS

Jim Schollmeyer and Ted Leeson

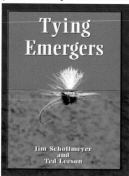

Two of fly-fishing's most well-respected writers collaborate once again, this time discussing emergers. Emergence is itself a behavior, and it puts the tier in a challenging and rather unusual position—not that of imitating a fixed and recognizable form of the insect, but rather of representing a process. This book shows you how, including: emerger design and materials, basic tying techniques, many specialized tying techniques, fly patterns, and more. When you buy a book by these two authors you know what you will get—up-to-the-minute information, well-written text, and superb photography, Tying Emergers will not let you down. 8 1/2 x 11 inches, 344 pages.

SB: $45.00   ISBN: 1-57188-306-1
UPC: 0-81127-00140-8

Spiral HB: $60.00   ISBN: 1-57188-307-X
UPC: 0-81127-00141-5

FEDERATION OF FLY FISHERS FLY PATTERN ENCYCLOPEDIA
Over 1600 of the Best Fly Patterns

Edited by Al & Gretchen Beatty

Simply stated, this book is a Federation of Fly Fishers' conclave taken to the next level, a level that allows the reader to enjoy the learning and sharing in the comfort of their own home. The flies, ideas, and techniques shared herein are from the "best of the best" demonstration fly tiers North America has to offer. The tiers are the famous as well as the unknown with one simple characteristic in common; they freely share their knowledge.

As you leaf through these pages, you will get from them just what you would if you spent time in the fly tying area at any FFF function. At such a show, if you dedicate time to observing the individual tiers, you can learn the information, tips, or tricks they are demonstrating. Full color, 8 1/2 x 11 inches, 232 pages.

SB: $39.95   ISBN: 1-57188-208-1
UPC: 0-66066-00422-2

ROD CRAFTING

Jeffrey L. Hatton

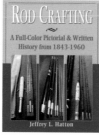

This unique, one-of-a-kind book is a must for anyone interested in the history of our great sport and collectors of antique fishing tackle. It takes a look at the history of fishing rods from the early 1800s to the 1970s, through text and hundreds of color photographs. With access to five private and extensive collections, Hatton covers the first three ages of rod-making: The smith age, up to 1870; the expansion era, 1870-1900; and the classic era, 1900-1970s. Forty-nine beautiful rods are featured, each with a description, history, notable features, and much more. Be warned: once you get into this book, you may look up to discover that several hours have gone by.

SB: $45.00   ISBN: 1-57188-356-8
UPC: 0-81127-00190-3

HB: $65.00   ISBN: 1-57188-357-6
UPC: 0-81127-00191-0

Limited HB: $150.00   ISBN: 1-57188-358-4
UPC: 0-81127-00192-7

MAYFLIES: TOP TO BOTTOM

Shane Stalcup

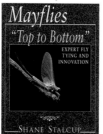

Shane Stalcup approaches fly-tying with the heart and mind of both a scientist and an artist. His realistic approach to imitating the mayfly is very popular and effective across the West, and can be applied to waters across North America. Mayflies are the most important insects to trout fishermen, and in this book, Shane shares his secrets for tying effective, life-like mayfly imitations that will bring fly-anglers more trout. Many tying techniques and materials are discussed, Mayflies: Top to Bottom is useful to beginner and expert tiers alike. 8 1/2 x 11 inches, 157 pages.

SB: $29.95   ISBN: 1-57188-242-1
UPC: 0-66066-00496-3

Spiral HB: $39.95   ISBN: 1-57188-243-X
UPC: 0-81127-00116-3

CURTIS CREEK MANIFESTO

Sheridan Anderson

Finest beginner fly-fishing guide due to its simple, straightforward approach. It is laced with outstanding humor provided in its hundreds of illustrations. All the practical information you need to know is presented in an extremely delightful way such as rod, reel, fly line and fly selection, casting, reading water, insect knowledge to determine which fly pattern to use, striking and playing fish, leaders and knot tying, fly tying, rod repairs, and many helpful tips. A great, easy-to-understand book. 8 1/2 x 11 inches, 48 pages.

SB: $7.95   ISBN: 0-936608-06-4
UPC: 0-81127-00113-2

WESTERN MAYFLY HATCHES

Rick Hafele & Dave Hughes

Western Mayfly Hatches introduces the mayflies important in the western states and provinces, shows how to recognize them, helps in the selection of fly patterns to match them, and provides the best presentation methods. Also included is: matching hatches, collecting and observing mayflies, recognizing species and stages, fly-tying techniques, and more. For each species there's a detailed illustration labeled with the characteristics of each life stage, and individual charts of emergence times and hatch importance provide even more information. Western Mayfly Hatches leaves no stone unturned. 8 1/2 x 11 inches, 268 pages.

SB: $39.95   ISBN: 1-57188-304-5
UPC: 0-81127-00138-5

HB: $60.00   ISBN: 1-57188-305-3
UPC: 0-81127-00139-2

Limited HB: $125.00   ISBN: 1-57188-337-1
UPC: 0-81127-00171-2

FLY TYING
MADE CLEAR AND SIMPLE

Skip Morris

With over 220 color photographs, expert tier show all the techniques you need to know. 73 different materials and 27 tools. Clear, precise advice tells you how to do it step-by-step. Dries, wets, streamers, nymphs, etc., included so that you can tie virtually any pattern. 8 1/2 x 11 inches, 80 pages.

SPIRAL SB: $19.95   ISBN: 1-878175-130
UPC: 0-66066-00103-0

SOFTBOUND: $19.95   ISBN: 1-57188-231-6
UPC: 0-81127-00131-6

INNOVATIVE FLIES
AND TECHNIQUES

Al & Gretchen Beatty

While working on The Federation of Fly Fishers Fly Pattern Encyclopedia it quickly became clear to the Beattys that another book was necessary. Many of the flies in the Encyclopedia were worthy of more than just a fly plate and dressing, so they are included in this book with step-by-step photos and descriptions. They've also included many new flies, but each is included for the same reasons: the pattern is an innovative design, a simple but effective idea, or makes improvements on an existing fly. This book is so much more than a fly pattern book, it's full of many creative and innovative ideas for creating productive fishing flies. 8 1/2 x 11 inches, 200 pages.

SB: $35.00   ISBN: 1-57188-347-9
UPC: 0-81127-00181-1

Spiral HB: $49.95   ISBN: 1-57188-348-7
UPC: 0-81127-00182-8

Limited HB: $125.00   ISBN: 1-57188-343-5
UPC: 0-81127-00183-5

ASK FOR THESE BOOKS AT YOUR LOCAL TACKLE OR FLY SHOP.
IF UNAVAILABLE CALL, FAX, OR ORDER ON THE WEB AT WWW.AMATOBOOKS.COM

Frank Amato Publications, Inc. • PO Box 82112 • Portland, Oregon 97282   0094

TOLL FREE 1-800-541-9498 (8-5 Pacific Time) • FAX (503) 653-2766